SYRIA

T0292819

INVESTMENT AND BUSINESS PROFILE

BASIC INFORMATION AND CONTACTS FOR SUCCESSFUL INVESTMENT AND BUSINESS ACTIVITY

International Business Publications, USA
Washington DC, USA - Syria

SYRIA
INVESTMENT AND BUSINESS PROFILE
BASIC INFORMATION AND CONTACTS FOR SUCCESSFUL INVESTMENT AND BUSINESS ACTIVITY

UPDATED ANNUALLY

We express our sincere appreciation to all government agencies and international organizations which provided information and other materials for this guide

Cover Design: International Business Publications, USA

2017 Updated Reprint International Business Publications, USA
ISBN 978-1-5145-1192-3

For additional analytical, business and investment opportunities information,
please contact Global Investment & Business Center, USA
at (703) 370-8082. Fax: (703) 370-8083. E-mail: ibpusa3@gmail.com
Global Business and Investment Info Databank - www.ibpus.com

Printed in the USA

For additional analytical, business and investment opportunities information,
please contact Global Investment & Business Center, USA
at (703) 370-8082. Fax: (703) 370-8083. E-mail: ibpusa3@gmail.com
Global Business and Investment Info Databank - www.ibpus.com

SYRIA
INVESTMENT AND BUSINESS PROFILE
BASIC INFORMATION AND CONTACTS FOR SUCCESSFUL INVESTMENT AND BUSINESS ACTIVITY

TABLE OF CONTENTS

**For additional analytical, business and investment opportunities information,
please contact Global Investment & Business Center, USA
at (703) 370-8082. Fax: (703) 370-8083. E-mail: ibpusa3@gmail.com
Global Business and Investment Info Databank - www.ibpus.com**

For additional analytical, business and investment opportunities information, please contact Global Investment & Business Center, USA at (703) 370-8082. Fax: (703) 370-8083. E-mail: ibpusa3@gmail.com Global Business and Investment Info Databank - www.ibpus.com

For additional analytical, business and investment opportunities information,
please contact Global Investment & Business Center, USA
at (703) 370-8082. Fax: (703) 370-8083. E-mail: ibpusa3@gmail.com
Global Business and Investment Info Databank - www.ibpus.com

For additional analytical, business and investment opportunities information,
please contact Global Investment & Business Center, USA
at (703) 370-8082. Fax: (703) 370-8083. E-mail: ibpusa3@gmail.com
Global Business and Investment Info Databank - www.ibpus.com

STRATEGIC AND DEVELOPMENT PROFILES

STRATEGIC AND BUSINESS PROFILE

Capital		Damascus 33°30′N 36°18′E33.500°N 36.300°E
	Largest city	Aleppo
	Official languages	Arabic
	Government	Dominant-party unitary semi-presidential state
-	President	Bashar al-Assad
-	Prime Minister	Wael Nader al-Halqi
-	Speaker of the People's Council	Mohammad Jihad al-Laham
	Legislature	People's Council
	Establishment	
-	Independence from Ottoman Empire	1 September 1918
-	Independence from France	17 April 1946
-	Secession from the United Arab Republic	28 September 1961
	Area	
-	Total	186,475 km^2 (89th) 71,479 sq mi
-	Water (%)	1.1
	Population	
-	estimate	22,530,746 (53rd)
-	Density	118.3/km^2 (101st) 306.5/sq mi
GDP (PPP)		estimate
-	Total	$107.831 billion
-	Per capita	$5,100
GDP (nominal)		2010 estimate
-	Total	$59.957 billion
-	Per capita	$2,802
Gini		35.8 medium
HDI		▼0.632 medium · 119th
	Currency	Syrian pound (SYP)
	Time zone	EET (UTC+2)
-	Summer (DST)	EEST (UTC+3)
	Drives on the	right
	Calling code	+963
	ISO 3166 code	SY
	Internet TLD	.sy, سوريا.

Syria officially the **Syrian Arab Republic**, is a country in Western Asia, bordering Lebanon and the Mediterranean Sea to the west, Turkey to the north, Iraq to the east, Jordan to the south, and Israel to the southwest. Its capital Damascus is among the oldest continuously-inhabited cities in the world. A country of fertile plains, high mountains, and deserts, it is home to diverse ethnic and religious groups, including Arabs, Greeks, Armenians, Assyrians, Kurds, Circassians, Mhallami, Mandeans and Turks. Religious groups include Sunni, Christians, Alawite, Druze religion, Mandeanism and Yezidi. Sunni Arabs make up the largest population group in Syria.

In English, the name "Syria" was formerly synonymous with the Levant (known in Arabic as *al-Sham*) while the modern state encompasses the sites of several ancient kingdoms and empires, including the Eblan civilization of the 3rd millennium BC. In the Islamic era, Damascus was the seat of the Umayyad Caliphate and a provincial capital of the Mamluk Sultanate in Egypt.

The modern Syrian state was established after World War I as a French mandate, and represented the largest Arab state to emerge from the formerly Ottoman-ruled Arab Levant. It gained independence in April 1946, as a parliamentary republic. The post-independence period was tumultuous, and a large number of military coups and coup attempts shook the country in the period 1949–1971. Between 1958-61, Syria entered a brief union with Egypt, which was terminated by a military coup. The Arab Republic of Syria came into being in 1963, transforming from the Republic of Syria in the Ba'athist coup d'état. Syria was under Emergency Law from 1963 to 2011, effectively suspending most constitutional protections for citizens, and its system of government is considered to be non-democratic. Bashar al-Assad has been president since 2000 and was preceded by his father Hafez al-Assad, who was in office from 1970 to 2000.

Syria is a member of one international organization other than the United Nations, the Non-Aligned Movement; it is currently suspended from the Arab League and the Organisation of Islamic Cooperation, and self-suspended from the Union for the Mediterranean. Since March 2011, Syria has been embroiled in an uprising against Assad and the Ba'athist government as part of the Arab Spring, a crackdown which contributed to the Syrian Civil War and Syria becoming among the least peaceful countries in the world. The Syrian Interim Government was formed by the opposition umbrella group, the Syrian National Coalition, in March 2013. Representatives of this government were subsequently invited to take up Syria's seat at the Arab League

GEOGRAPHY

Location: Middle East, bordering the Mediterranean Sea, between Lebanon and Turkey
Geographic coordinates: 35 00 N, 38 00 E
Map references: Middle East

Area:
total: 185,180 sq km
land: 184,050 sq km
water: 1,130 sq km
note: includes 1,295 sq km of Israeli-occupied territory

Area—comparative: slightly larger than North Dakota

Land boundaries:
total: 2,253 km
border countries: Iraq 605 km, Israel 76 km, Jordan 375 km, Lebanon 375 km, Turkey 822 km

Coastline: 193 km

For additional analytical, business and investment opportunities information,
please contact Global Investment & Business Center, USA
at (703) 370-8082. Fax: (703) 370-8083. E-mail: ibpusa3@gmail.com
Global Business and Investment Info Databank - www.ibpus.com

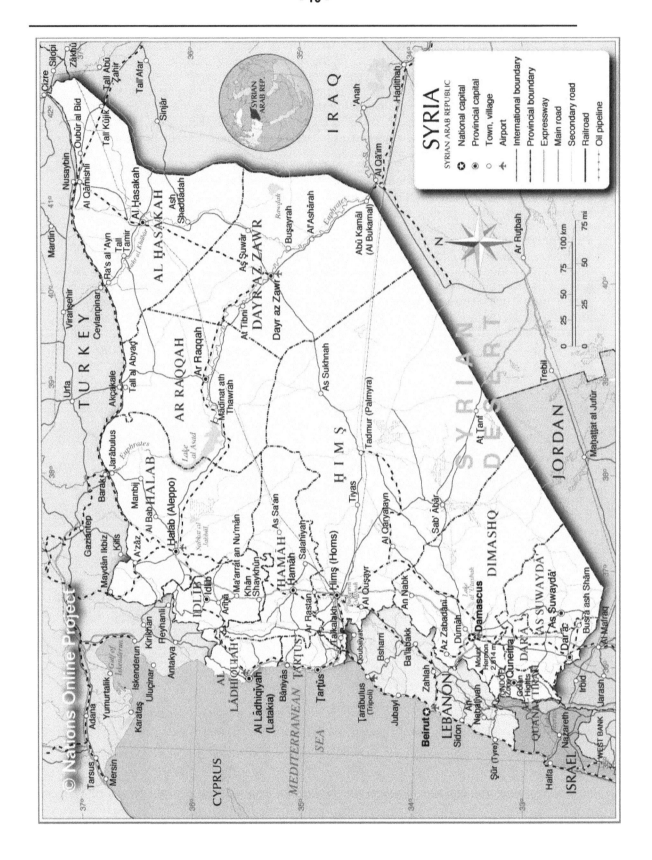

For additional analytical, business and investment opportunities information,
please contact Global Investment & Business Center, USA
at (703) 370-8082. Fax: (703) 370-8083. E-mail: ibpusa3@gmail.com
Global Business and Investment Info Databank - www.ibpus.com

Maritime claims:
contiguous zone: 41 nm
territorial sea: 35 nm

Climate: mostly desert; hot, dry, sunny summers (June to August) and mild, rainy winters (December to February) along coast; cold weather with snow or sleet periodically hitting Damascus

Terrain: primarily semiarid and desert plateau; narrow coastal plain; mountains in west

Elevation extremes:
lowest point: unnamed location near Lake Tiberias -200 m
highest point: Mount Hermon 2,814 m

Natural resources: petroleum, phosphates, chrome and manganese ores, asphalt, iron ore, rock salt, marble, gypsum

Land use:
arable land: 28%
permanent crops: 4%
permanent pastures: 43%
forests and woodland: 3%
other: 22%

Irrigated land: 9,060 sq km

Natural hazards: dust storms, sandstorms

Environment—current issues: deforestation; overgrazing; soil erosion; desertification; water pollution from dumping of raw sewage and wastes from petroleum refining; inadequate supplies of potable water

Environment—international agreements:
party to: Biodiversity, Climate Change, Desertification, Hazardous Wastes, Nuclear Test Ban, Ozone Layer Protection, Ship Pollution
signed, but not ratified: Environmental Modification

Geography—note: there are 42 Israeli settlements and civilian land use sites in the Israeli-occupied Golan Heights (August 1997 est.)

PEOPLE

Population: 16,673,282
note: in addition, there are 35,150 people living in the Israeli-occupied Golan Heights—18,150 Arabs (16,500 Druze and 1,650 Alawites) and 17,000 Israeli settlers

Age structure:
0-14 years: 46% (male 3,937,575; female 3,748,881)
15-64 years: 51% (male 4,342,022; female 4,157,268)
65 years and over: 3% (male 240,603; female 246,933) (July 1998 est.)

Population growth rate: 3.23%
Birth rate: 37.83 births/1,000 population
Death rate: 5.55 deaths/1,000 population
Net migration rate: 0 migrant(s)/1,000 population

For additional analytical, business and investment opportunities information, please contact Global Investment & Business Center, USA at (703) 370-8082. Fax: (703) 370-8083. E-mail: ibpusa3@gmail.com
Global Business and Investment Info Databank - www.ibpus.com

Sex ratio:
at birth: 1.05 male(s)/female
under 15 years: 1.05 male(s)/female
15-64 years: 1.04 male(s)/female
65 years and over: 0.97 male(s)/female

Infant mortality rate: 37.6 deaths/1,000 live births

Life expectancy at birth:
total population: 67.76 years
male: 66.48 years
female: 69.11 years

Total fertility rate: 5.55 children born/woman

Nationality:
noun: Syrian(s)
adjective: Syrian

Ethnic groups: Arab 90.3%, Kurds, Armenians, and other 9.7%

Religions: Sunni Muslim 74%, Alawite, Druze, and other Muslim sects 16%, Christian (various sects) 10%, Jewish (tiny communities in Damascus, Al Qamishli, and Aleppo)

Languages: Arabic (official); Kurdish, Armenian, Aramaic, Circassian widely understood; French, English somewhat understood

Literacy:
definition: age 15 and over can read and write
total population: 70.8%
male: 85.7%
female: 55.8%

GOVERNORATES OF SYRIA

Syria has fourteen governorates, or *muhafazat* (singular: *muhafazah*). The governorates are divided into sixty districts, or *manatiq* (sing. *mintaqah*), which are further divided into subdistricts, or *nawahi* (sing. *nahia*). The *nawahi* contain villages, which are the smallest administrative units.

A governor, whose appointment is proposed by the minister of the interior, approved by the cabinet, and announced by executive decree, heads each governorate. The governor is responsible for administration, health, social services, education, tourism, public works, transportation, domestic trade, agriculture, industry, civil defense, and maintenance of law and order in the province. The minister of local administration works closely with each governor to coordinate and supervise local development projects. The governor is assisted by a provincial council, three-quarters of whose members are popularly elected for a term of four years, the remainder being appointed by the minister of the interior and the governor. In addition, each council has an executive arm consisting of six to ten officers appointed by the central government from among the council's elected members. Each executive officer is charged with specific functions.

Districts and subdistricts are administered by officials appointed by the governor, subject to the approval of the minister of the interior. These officials work with elected district councils to attend to assorted local needs and serve as intermediaries between central government authority and traditional local leaders, such as village chiefs, clan leaders, and councils of elders.

Syria is divided into 14 governorates, which are sub-divided into 61 districts, which are further divided into sub-districts.

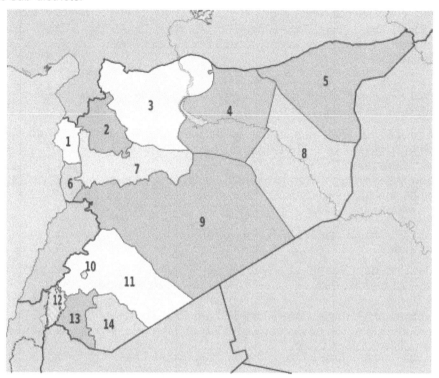

No.	Governorate	Capital
1	Latakia	Latakia
2	Idlib	Idlib
3	Aleppo	Aleppo
4	Al-Raqqah	Al-Raqqah
5	Al-Hasakah	Al-Hasakah
6	Tartus	Tartus
7	Hama	Hama
8	Deir ez-Zor	Deir ez-Zor
9	Homs	Homs
10	Damascus	–
11	Rif Dimashq	–
12	Quneitra	Quneitra
13	Daraa	Daraa
14	Al-Suwayda	Al-Suwayda

GOVERNMENT

Country name:
conventional long form: Syrian Arab Republic
conventional short form: Syria
local long form: Al Jumhuriyah al Arabiyah as Suriyah
local short form: Suriyah
former: United Arab Republic (with Egypt)
Data code: SY
Government type: republic under military regime since March 1963
National capital: Damascus

Administrative divisions: 14 provinces (muhafazat, singular—muhafazah); Al Hasakah, Al Ladhiqiyah, Al Qunaytirah, Ar Raqqah, As Suwayda', Dar'a, Dayr az Zawr, Dimashq, Halab, Hamah, Hims, Idlib, Rif Dimashq, Tartus

Independence: 17 April 1946 (from League of Nations mandate under French administration)
National holiday: National Day, 17 April (1946)
Constitution: 13 March 1973
Legal system: based on Islamic law and civil law system; special religious courts; has not accepted compulsory ICJ jurisdiction
Suffrage: 18 years of age; universal

Executive branch:

chief of state: President Bashar al-ASAD (since 17 July 2000); Vice President Najah al-ATTAR (since 23 March 2006)

head of government: Prime Minister Imad Muhammad Dib KHAMIS (since 22 June 2016); Deputy Prime Ministers Fahd Jasim al-FURAYJ, Lt. Gen.(since 23 June 2012) and Walid al-MUALEM (since 23 June 2012)
cabinet: Council of Ministers appointed by the president
elections/appointments: president directly elected by simple majority popular vote for a 7-year term (eligible for a second term); election last held on 3 June 2014 (next to be held in June 2021); the president appoints the vice presidents, prime minister, and deputy prime ministers

election results: Bashar al-ASAD elected president; percent of vote - Bashar al-ASAD (Ba'th Party) 88.7%, Hassan al-NOURI (independent) 4.3%, Maher HAJJER (independent) 3.2%, other/invalid 3.8%

Legislative branch:
description: unicameral People's Assembly or Majlis al-Shaab (250 seats; members directly elected in multi-seat constituencies by proportional representation vote to serve 4-year terms)

elections: last held on 13 April 2016 (next to be held in 2020)
election results: percent of vote by party - NPF 80%, other 20%; seats by party - NPF 200, other 50

Judicial branch:
highest court(s): Court of Cassation (organized into civil, criminal, religious, and military divisions, each with 3 judges); Supreme Constitutional Court (consists of 7 members)
judge selection and term of office: Court of Cassation judges appointed by the Supreme Judicial Council or SJC, a judicial management body headed by the minister of justice with 7 members including the national president; judge tenure NA; Supreme Constitutional

Court judges nominated by the president and appointed by the SJC; judges appointed for 4-year renewable terms
subordinate courts: courts of first instance; magistrates' courts; religious and military courts; Economic Security Court; Counterterrorism Court (established June 2012)

Political parties and leaders:
legal parties/alliances: Arab Socialist Ba'ath Party [Bashar al-ASAD, regional secretary] Arab Socialist Union of Syria or ASU [Safwan al-QUDSI]
National Progressive Front or NPF [Bashar al-ASAD, Suleiman QADDAH] (alliance includes Arab Socialist Renaissance (Ba'th) Party [President Bashar al-ASAD], Socialist Unionist Democratic Party [Fadlallah Nasr al-DIN])
Syrian Communist Party (two branches) [Wissal Farha BAKDASH, Yusuf Rashid FAYSAL]
Syrian Social Nationalist Party or SSNP [Ali HAIDAR]
Unionist Socialist Party [Fayez ISMAIL]
Kurdish parties (considered illegal): Kurdish Azadi Party
Kurdish Democratic Accord Party (al Wifaq) [Fowzi SHINKALI]
Kurdish Democratic Left Party [Saleh KIDDO]
Kurdish Democratic Party (al Parti-Ibrahim wing) [Nasr al-Din IBRAHIM]
Kurdish Democratic Party (al Parti-Mustafa wing)
Kurdish Democratic Party in Syria or KDP-S [Saud AL-MALA]
Kurdish Democratic Patriotic/National Party
Kurdish Democratic Peace Party [Talal MOHAMMED]
Kurdish Democratic Progressive Party or KDPP-Darwish
Kurdish Democratic Progressive Party or KDPP-Muhammad
Kurdish Democratic Union Party or PYD [Salih Muslim MOHAMMAD]
Kurdish Democratic Unity Party [Kamiron Haj ABDU]
Kurdish Democratic Yekiti Party [Mahi al-Din Sheikh ALI]
Kurdish Equality Party [Namet DAOUD]
Kurdish Future Party [Rezan HASSAN]
Kurdish Green Party [Laqman AHMI]
Kurdish Left Party [Shallal KIDDO]
Kurdish National Democratic Rally in Syria
Kurdish Reform Movement in Syria [Amjad OTHMAN]
Kurdish Reform Movement Party [Feisal AL-YUSSEF]
Kurdish Yekiti (Union) Party
Kurdistan Communist Party [Nejm al-Sin MALA'AMIR]
Kurdistan Democratic Party in Syria [Abdul Karim SAKKO]
Kurdistan Liberal Union [Farhad TILO]
Syrian Kurdish Democratic Party
Tiyar al-Mustaqbal [Narin MATINI]
other: Syrian Democratic Party [Mustafa QALAAJI]

Political pressure groups and leaders:
Free Syrian Army
Syrian Muslim Brotherhood or SMB [Mohamed Hekmat WALID] (operates in exile in London)
Syrian Opposition Coalition or National Coalition of Syrian Revolutionary and Opposition Forces [Riad SEIF]
note: there are also hundreds of local and provincial political and armed opposition groups that organize protests, provide civilian services, and stage armed attacks

International organization participation:

For additional analytical, business and investment opportunities information, please contact Global Investment & Business Center, USA at (703) 370-8082. Fax: (703) 370-8083. E-mail: ibpusa3@gmail.com Global Business and Investment Info Databank - www.ibpus.com

ABEDA, AFESD, AMF, CAEU, FAO, G-24, G-77, IAEA, IBRD, ICAO, ICC (national committees), ICRM, IDA, IDB, IFAD, IFC, IFRCS, IHO, ILO, IMF, IMO, Interpol, IOC, IPU, ISO, ITSO, ITU, LAS, MIGA, NAM, OAPEC, OIC, OPCW, UN, UNCTAD, UNESCO, UNIDO, UNRWA, UNWTO, UPU, WCO, WFTU (NGOs), WHO, WIPO, WMO, WTO (observer)

Diplomatic representation in the US:
note: Embassy ceased operations and closed on 18 March 2014
chief of mission: Ambassador (vacant); Charge d'Affaires Mounir KOUDMANI (since 1 June 2012)
chancery: 2215 Wyoming Avenue NW, Washington, DC 20008
telephone: [1] (202) 232-6313
FAX: [1] (202) 234-9548

Diplomatic representation from the US:
chief of mission: ambassador (vacant); US Special Envoy for Syria Michael RATNEY (since 27 July 2015); note - on 6 February 2012, the US closed its embassy in Damascus; Czechia serves as protecting power for US interests in Syria
embassy: Abou Roumaneh, 2 Al Mansour Street, Damascus
mailing address: P. O. Box 29, Damascus
telephone: [963] (11) 3391-4444
FAX: [963] (11) 3391-3999

Flag description: three equal horizontal bands of red (top), white, and black with two small green five-pointed stars in a horizontal line centered in the white band; similar to the flag of Yemen, which has a plain white band and of Iraq, which has three green stars (plus an Arabic inscription) in a horizontal line centered in the white band; also similar to the flag of Egypt, which has a symbolic eagle centered in the white band

ECONOMY

Syria's economy continues to deteriorate amid the ongoing conflict that began in 2011, declining by more than 70% from 2010 to 2016. The government has struggled to address the effects of international sanctions, widespread infrastructure damage, diminished domestic consumption and production, reduced subsidies, and high inflation, which have caused dwindling foreign exchange reserves, rising budget and trade deficits, a decreasing value of the Syrian pound, and falling household purchasing power.

During 2014, the ongoing conflict and continued unrest and economic decline worsened the humanitarian crisis and elicited a greater need for international assistance, as the number of people in need inside Syria increased from 9.3 million to 12.2 million, and the number of Syrian refugees increased from 2.2 million to more than 3.3 million.

Prior to the turmoil, Damascus had begun liberalizing economic policies, including cutting lending interest rates, opening private banks, consolidating multiple exchange rates, raising prices on some subsidized items, and establishing the Damascus Stock Exchange, but the economy remains highly regulated. Long-run economic constraints include foreign trade barriers, declining oil production, high unemployment, rising budget deficits, increasing pressure on water supplies caused by heavy use in agriculture, rapid population growth, industrial expansion, water pollution, and widespread infrastructure damage.

GDP (purchasing power parity):

$NA (2015 est.)
$55.8 billion (2014 est.)
$61.9 billion (2013 est.)
notes: data are in 2015 US dollars
the war-driven deterioration of the economy resulted in a disappearance of quality national level statistics in the 2012-13 period
country comparison to the world: 110

GDP (official exchange rate):
$24.6 billion (2014 est.)

GDP - real growth rate:
NA% (2016 est.)
-9.9% (2014 est.)
-36.5% (2013 est.)
note: data are in 2015 dollars
country comparison to the world: 219

GDP - per capita (PPP):
$2,900 (2015 est.)
$3,300 (2014 est.)
$2,800 (2013 est.)
note: data are in 2015 US dollars
country comparison to the world: 194

Gross national saving:
19.1% of GDP (2016 est.)
20.1% of GDP (2015 est.)
18.2% of GDP (2014 est.)
country comparison to the world: 105

GDP - composition, by end use:
household consumption: 65.6%
government consumption: 23.5%
investment in fixed capital: 17.6%
investment in inventories: 11.4%
exports of goods and services: 10.8%
imports of goods and services: -29% (2016 est.)

GDP - composition, by sector of origin:
agriculture: 19.5%
industry: 19%
services: 61.5% (2016 est.)

Agriculture - products:
wheat, barley, cotton, lentils, chickpeas, olives, sugar beets; beef, mutton, eggs, poultry, milk

Industries:
petroleum, textiles, food processing, beverages, tobacco, phosphate rock mining, cement, oil seeds crushing, automobile assembly
Industrial production growth rate:
-2.4% (2016 est.)

For additional analytical, business and investment opportunities information,
please contact Global Investment & Business Center, USA
at (703) 370-8082. Fax: (703) 370-8083. E-mail: ibpusa3@gmail.com
Global Business and Investment Info Databank - www.ibpus.com

country comparison to the world: 177

Labor force:
3.871 million (2016 est.)
country comparison to the world: 96

Labor force - by occupation:
agriculture: 17%
industry: 16%
services: 67% (2008 est.)

Unemployment rate:
50% (2016 est.)
50% (2015 est.)
country comparison to the world: 214

Population below poverty line:
82.5% (2014 est.)

Budget:
revenues: $496.6 million
expenditures: $2.889 billion
note: government projections for FY2016 (2016 est.)

Taxes and other revenues:
2% of GDP (2016 est.)
country comparison to the world: 220

Budget surplus (+) or deficit (-):
-9.7% of GDP (2016 est.)
country comparison to the world: 197

Public debt:
55.7% of GDP (2016 est.)
48.9% of GDP (2015 est.)
country comparison to the world: 84

Fiscal year:
calendar year

Inflation rate (consumer prices):
43.9% (2016 est.)
38.1% (2015 est.)
country comparison to the world: 224

Central bank discount rate:
0.75% (31 December 2016)
5% (31 December 2015)
country comparison to the world: 130

Commercial bank prime lending rate:
32% (31 December 2016 est.)
27% (31 December 2015 est.)

For additional analytical, business and investment opportunities information,
please contact Global Investment & Business Center, USA
at (703) 370-8082. Fax: (703) 370-8083. E-mail: ibpusa3@gmail.com
Global Business and Investment Info Databank - www.ibpus.com

country comparison to the world: 4

Stock of narrow money:
$4.488 billion (31 December 2016 est.)
$5.254 billion (31 December 2015 est.)
country comparison to the world: 106

Stock of broad money:
$5.522 billion (31 December 2016 est.)
$6.98 billion (31 December 2015 est.)
country comparison to the world: 124

Stock of domestic credit:
$5.993 billion (31 December 2016 est.)
$7.225 billion (31 December 2015 est.)
country comparison to the world: 120

Current account balance:
$-2.077 billion (2016 est.)
$-2.955 billion (2015 est.)
country comparison to the world: 156

Exports:
$1.705 billion (2016 est.)
$1.587 billion (2015 est.)
country comparison to the world: 142

Exports - commodities:
crude oil, minerals, petroleum products, fruits and vegetables, cotton fiber, textiles, clothing, meat and live animals, wheat

Exports - partners:
Lebanon 34.6%, Jordan 11.6%, China 9.4%, Turkey 8.2%, Iraq 7.7%, Tunisia 4.9% (2016)
Imports:
$5.496 billion (2016 est.)
$6.076 billion (2015 est.)
country comparison to the world: 118

Imports - commodities:
machinery and transport equipment, electric power machinery, food and livestock, metal and metal products, chemicals and chemical products, plastics, yarn, paper

Imports - partners:
Russia 22%, Turkey 20%, China 11.3% (2016)

Reserves of foreign exchange and gold:
$504.6 million (31 December 2016 est.)
$772.9 million (31 December 2015 est.)
country comparison to the world: 145

Debt - external:
$5.085 billion (31 December 2016 est.)
$4.42 billion (31 December 2015 est.)

country comparison to the world: 133

Exchange rates:
Syrian pounds (SYP) per US dollar -
459.2 (2016 est.)
459.2 (2015 est.)
236.41 (2014 est.)
153.695 (2013 est.)
64.39 (2012 est.)

ENERGY

Electricity - production:

43.76 billion kWh
country comparison to the world: 55

Electricity - consumption:

35.61 billion kWh
country comparison to the world: 57

Electricity - exports:

1.043 billion kWh
country comparison to the world: 57

Electricity - imports:

0 kWh
country comparison to the world: 203

Electricity - installed generating capacity:

8.323 million kW
country comparison to the world: 63

Electricity - from fossil fuels:

89.2% of total installed capacity
country comparison to the world: 78

Electricity - from nuclear fuels:

0% of total installed capacity
country comparison to the world: 182

Electricity - from hydroelectric plants:

10.8% of total installed capacity

country comparison to the world: 111

Electricity - from other renewable sources:

0% of total installed capacity
country comparison to the world: 125

Crude oil - production:

182,500 bbl/day
country comparison to the world: 40

Crude oil - exports:

152,400 bbl/day
country comparison to the world: 34

Crude oil - imports:

0 bbl/day
country comparison to the world: 124

Crude oil - proved reserves:

2.5 billion bbl
country comparison to the world: 33

Refined petroleum products - production:

253,600 bbl/day
country comparison to the world: 48

Refined petroleum products - consumption:

258,800 bbl/day
country comparison to the world: 49

Refined petroleum products - exports:

36,210 bbl/day
country comparison to the world: 65

Refined petroleum products - imports:

104,800 bbl/day
country comparison to the world: 50

Natural gas - production:

For additional analytical, business and investment opportunities information,
please contact Global Investment & Business Center, USA
at (703) 370-8082. Fax: (703) 370-8083. E-mail: ibpusa3@gmail.com
Global Business and Investment Info Databank - www.ibpus.com

7.87 billion cu m
country comparison to the world: 45

Natural gas - consumption:

9.63 billion cu m
country comparison to the world: 48

Natural gas - exports:

0 cu m
country comparison to the world: 187

Natural gas - imports:

250 million cu m
country comparison to the world: 69

Natural gas - proved reserves:

240.7 billion cu m
country comparison to the world: 45

Carbon dioxide emissions from consumption of energy:

63.14 million Mt

COMMUNICATIONS

Telephones - main lines in use:

4.425 million
country comparison to the world: 36

Telephones - mobile cellular:

12.928 million
country comparison to the world: 66

Telephone system:

general assessment: fair system currently undergoing significant improvement and digital upgrades, including fiber-optic technology and expansion of the network to rural areas; the armed insurgency that began in 2011 has led to major disruptions to the network and has caused telephone and Internet outages throughout the country
domestic: the number of fixed-line connections has increased markedly since 2000; mobile-cellular service growing with telephone subscribership nearly 60 per 100 persons in 2011
international: country code - 963; submarine cable connection to Egypt, Lebanon, and Cyprus; satellite earth stations - 1 Intelsat (Indian Ocean) and 1 Intersputnik (Atlantic

Ocean region); coaxial cable and microwave radio relay to Iraq, Jordan, Lebanon, and Turkey; participant in Medarabtel

Broadcast media:

state-run TV and radio broadcast networks; state operates 2 TV networks and a satellite channel; roughly two-thirds of Syrian homes have a satellite dish providing access to foreign TV broadcasts; 3 state-run radio channels; first private radio station launched in 2005; private radio broadcasters prohibited from transmitting news or political content

Internet country code:

.sy

Internet hosts:

416
country comparison to the world: 187

Internet users:

4.469 million
country comparison to the world: 52

TRANSPORTATION

Airports:

90
country comparison to the world: 62

Airports - with paved runways:

total: 29
over 3,047 m: 5
2,438 to 3,047 m: 16
914 to 1,523 m: 3
under 914 m: 5

Airports - with unpaved runways:

total: 61
1,524 to 2,437 m: 1
914 to 1,523 m: 12
under 914 m:
48

Heliports:

6

Pipelines:

gas 3,170 km; oil 2,029 km

Railways:

total: 2,052 km
country comparison to the world: 72
standard gauge: 1,801 km 1.435-m gauge
narrow gauge: 251 km 1.050-m gauge

Roadways:

total: 69,873 km
country comparison to the world: 67
paved: 63,060 km
unpaved: 6,813 km

Waterways:

900 km (navigable but not economically significant) (2011)
country comparison to the world: 69

Merchant marine:

total: 19
country comparison to the world: 95
by type: bulk carrier 4, cargo 14, carrier 1
registered in other countries: 166 (Barbados 1, Belize 4, Bolivia 4, Cambodia 22, Comoros 5, Dominica 4, Georgia 24, Lebanon 2, Liberia 1, Malta 4, Moldova 5, North Korea 4, Panama 34, Saint Vincent and the Grenadines 9, Sierra Leone 13, Tanzania 23, Togo 6, unknown 1)

Ports and terminals:

major seaport(s): Baniyas, Latakia, Tartus

MILITARY

Military branches:

Syrian Armed Forces: Land Forces, Naval Forces, Air Forces (includes Air Defense Forces)

Military service age and obligation:

18 years of age for compulsory and voluntary military service; conscript service obligation is 18 months; women are not conscripted but may volunteer to serve; re-enlistment obligation 5 years, with retirement after 15 years or age 40 (enlisted) or 20 years or age 45 (NCOs)

Manpower available for military service:

males age 16-49: 5,889,837
females age 16-49: 5,660,751

Manpower fit for military service:

males age 16-49: 5,055,510
females age 16-49: 4,884,151

Manpower reaching militarily significant age annually:

male: 256,698
female: 244,712

TRANSNATIONAL ISSUES

Disputes - international:

Golan Heights is Israeli-occupied with the almost 1,000-strong UN Disengagement Observer Force patrolling a buffer zone since 1964; lacking a treaty or other documentation describing the boundary, portions of the Lebanon-Syria boundary are unclear with several sections in dispute; since 2000, Lebanon has claimed Shab'a Farms in the Golan Heights; 2004 Agreement and pending demarcation settles border dispute with Jordan

Refugees and internally displaced persons:

refugees (country of origin): 146,200 (Iraq) (2013); 517,255 (Palestinian Refugees (UNRWA)) (2014)
note: the ongoing civil war had created more than 2.8 million Syrian refugees - dispersed in Egypt, Iraq, Jordan, Lebanon, and Turkey - as of February 2014
IDPs: 6.5 million (ongoing civil war since 2011) (2014)
stateless persons: 221,000 (); note - Syria's stateless population is composed of Kurds and Palestinians; stateless persons are prevented from voting, owning land, holding certain jobs, receiving food subsidies or public healthcare, enrolling in public schools, or being legally married to Syrian citizens; in 1962, some 120,000 Syrian Kurds were stripped of their Syrian citizenship, rendering them and their descendants stateless; in 2011, the Syrian Government granted citizenship to thousands of Syrian Kurds as a means of appeasement; however, resolving the question of statelessness is not a priority given Syria's ongoing civil war

Trafficking in persons:

current situation: due to Syria's political uprising and violent unrest, hundreds of thousands of Syrians, foreign migrant workers, and refugees have fled the country and are vulnerable to human trafficking; the lack of security and inaccessibility of the majority of the country makes it impossible to conduct a thorough analysis of the ongoing conflict and the scope and magnitude of Syria's human trafficking situation; prior to the uprising, Syria was principally a destination country for women and children subjected to forced labor or sex trafficking; thousands of women - the majority from Indonesia, the Philippines, Somalia,

For additional analytical, business and investment opportunities information,
please contact Global Investment & Business Center, USA
at (703) 370-8082. Fax: (703) 370-8083. E-mail: ibpusa3@gmail.com
Global Business and Investment Info Databank - www.ibpus.com

and Ethiopia - were recruited to work as domestic servants but were subsequently subjected to forced labor; Filipina domestic workers continue to be sent to Syria and are vulnerable to forced labor; the Syrian armed forces and opposition forces are using Syrian children in combat and support roles and as human shields; Iraqi women and girls continue to be sexually exploited, and Syrian children still face conditions of forced labor
tier rating: Tier 3 - the government does not fully comply with the minimum standards for the elimination of trafficking and is not making significant efforts to do so; the government does not demonstrate evidence of increasing efforts to investigate and punish trafficking offenses, provide protective services to victims, inform the public about human trafficking, or provide much-needed anti-trafficking training to law enforcement and social welfare officials; the government does not refer any victims to NGO-operated shelters and has failed to institute procedures for the identification, interview, and referral of trafficking victims; the status of the national plan of action against trafficking is unknown (2013)

Illicit drugs:

a transit point for opiates, hashish, and cocaine bound for regional and Western markets; weak anti-money-laundering controls and bank privatization may leave it vulnerable to money laundering

IMPORTANT INFORMATION FOR UNDERSTANDING SYRIA

BASIC INFORMATION

Geography
Area: 185,170 sq. km. (71,504 sq. mi.), including 1,295 sq. km. of Israeli-occupied territory; about the size of North Dakota.
Cities: *Capital*--Damascus (1.7 million). *Other cities*--Metropolitan Damascus (excluding city) (2.7 million), Aleppo (4.6 million), Homs (1.7 million), Hama (1.5 million), Idleb (1.4 million), al-Hasakeh (1.4 million), Dayr al-Zur (1.1 million), Latakia (1 million), Dar'a (1 million), al-Raqqa (900,000), and Tartus (800,000).
Terrain: Narrow coastal plain with a double mountain belt in the west; large, semiarid and desert plateau to the east.
Climate: Mostly desert; hot, dry, sunny summers (June to August) and mild, rainy winters (December to February) along coast.

People
Nationality: *Noun and adjective*--Syrian(s).
Population (2009 est.)*: 21 million.
Population growth rate (2009 est.): 2.37%.
Major ethnic groups: Arabs (90%), Kurds (9%), Armenians, Circassians, Turkomans.
Religions: Sunni Muslims (74%), Alawis (12%), Christians (10%), Druze (3%), and small numbers of other Muslim sects, Jews, and Yazidis.
Languages: Arabic (official), Kurdish, Armenian, Aramaic, Circassian widely understood, French, English somewhat understood, principally in major cities.
Education (2008 est.): *Years compulsory*--primary, 6 yrs. *Attendance*--97.9%. *Literacy*--90.8%, *illiteracy*--9.2%.
Health (2009 est.): *Infant mortality rate*--17/1,000. *Life expectancy*--69.8 yrs. male, 72.68 yrs. female.
Work force (5.5 million, 2008 est.): Services (including government) 26%, agriculture 19%, industry 14%, commerce 16%, construction 15%, transportation 7%, and finance 3%.
Unemployment (2008 est.): 9.8%.

Government
Type: Republic, under authoritarian military-dominated Arab Socialist Ba'ath Party regimes since March 1963.
Independence: April 17, 1946.
Constitution: March 13, 1973. Since 1963, Syria has been under Emergency Law, which effectively suspends most constitutional protections.
Branches: *Executive*--president, two vice presidents, prime minister, Council of Ministers (cabinet). *Legislative*--unicameral People's Council. *Judicial*--Supreme Judicial Council, Supreme Constitutional Court, Court of Cassation, Appeals Courts, Economic Security Courts, Supreme State Security Court, Personal Status and local levels courts.
Administrative subdivisions: 14 provinces
Political parties: The National Progressive Front, an umbrella organization for several parties permitted by the government including the Arab Socialist Renaissance (Ba'ath) Party; Socialist Unionist Democratic Party; Syrian Arab Socialist Union or ASU, Syrian Communist Party (two branches); Syrian Social Nationalist Party; Unionist Socialist Party; and other parties not legally recognized but quasi-tolerated, generally considered opposition-oriented but enfeebled and

reluctant to challenge the government. There are also several illegal Kurdish parties.
Suffrage: Universal at 18.

PEOPLE

Ethnic Syrians are of Semitic stock. Syria's population is 90% Muslim--74% Sunni, and 16% other Muslim groups, including the Alawi, Shi'a, and Druze--and 10% Christian. There also is a tiny Syrian Jewish community.

Arabic is the official, and most widely spoken, language. Arabs, including some 500,000 Palestinian and up to 1 million Iraqi refugees, make up 90% of the population. Many educated Syrians also speak English or French, but English is the more widely understood. The Kurds, many of whom speak the banned Kurdish language, make up 9% of the population and live mostly in the northeast corner of Syria, though sizable Kurdish communities live in most major Syrian cities as well. Armenian and Turkic are spoken among the small Armenian and Turkoman populations.

Most people live in the Euphrates River valley and along the coastal plain, a fertile strip between the coastal mountains and the desert. Education is free and compulsory from ages 6 to 12. Schooling consists of 6 years of primary education followed by a 3-year preparatory or vocational training period and a 3-year secondary or vocational program. The second 3-year period of secondary schooling is required for university admission. Total enrollment at post-secondary schools is over 150,000. The illiteracy rate of Syrians aged 15 and older is 9.3% for males and 17.8% for females.

Ancient Syria's cultural and artistic achievements and contributions are many. Archaeologists have discovered extensive writings and evidence of a brilliant culture rivaling those of Mesopotamia and Egypt in and around the ancient city of Ebla. Later Syrian scholars and artists contributed to Hellenistic and Roman thought and culture. Zeno of Sidon founded the Epicurean school; Cicero was a pupil of Antiochus of Ascalon at Athens; and the writings of Posidonius of Apamea influenced Livy and Plutarch. Syrians have contributed to Arabic literature and music and have a proud tradition of oral and written poetry. Although declining, the world-famous handicraft industry still employs thousands.

HISTORY

Archaeologists have demonstrated that Syria was the center of one of the most ancient civilizations on earth. Around the excavated city of Ebla in northern Syria, discovered in 1975, a great Semitic empire spread from the Red Sea north to Turkey and east to Mesopotamia from 2500 to 2400 B.C. The city of Ebla alone during that time had a population estimated at 260,000. Scholars believe the language of Ebla to be the oldest Semitic language.

Syria was occupied successively by Canaanites, Phoenicians, Hebrews, Arameans, Assyrians, Babylonians, Persians, Greeks, Romans, Nabataeans, Byzantines, and, in part, Crusaders before finally coming under the control of the Ottoman Turks. Syria is significant in the history of Christianity; Paul was converted on the road to Damascus and established the first organized Christian Church at Antioch in ancient Syria, from which he left on many of his missionary journeys.

Damascus, settled about 2500 B.C., is one of the oldest continuously inhabited cities in the world. It came under Muslim rule in A.D. 636. Immediately thereafter, the city's power and prestige reached its peak, and it became the capital of the Omayyad Empire, which extended from Spain to India from A.D. 661 to A.D. 750, when the Abbasid caliphate was established at Baghdad, Iraq.

For additional analytical, business and investment opportunities information, please contact Global Investment & Business Center, USA at (703) 370-8082. Fax: (703) 370-8083. E-mail: ibpusa3@gmail.com Global Business and Investment Info Databank - www.ibpus.com

Damascus became a provincial capital of the Mameluke Empire around 1260. It was largely destroyed in 1400 by Tamerlane, the Mongol conqueror, who removed many of its craftsmen to Samarkand. Rebuilt, it continued to serve as a capital until 1516. In 1517, it fell under Ottoman rule. The Ottomans remained for the next 400 years, except for a brief occupation by Ibrahim Pasha of Egypt from 1832 to 1840.

French Occupation

In 1920, an independent Arab Kingdom of Syria was established under King Faysal of the Hashemite family, who later became King of Iraq. However, his rule over Syria ended after only a few months, following the clash between his Syrian Arab forces and regular French forces at the battle of Maysalun. French troops occupied Syria later that year after the League of Nations put Syria under French mandate. With the fall of France in 1940, Syria came under the control of the Vichy Government until the British and Free French occupied the country in July 1941. Continuing pressure from Syrian nationalist groups forced the French to evacuate their troops in April 1946, leaving the country in the hands of a republican government that had been formed during the mandate.

Independence to 1970

Although rapid economic development followed the declaration of independence of April 17, 1946, Syrian politics from independence through the late 1960s were marked by upheaval. A series of military coups, begun in 1949, undermined civilian rule and led to army colonel Adib Shishakli's seizure of power in 1951. After the overthrow of President Shishakli in a 1954 coup, continued political maneuvering supported by competing factions in the military eventually brought Arab nationalist and socialist elements to power.

Syria's political instability during the years after the 1954 coup, the parallelism of Syrian and Egyptian policies, and the appeal of Egyptian President Gamal Abdel Nasser's leadership in the wake of the 1956 Suez crisis created support in Syria for union with Egypt. On February 1, 1958, the two countries merged to create the United Arab Republic, and all Syrian political parties ceased overt activities.

The union was not a success, however. Following a military coup on September 28, 1961, Syria seceded, reestablishing itself as the Syrian Arab Republic. Instability characterized the next 18 months, with various coups culminating on March 8, 1963, in the installation by leftist Syrian Army officers of the National Council of the Revolutionary Command (NCRC), a group of military and civilian officials who assumed control of all executive and legislative authority. The takeover was engineered by members of the Arab Socialist Resurrection Party (Ba'ath Party), which had been active in Syria and other Arab countries since the late 1940s. The new cabinet was dominated by Ba'ath members.

The Ba'ath takeover in Syria followed a Ba'ath coup in Iraq the previous month. The new Syrian Government explored the possibility of federation with Egypt and Ba'ath-controlled Iraq. An agreement was concluded in Cairo on April 17, 1963, for a referendum on unity to be held in September 1963. However, serious disagreements among the parties soon developed, and the tripartite federation failed to materialize. Thereafter, the Ba'ath regimes in Syria and Iraq began to work for bilateral unity. These plans foundered in November 1963, when the Ba'ath regime in Iraq was overthrown. In May 1964, President Amin Hafiz of the NCRC promulgated a provisional constitution providing for a National Council of the Revolution (NCR), an appointed legislature composed of representatives of mass organizations--labor, peasant, and professional unions--a presidential council, in which executive power was vested, and a cabinet. On February 23, 1966, a group of army officers carried out a successful, intra-party coup, imprisoned President Hafiz, dissolved the cabinet and the NCR, abrogated the provisional constitution, and designated a

For additional analytical, business and investment opportunities information, please contact Global Investment & Business Center, USA at (703) 370-8082. Fax: (703) 370-8083. E-mail: ibpusa3@gmail.com Global Business and Investment Info Databank - www.ibpus.com

regionalist, civilian Ba'ath government. The coup leaders described it as a "rectification" of Ba'ath Party principles. The defeat of the Syrians and Egyptians in the June 1967 war with Israel weakened the radical socialist regime established by the 1966 coup. Conflict developed between a moderate military wing and a more extremist civilian wing of the Ba'ath Party. The 1970 retreat of Syrian forces sent to aid the PLO during the "Black September" hostilities with Jordan reflected this political disagreement within the ruling Ba'ath leadership. On November 13, 1970, Minister of Defense Hafiz al-Asad affected a bloodless military coup, ousting the civilian party leadership and assuming the role of prime minister.

1970 to 2000
Upon assuming power, Hafiz al-Asad moved quickly to create an organizational infrastructure for his government and to consolidate control. The Provisional Regional Command of Asad's Arab Socialist Ba'ath Party nominated a 173-member legislature, the People's Council, in which the Ba'ath Party took 87 seats. The remaining seats were divided among "popular organizations" and other minor parties. In March 1971, the party held its regional congress and elected a new 21-member Regional Command headed by Asad. In the same month, a national referendum was held to confirm Asad as President for a 7-year term. In March 1972, to broaden the base of his government, Asad formed the National Progressive Front, a coalition of parties led by the Ba'ath Party, and elections were held to establish local councils in each of Syria's 14 governorates. In March 1973, a new Syrian constitution went into effect followed shortly thereafter by parliamentary elections for the People's Council, the first such elections since 1962.

The authoritarian regime was not without its critics, though most were quickly dealt with. A serious challenge arose in the late 1970s, however, from fundamentalist Sunni Muslims, who reject the basic values of the secular Ba'ath program and object to rule by the Alawis, whom they consider heretical. From 1976 until its suppression in 1982, the archconservative Muslim Brotherhood led an armed insurgency against the regime. In response to an attempted uprising by the brotherhood in February 1982, the government crushed the fundamentalist opposition centered in the city of Hama, leveling parts of the city with artillery fire and causing many thousands of dead and wounded. Since then, public manifestations of anti-regime activity have been very limited.

Syria's 1990 participation in the U.S.-led multinational coalition aligned against Saddam Hussein marked a dramatic watershed in Syria's relations both with other Arab states and with the West. Syria participated in the multilateral Middle East Peace Conference in Madrid in October 1991. During the 1990s, Syria engaged in direct, face-to-face negotiations with Israel; these negotiations failed.

Hafiz Al-Asad died on June 10, 2000, after 30 years in power. Immediately following Al-Asad's death, the parliament amended the constitution, reducing the mandatory minimum age of the president from 40 to 34 years old, which allowed his son, Bashar Al-Asad legally to be eligible for nomination by the ruling Ba'ath Party. On July 10, 2000, Bashar Al-Asad was elected President by referendum in which he ran unopposed, garnering 97.29% of the vote, according to Syrian Government statistics. He was inaugurated into office on July 17, 2000 for a 7-year term.

2000 to 2011
In the aftermath of the September 11, 2001 terrorist attacks in the United States, the Syrian Government began limited cooperation with U.S. counterterrorism efforts. However, Syria opposed the Iraq war in March 2003, and bilateral relations with the United States swiftly deteriorated. In December 2003, President George W. Bush signed into law the Syria Accountability and Lebanese Sovereignty Restoration Act of 2003, which provided for the imposition of a series of sanctions against Syria if Syria did not end its support for Palestinian terrorist groups, curtail its military and security interference in Lebanon, cease its pursuit of

weapons of mass destruction, and meet its obligations under United Nations Security Council resolutions regarding the stabilization and reconstruction of Iraq. In May 2004, the President determined that Syria had not met these conditions and implemented sanctions that prohibit the export to Syria of U.S. products except for food and medicine, and the taking off from or landing in the United States of Syrian Government-owned aircraft. At the same time, the U.S. Department of the Treasury announced its intention to order U.S. financial institutions to sever correspondent accounts with the Commercial Bank of Syria based on money-laundering concerns, pursuant to Section 311 of the USA PATRIOT Act. Acting under the International Emergency Economic Powers Act (IEEPA), the President also authorized the Secretary of the Treasury, in consultation with the Secretary of State, to freeze assets belonging to certain Syrian individuals and entities.

Tensions between Syria and the United States intensified from mid-2004 to early 2009, primarily over issues relating to Iraq and Lebanon. The U.S. Government recalled its ambassador to Syria in February 2005, after the assassination of former Lebanese Prime Minister Rafiq Hariri. Prior to the assassination, France and the U.S. in 2004 had co-authored UN Security Council Resolution (UNSCR) 1559 calling for "all remaining foreign forces to withdraw from Lebanon." Under pressure following the assassination, Syrian troops stationed in Lebanon since 1976 were withdrawn by April 2005. Sensing its international isolation, the Syrians strengthened their relations with Iran and radical Palestinians groups based in Damascus, and cracked down on any signs of internal dissent. However, during the July-August 2006 conflict between Israel and Hizballah, Syria placed its military forces on alert but did not intervene directly on behalf of its ally Hizballah.

On May 27, 2007, President Al-Asad was reaffirmed by referendum for a second 7-year term with 97.6% of the vote. During 2008, though Syria's relations with the U.S. remained strained, Syria's international isolation was slowly being overcome as indirect talks between Israel and Syria, mediated by Turkey, were announced and a Qatar-brokered deal in Lebanon was reached. Shortly thereafter, French president Nicolas Sarkozy invited President Asad to participate in the Euro-Mediterranean summit in Paris, spurring a growing stream of diplomatic visits to Damascus. Since January 2009, President Barack Obama's administration has continued to review Syria policy, and there have been a succession of congressional and U.S. administration officials who have visited Syria while in the region.

Despite high hopes when President Al-Asad first took power in 2000, there has been little movement on political reform, with more public focus on limited economic liberalizations. The Syrian Government provided some cooperation to the UN Independent International Investigation Commission, which investigated the killing of Hariri until superseded by the Special Tribunal for Lebanon. Since the 34-day conflict in Lebanon in July and August 2006, evidence of Syrian compliance with its obligations under UN Security Council Resolution 1701 not to rearm the Lebanese group Hizballah is unpersuasive. On April 17, 2007, the United Nations Security Council welcomed the Secretary General's intention to evaluate the situation along the entire Syria-Lebanon border and invited the Secretary General to dispatch an independent mission to fully assess the monitoring of the border, and to report back on its findings and recommendations. As of March 2011, the border had yet to be demarcated.

Since 2009, the U.S. has attempted to engage with Syria to find areas of mutual interest, reduce regional tensions, and promote Middle East peace. These efforts have included congressional and executive meetings with senior Syrian officials, including President Asad, and the return of a U.S. Ambassador to Damascus.

GOVERNMENT

The Syrian constitution vests the Arab Socialist Ba'ath Party with leadership functions in the state and society and provides broad powers to the president. The president, approved by referendum for a 7-year term, is also Secretary General of the Ba'ath Party and leader of the National Progressive Front, which is a coalition of 10 political parties authorized by the regime. The president has the right to appoint ministers, to declare war and states of emergency, to issue laws (which, except in the case of emergency, require ratification by the People's Council), to declare amnesty, to amend the constitution, and to appoint civil servants and military personnel. The Emergency Law, which effectively suspends most constitutional protections for Syrians, has been in effect since 1963.

The National Progressive Front also acts as a forum in which economic policies are debated and the country's political orientation is determined. However, because of Ba'ath Party dominance, the National Progressive Front has traditionally exercised little independent power.

The Syrian constitution of 1973 requires that the president be Muslim but does not make Islam the state religion. Islamic jurisprudence, however, is required to be a main source of legislation. The judicial system in Syria is an amalgam of Ottoman, French, and Islamic laws, with three levels of courts: courts of first instance, courts of appeals, and the constitutional court, the highest tribunal. In addition, religious courts handle questions of personal and family law.

The Ba'ath Party emphasizes socialism and secular Arabism. Although Ba'ath Party doctrine seeks to build pan-Arab rather than ethnic identity, ethnic, religious, and regional allegiances remain important in Syria.

Members of President Asad's own minority sect, the Alawis, hold most of the important military and security positions, while Sunnis (in 2006) controlled ten of 14 positions on the powerful Ba'ath Party Regional Command. In recent years there has been a gradual decline in the party's preeminence. The party also is heavily influenced by the security services and the military, the latter of which consumes a large share of Syria's economic resources.

Syria is divided administratively into 14 provinces, one of which is Damascus. A governor for each province is appointed by the president. The governor is assisted by an elected provincial council.

Principal Government Officials

Pres., **Bashar al-ASAD**
Vice Pres., **Farouk al-SHARA**
Vice Pres., **Najah al-ATTAR**
Prime Min., **Wael al-HALQI**
Dep. Prime Min., **Fahd Jasim al-FURAYJ,** *Lt. Gen.*
Dep. Prime Min., **Walid al-MUALEM**
Dep. Prime Min. for Economic Affairs, **Qadri JAMIL**
Dep. Prime Min. for Services Affairs, **Umar Ibrahim GHALAWANJI**
Min. of Agriculture, **Subhi Ahmad al-ABDALLAH**
Min. of Culture, **Lubanah MUSHAWEH**
Min. of Defense, **Fahd Jasim al-FURAYJ,** *Lt. Gen.*
Min. of Domestic Trade & Consumer Protection, **Qadri JAMIL**
Min. of Economy & Foreign Trade, **Muhammad Zafir MAHABIK**
Min. of Education, **Hazwan al-WAZZ**
Min. of Electricity, **Imad Muhammad Deeb KHAMIS**
Min. of Finance, **Muhammad al-JULAYLATI**
Min. of Foreign & Expatriate Affairs, **Walid al-MUALEM**
Min. of Health, **Wael Nader al-HALAQI**

Min. of Higher Education, **Muhammad Yahya MU'ALLA**
Min. of Housing & Urban Development, **Safwan al-ASSAF**
Min. of Industry, **Fuad Shukri KURDI**
Min. of Information, **Umran Ahid al-ZA'BI**
Min. of the Interior, **Muhammad Ibrahim al-SHA'AR**
Min. of Justice, **Radwan HABIB**
Min. of Local Admin., **Umar Ibrahim GHALAWANJI**
Min. of Petroleum & Mineral Wealth, **Said Ma'za HANIDI**
Min. of Presidential Affairs, **Mansur Fadlallah AZZAM**
Min. of Public Works, **Yasser al-SIBA'I**
Min. of Religious Endowments, **Muhammad Abd al-Sattar al-SAYYID**
Min. of Social Affairs & Labor, **Jasim Muhammad ZAKARIYA**
Min. of Telecommunication & Technology, **Imad SABBUNI**
Min. of Tourism, **Hala Muhammad al-NASER**
Min. of Transport, **Mahmoud Ibrahim SAID**
Min. of Water Resources, **Bassam HANNA**
Min. of State, **Husayn Mahmoud FARZAT**
Min. of State, **Abdallah Khalil HUSAYN**
Min. of State, **Najm al-Din KHRIIT**
Min. of State, **Muhammad Turki al-SAYYID**
Min. of State, **Jamal Shaaban SHAHEEN**
Min. of State, **Joseph SUWAYD**
Min. of State for Environmental Affairs, **Nazira Farah SARKIS**
Min. of State for National Reconciliation Affairs, **Ali HAYDAR**
Governor, Central Bank, **Adib MAYALA**
Ambassador to the US,
Permanent Representative to the UN, New York, **Bashar al-JAFARI**

Syria maintains an **embassy** in the United States at 2215 Wyoming Avenue, NW, Washington, DC 20008 (tel. 202-232-6313; fax 202-234-9548). Consular section hours are 9:15 a.m.-3:15 p.m., Monday-Friday. Syria also has three honorary consuls: 1022 Wirt Rd., Suite 300, Houston, TX 77055 (tel. 713-622-8860; fax 713-622-8872); 3 San Joaquin Plaza, #190, Newport Beach, CA 92660 (tel. 949-640-9888; fax 949-640-9292); and P.O. Box 2392, Birmingham, MI 48012-2392 (tel. 248-519-2496; fax 248-519-2399).

POLITICAL CONDITIONS

Officially, Syria is a republic. In reality, however, it is an authoritarian regime that exhibits only the forms of a democratic system. Although citizens ostensibly vote for the president and members of parliament, they do not have the right to change their government. The late President Hafiz Al-Asad was confirmed by unopposed referenda five times. His son, Bashar Al-Asad, also was confirmed by an unopposed referendum in July 2000 and May 2007. The President and his senior aides, particularly those in the military and security services, ultimately make most basic decisions in political and economic life, with a very limited degree of public accountability. Political opposition to the President is not tolerated. Syria has been under a state of emergency since 1963. Syrian governments have justified martial law by the state of war that continues to exist with Israel and by continuing threats posed by terrorist groups.

The Asad regime (little has changed since Bashar Al-Asad succeeded his father) has held power longer than any other Syrian government since independence; its survival is due partly to a strong desire for stability and the regime's success in giving groups such as religious minorities and peasant farmers a stake in society. The expansion of the government bureaucracy has also created a large class loyal to the regime. The President's continuing strength is due also to the army's continued loyalty and the effectiveness of Syria's large internal security apparatus. The leadership of both is comprised largely of members of Asad's own Alawi sect. The several main branches of the security services operate independently of each other and outside of the legal system. Each continues to be responsible for human rights violations.

All three branches of government are guided by the views of the Ba'ath Party, whose primacy in state institutions is assured by the constitution. The Ba'ath platform is proclaimed succinctly in the party's slogan: "Unity, freedom, and socialism." The party has traditionally been considered both socialist, advocating state ownership of the means of industrial production and the redistribution of agricultural land, and revolutionary, dedicated to carrying a socialist revolution to every part of the Arab world. Founded by Michel 'Aflaq, a Syrian Christian and Salah al-Din Al-Bitar, a Syrian Sunni, the Ba'ath Party embraces secularism and has attracted supporters of all faiths in many Arab countries, especially Iraq, Jordan, and Lebanon. Since August 1990, however, the party has tended to de-emphasize socialism and to stress both pan-Arab unity and the need for gradual reform of the Syrian economy.

Nine smaller political parties are permitted to exist and, along with the Ba'ath Party, make up the National Progressive Front (NPF), a grouping of parties that represents the sole framework of legal political party participation for citizens. Created to give the appearance of a multi-party system, the NPF is dominated by the Ba'ath Party and does not change the essentially one-party character of the political system. Non-Ba'ath parties included in the NPF represent small political groupings of a few hundred members each and conform strictly to Ba'ath Party and government policies. There were reports in 2005, in the wake of the June Ba'ath Party Congress, that the government was considering legislation to permit the formation of new political parties and the legalization of parties previously banned. These changes have not taken place. In addition, some 15 small independent parties outside the NPF operate without government sanction.

The Ba'ath Party dominates the parliament, which is known as the People's Council. With members elected every 4 years, the Council has no independent authority. The executive branch retains ultimate control over the legislative process, although parliamentarians may criticize policies and modify draft laws; according to the constitution and its bylaws, a group of 10 parliamentarians can propose legislation. During 2001, two independent members of parliament, Ma'mun al-Humsy and Riad Seif, who had advocated political reforms, were stripped of their parliamentary immunity and tried and convicted of charges of "attempting to illegally change the constitution." Seif was released from prison in early 2006, but was detained and sentenced to prison again in January 2008.

The government has allowed independent non-NPF candidates to run for a limited allotment of seats in the 250-member People's Council. Following the April 22-23, 2007 parliamentary elections, the NPF strengthened its hold on parliament, with the number of non-NPF deputies shrinking from 83 to 80, ensuring a permanent absolute majority for the Ba'ath Party-dominated NPF.

There was a surge of interest in political reform after Bashar al-Asad assumed power in 2000. Human rights activists and other civil society advocates, as well as some parliamentarians, became more outspoken during a period referred to as "Damascus Spring" (July 2000-February 2001). Asad also made a series of appointments of reform-minded advisors to formal and less formal positions, and included a number of similarly oriented individuals in his cabinet. The 2001 arrest and long-term detention of the two reformist parliamentarians and the apparent marginalizing of some of the reformist advisors in the past 10 years, indicate that the pace of any political reform in Syria is likely to be much slower than the short-lived Damascus Spring promised. A crackdown on civil society in 2005, in the wake of Syria's withdrawal from Lebanon, and again in the late winter and spring of 2006, coupled with the early-2011 mobilization of security forces to prevent protests and demonstrations have reinforced the perception that any steps toward political reform were likely to be halting and piecemeal at best.

In October 2008, 12 members of the Damascus Declaration National Council were sentenced to 2-1/2 years in prison. The Damascus Declaration is a civil society reform document written in 2005 and signed by a confederation of opposition parties and individual activists who seek to work with the government to ensure greater civil liberties and democratic political reform. The government has shown no hesitation in suppressing those who advocate for human, legal, or minority rights.

Although Internet access is increasing and non-political private media is slowly being introduced, the government continues to ban numerous newspaper and news journal publications from circulating in the country, including Al-Hayat and Al-Sharq Al-Auwsat (both Saudi owned). It has recently allowed access to previously blocked websites, including YouTube.com, Amazon.com, and Facebook.com, but since many computer users in Syria had already learned to circumvent these restrictions, the move is largely cosmetic.

ECONOMY

The **economy of Syria** is based on agriculture, oil, industry and services. Its GDP per capita expanded 80% in the 1960s reaching a peak of 336% of total growth during the 1970s. This proved unsustainable for Syria and the economy shrank by 33% during the 1980s. However the GDP per capita registered a very modest total growth of 12% (1.1% per year on average) during the 1990s due to successful diversification. More recently, the International Monetary Fund (IMF) projected real GDP growth at 3.9% in 2009 from close to 6% in 2008. The two main pillars of the Syrian economy used to be agriculture and oil, which together accounted for about one-half of GDP. Agriculture, for instance, accounted for about 25% of GDP and employed 25% of the total labor force. However, poor climatic conditions and severe drought badly affected the agricultural sector, thus reducing its share in the economy to about 17% of 2008 GDP, down from 20.4% in 2007, according to preliminary data from the Central Bureau of Statistics. On the other hand, higher crude oil prices countered declining oil production and led to higher budgetary and export receipts.

Since the out break of the Syrian civil war, the Syrian economy has been hit by massive economic sanctions restricting trade with the Arab League, Australia, Canada, the European Union, (as well as the European countries of Albania, Iceland, Liechtenstein, Macedonia, Moldova, Montenegro, Norway, Serbia, and Switzerland) Georgia, Japan, Turkey, and the United States. These sanctions and the instability associated with the civil war have reversed previous growth in the Syrian economy to a state of decline for the years 2011 and . According to the UN, total economic damages of the Syrian civil war are estimated at $143 billion as of late 2013

Syria is a middle-income, developing country with an economy based on agriculture, oil, industry, and tourism. However, Syria's economy faces serious challenges and impediments to growth, including: a large and poorly performing public sector; declining rates of oil production; widening non-oil deficit; widescale corruption; weak financial and capital markets; and high rates of unemployment tied to a high population growth rate. In addition, Syria currently is subject to U.S. economic sanctions under the Syria Accountability Act, which prohibits or restricts the export and re-export of most U.S. products to Syria.

As a result of an inefficient and corrupt centrally planned economy, Syria has low rates of investment, and low levels of industrial and agricultural productivity. The IMF projected real GDP growth at 3.9% in 2009 from close to 6% in 2008. The two main pillars of the Syrian economy used to be agriculture and oil, which together accounted for about one-half of GDP. Agriculture, for instance, accounted for about 25% of GDP and employed 25% of the total labor force.

However, poor climatic conditions and severe drought badly affected the agricultural sector, thus reducing its share in the economy to about 17% of 2008 GDP, down from 20.4% in 2007, according to preliminary data from the Central Bureau of Statistics. On the other hand, higher crude oil prices countered declining oil production and led to higher budgetary and export receipts.

Water and energy are among the most pervasive issues facing the agriculture sector. Another difficulty the agricultural sector suffered from is the government's decision to liberalize the prices of fertilizers, which have increased between 100% and 400%. Drought was an alarming problem in 2008; however, the drought situation slightly improved in 2009. Wheat and barley production about doubled in 2009 compared to 2008. In spite of that, the livelihoods of up to 1 million agricultural workers have been threatened. In response, the UN launched an emergency appeal for $20.2 million. Wheat has been one of the crops most affected, and for the first time in 2 decades Syria has moved from being a net exporter of wheat to a net importer.

Damascus has implemented modest economic reforms in the past few years, including cutting lending interest rates; opening private banks; consolidating all of the multiple exchange rates; raising prices on some subsidized items, most notably diesel, other oil derivatives, and fertilizers; and establishing the Damascus Stock Exchange, which began operations in 2009. In May 2008, Damascus raised the price of subsidized diesel by 357%, and in January 2009 the price of fuel oil was raised by 50%. In addition, President Asad signed legislative decrees to encourage corporate ownership reform and allowed the Central Bank to issue Treasury bills and bonds for government debt. Despite these reforms, the economy remains highly controlled by the government. Long-run economic constraints include declining oil production, high unemployment and inflation rates, rising budget deficits, increasing pressure on water supplies caused by heavy use in agriculture, increasing demand for electricity, rapid population growth, industrial expansion, and water pollution.

The government hopes to attract new investment in the tourism, natural gas, and service sectors to diversify its economy and reduce its dependence on oil and agriculture. The government has begun to institute economic reforms aimed at liberalizing most markets, but reform thus far has been slow and ad hoc. For ideological reasons, privatization of government enterprises is still not widespread, but is in its initial stage for port operations, power generation, and air transport. Most sectors are open for private investment except for cotton mills, land telecommunications, and bottled water.

The Bashar al-Asad government started its reform efforts by changing the regulatory environment in the financial sector, including the introduction of private banks and the opening of a stock exchange in March 2009. In 2001, Syria legalized private banking and the sector, while still nascent, has been growing. As of January 2010, 13 private banks had opened, including two Islamic banks. Syria has taken gradual steps to loosen controls over foreign exchange. In 2003, the government canceled a law that criminalized private sector use of foreign currencies, and in 2005 it issued legislation that allowed licensed private banks to sell specific amounts of foreign currency to Syrian citizens under certain circumstances and to the private sector to finance imports. In October 2009, the Syrian Government further loosened its restrictions on foreign currency transfers by allowing Syrians travelling abroad to withdraw the equivalent of up to U.S. $10,000 from their Syrian Pound accounts. In practice, the decision allows local banks to open accounts of a maximum of U.S. $10,000 that their clients can use for their international payment cards. The holders of these accounts will be able to withdraw up to U.S. $10,000 per month while travelling abroad.

To attract investment and to ease access to credit, the government allowed investors in 2007 to receive loans and other credit instruments from foreign banks, and to repay the loans and any

For additional analytical, business and investment opportunities information,
please contact Global Investment & Business Center, USA
at (703) 370-8082. Fax: (703) 370-8083. E-mail: ibpusa3@gmail.com
Global Business and Investment Info Databank - www.ibpus.com

accrued interest through local banks using project proceeds. In February 2008, the government permitted investors to receive loans in foreign currencies from local private banks to finance capital investment. Syria's exchange rate is fixed, and the government maintains two official rates--one rate on which the budget and the value of imports, customs, and other official transactions are based, and a second set by the Central Bank on a daily basis that covers all other financial transactions. The government passed a law in 2006 which permits the operation of private money exchange companies. However, a small black market for foreign currency is still active.

Given the policies adopted from the 1960s through the late 1980s, which included nationalization of companies and private assets, Syria failed to join an increasingly interconnected global economy. Syria withdrew from the General Agreement on Tariffs and Trade (GATT) in 1951 because of Israel's accession. It is not a member of the World Trade Organization (WTO), although it submitted a request to begin the accession process in 2001 and again in 2004. Syria is developing regional free trade agreements. As of January 1, 2005, the Greater Arab Free Trade Agreement (GAFTA) came into effect and customs duties were eliminated between Syria and all other members of GAFTA. Syria's free trade agreement with Turkey came into force in January 2007. Syria is a signatory to free trade agreements with Jordan, India, Belarus, and Slovakia. In 2004 Syria and the European Union initialed an Association Agreement; the ratification process had not been finalized as of March 2011. Although Syria claims a recent boom in non-oil exports, its trade numbers are notoriously inaccurate and out-of-date. Syria's main exports include crude oil, refined products, rock phosphate, raw cotton, clothing, fruits and vegetables, and spices. The bulk of Syrian imports are raw materials essential for industry, petroleum products, vehicles, agricultural equipment, and heavy machinery. Earnings from oil exports as well as remittances from Syrian workers are the government's most important sources of foreign exchange.

Syria has produced heavy-grade oil from fields located in the northeast since the late 1960s. In the early 1980s, light-grade, low-sulphur oil was discovered near Dayr al-Zur in eastern Syria. Syria's rate of oil production has been decreasing steadily, from a peak close to 610,000 barrels per day (bpd) in 1995 down to approximately 379,000 bpd in 2008. In parallel, Syria's oil reserves are being gradually depleted and reached 2.5 billion barrels in January 2009. Recent developments have helped revitalize the energy sector, including new discoveries and the successful development of its hydrocarbon reserves. According to the 2009 Syria Report of the Oxford Business Group, the oil sector accounted for 23% of government revenues, 20% of exports, and 22% of GDP in 2008. Experts generally agree that Syria will become a net importer of petroleum by the end of the next decade. Syria exported roughly 150,000 bpd in 2008, and oil still accounts for a majority of the country's export income. Syria also produces about 22 million cubic meters of gas per day, with estimated reserves around 240 billion cubic meters or 8.5 trillion cubic feet. While the government has begun to work with international energy companies in the hopes of eventually becoming a gas exporter, all gas currently produced is consumed domestically. Demand for electricity is growing at a rate of about 10% per year and is barely met by current generation capacity, and ongoing and planned projects are not expected to be sufficient to meet future demand.

Some basic commodities, such as bread, continue to be heavily subsidized, and social services are provided for nominal charges. The subsidies are becoming harder to sustain as the gap between consumption and production continues to increase. Syria has a population of approximately 21 million people, and Syrian Government figures place the population growth rate at 2.37%, with 65% of the population under the age of 35 and more than 40% under the age of 15. Approximately 200,000 people enter the labor market every year. According to Syrian Government statistics, the unemployment rate in 2009 was 12.6%; however, more accurate independent sources placed it closer to 20%. Government and public sector employees constitute about 30% of the total labor force and are paid very low salaries and wages. Government officials acknowledge that the economy is not growing at a pace sufficient to create enough new jobs annually to match population growth. The UN Development Program announced in 2005 that 30% of the Syrian population lives in poverty and 11.4% live below the subsistence level.

Syria has made progress in easing its heavy foreign debt burden through bilateral rescheduling deals with its key creditors in Europe, most importantly Russia, Germany, and France. Syria has also settled its debt with Iran and the World Bank. In December 2004, Syria and Poland reached an agreement by which Syria would pay $27 million out of the total $261.7 million debt. In January 2005, Russia forgave 73% of Syria's $14.5 billion long-outstanding debt and in June 2008, Russia's parliament ratified the agreement. In 2007, Syria and Romania reached an agreement by which Syria will pay 35% of the $118.1 million debt. In May 2008, Syria settled all the debt it owed to the Czech Republic and Slovakia.

NATIONAL SECURITY

President Bashar Al-Asad is commander in chief of the Syrian armed forces, comprised of some 400,000 troops upon mobilization. The military is a conscripted force; males serve 18 months in the military upon reaching the age of 18, though exemptions do exist. Some 17,000 Syrian soldiers formerly deployed in Lebanon were withdrawn to Syria in 2005 in accordance with UNSCR 1559.

Syria's military remains one of the largest in the region, although the breakup of the Soviet Union--long the principal source of training, material, and credit for the Syrian forces--slowed Syria's ability to acquire modern military equipment. Syria received significant financial aid from Gulf Arab states in the 1990s as a result of its participation in the first Gulf War, with a sizable portion of these funds earmarked for military spending. Besides sustaining its conventional forces, Syria seeks to develop its weapons of mass destruction (WMD) capability, including chemical munitions and delivery systems.

In September 2007 Israeli warplanes attacked a purported nuclear facility in Syria. Investigation by the International Atomic Energy Agency (IAEA) discovered particles of enriched uranium at the site, with a low probability they were introduced by the missiles used to attack the facility. As of March 2011, the IAEA continued to investigate the issue with only limited cooperation from the Syrian Government.

FOREIGN RELATIONS

Ensuring regime survival, increasing influence among its Arab neighbors, and achieving a comprehensive Arab-Israeli peace settlement, which includes the return of the Golan Heights, are the primary goals of President Asad's foreign policy.

Relations with Other Arab Countries
Syria reestablished full diplomatic relations with Egypt in 1989. In the 1990-91 Gulf War, Syria joined other Arab states in the U.S.-led multinational coalition against Iraq. In 1998, Syria began a slow rapprochement with Iraq, driven primarily by economic needs. Syria continues to play an active pan-Arab role and has emerged from its relative isolation following the Hariri assassination, to assert its influence regionally and expand diplomatic relations with Europe, Latin America, and China.

Though it voted in favor of UNSCR 1441 in 2002, Syria was against coalition military action in Iraq in 2003. However, the Syrian Government accepted UNSCR 1483 (after being absent for the actual vote), which lifted sanctions on Iraq and established a framework to assist the Iraqi people in determining their political future and rebuilding their economy. Syria also voted for UNSCR 1511, which called for greater international involvement in Iraq and addressed the transfer of sovereignty from the U.S.-led coalition. Since the transfer of sovereignty in Iraq on June 28, 2004, Syria extended qualified support to the Iraqi Government and pledged to cooperate in the areas of border security, repatriation of Iraqi assets, and eventual restoration of formal diplomatic relations.

While Syria has taken some steps to tighten controls along the Syria-Iraq border, Syria remains one of the primary transit points for foreign fighters entering Iraq. Consequently, relations between Syria and the Iraqi Government remained strained. Following a series of visits between high-level officials from both governments--including Foreign Minister Mu'allim's November 2006 visit to Baghdad and Iraqi President Talabani's subsequent visit to Damascus--formal diplomatic relations were established in December 2006. That same month, the Ministers of Interior from both countries signed a Memorandum of Security Understanding aimed at improving border security and combating terrorism and crime. However, both nations withdrew their ambassadors following August 2009 bombings in Baghdad. While Iraq continues to call for more action on the part of Syria to control its border and to prevent Iraqi and Arab elements residing in--or transiting--Syria from contributing financially, politically, or militarily to the insurgency in Iraq, relations have improved. Both countries returned their ambassadors in 2010.

Up to an estimated 1 million Iraqi refugees live in Syria since the 2003 U.S.-led intervention in Iraq, of which more than 224,000 have officially registered with the UN High Commissioner for Refugees. The U.S. remains the largest single contributor to UN and non-governmental organization (NGO) efforts to assist Iraqi refugees in the region. Total U.S. support region-wide in 2008 approached $400 million--up from $171 million in 2007. By the end of September 2008, 13,823 Iraqi refugees had arrived for resettlement in the United States, surpassing the target of 12,000. This figure represents a more than eightfold increase over the 1,608 Iraqis admitted in the previous year. Most of the Iraqis who arrived in the U.S.--over 9,000--came from Jordan and Syria, the two countries hosting the most Iraqi refugees. Smaller groups came from Turkey, Lebanon, and Egypt. The U.S. remains committed to assisting Iraqi refugees and plans to continue to help meet the needs of Iraq's displaced population. Between October 2008 and September 2009 the U.S. pledged to admit a minimum of 17,000 of the most vulnerable Iraqis for resettlement in the U.S. through the U.S. Refugee Admissions Program.

Involvement in Lebanon
Syria has played an important role in Lebanon by virtue of its history, size, power, and economy. Lebanon was part of post-Ottoman Syria until 1926. The presence of Syrian troops in Lebanon dated to 1976, when President Hafiz al-Asad intervened in the Lebanese civil war on behalf of Maronite Christians. Following the 1982 Israeli invasion of Lebanon, Syrian and Israeli forces clashed in eastern Lebanon. However, Syrian opposition blocked implementation of the May 17, 1983, Lebanese-Israeli accord on the withdrawal of Israeli forces from Lebanon.

In 1989, Syria endorsed the Charter of National Reconciliation, or "Taif Accord," a comprehensive plan for ending the Lebanese conflict negotiated under the auspices of Saudi Arabia, Algeria, and Morocco. In May 1991, Lebanon and Syria signed the treaty of brotherhood, cooperation, and coordination called for in the Taif Accord.

According to the U.S. interpretation of the Taif Accord, Syria and Lebanon were to have decided on the redeployment of Syrian forces from Beirut and other coastal areas of Lebanon by September 1992. Israeli occupation of Lebanon until May 2000, the breakdown of peace negotiations between Syria and Israel that same year, and intensifying Arab/Israeli tensions since the start of the second Palestinian uprising in September 2000 helped delay full implementation of the Taif Accords.

For additional analytical, business and investment opportunities information,
please contact Global Investment & Business Center, USA
at (703) 370-8082. Fax: (703) 370-8083. E-mail: ibpusa3@gmail.com
Global Business and Investment Info Databank - www.ibpus.com

The United Nations declared that Israel's May 2000 withdrawal from southern Lebanon fulfilled the requirements of UN Security Council Resolution 425. However, Syria and Lebanon claimed that UNSCR 425 had not been fully implemented because Israel did not withdraw from an area of the Golan Heights called Sheba Farms, which had been occupied by Israel in 1967, and which Syria now claimed was part of Lebanon. The United Nations does not recognize this claim. However, Hizballah uses it to justify attacks against Israeli forces in that region. The danger of Hizballah's tactics was highlighted when Hizballah's abduction of two Israeli soldiers on July 12, 2006 sparked a 34-day conflict in Lebanon. After the conflict, the passing of UNSCR 1701 authorized the enhancement of the UN Interim Force in Lebanon (UNIFIL). Before the conflict, UNIFIL authorized a presence of 2,000 troops in southern Lebanon; post-conflict, this ceiling was raised to 15,000. UNIFIL is tasked with ensuring peace and security along the frontier and overseeing the return of effective Lebanese government and military authority throughout the border region.

Until its withdrawal in April 2005, Syria maintained approximately 17,000 troops in Lebanon. A September 2004 vote by Lebanon's Chamber of Deputies to amend the constitution to extend Lebanese President Lahoud's term in office by 3 years amplified the question of Lebanese sovereignty and the continuing Syrian presence. The vote was clearly taken under Syrian pressure, exercised in part through Syria's military intelligence service, whose chief in Lebanon had acted as a virtual proconsul for many years. The UN Security Council expressed its concern over the situation by passing Resolution 1559, which called for the withdrawal of all remaining foreign forces from Lebanon, disbanding and disarmament of all Lebanese and non-Lebanese militias in accordance with the Taif Accord, the deployment of the Lebanese Armed Forces throughout the country, and a free and fair electoral process in the presidential election.

Former Prime Minister Rafiq Hariri and 19 others were assassinated in Beirut by a car bomb on February 14, 2005. The assassination spurred massive protests in Beirut and international pressure that led to the withdrawal of the remaining Syrian military troops from Lebanon on April 26, 2005. Rafiq Hariri's assassination was just one of a number of attacks that targeted high-profile Lebanese critics of Syria. The UN International Independent Investigative Commission (UNIIIC) investigated Hariri's assassination until the Special Tribunal for Lebanon (STL) was established by the UN Security Council. The STL began operating in March 2009, continuing UNIIIC's work with an aim toward prosecuting the individuals suspected of being behind the attacks.

Syrian-Lebanese relations have improved since 2008 when, in response to French and Saudi engagement with Syria, Damascus recognized Lebanon's sovereignty and the two countries agreed to exchange ambassadors. Syria sent Ali Abdul Karim Ali to Beirut as its ambassador to Lebanon in May 2009. Following his election in November 2009, Prime Minister Saad Hariri, son of the slain leader, traveled to Damascus for discussions with President Asad. During the visit, the two countries agreed to demarcate their border for the first time. As of March 2011, the border had yet to be demarcated.

Syrian relations with Prime Minister Saad Hariri became strained due to his support for the STL and Syria's continued support of Hizballah. Hizballah and its parliamentary allies engineered the fall of the Hariri government on January 12, 2011 when they resigned from the cabinet en masse, triggering a constitutional crisis. The new Prime Minister-designate, Najib Mikati, has strong connections to the Syrian regime.

The United States supports a sovereign, independent Lebanon, free of all foreign forces, and believes that the best interests of both Lebanon and Syria are served by a positive and constructive relationship based upon principles of mutual respect and non-intervention between two neighboring sovereign and independent states. The United States calls for Syrian non-

For additional analytical, business and investment opportunities information,
please contact Global Investment & Business Center, USA
at (703) 370-8082. Fax: (703) 370-8083. E-mail: ibpusa3@gmail.com
Global Business and Investment Info Databank - www.ibpus.com

interference in Lebanon, consistent with UNSCR 1559 and 1701.

Arab-Israeli Relations

Syria was an active belligerent in the 1967 Arab-Israeli War, which resulted in Israel's occupation of the Golan Heights and the city of Quneitra. Following the October 1973 Arab-Israeli War, which left Israel in occupation of additional Syrian territory, Syria accepted UN Security Council Resolution 338, which signaled an implicit acceptance of Resolution 242. Resolution 242, which became the basis for the peace process negotiations begun in Madrid in 1981, calls for a just and lasting Middle East peace to include withdrawal of Israeli armed forces from territories occupied in 1967; termination of the state of belligerency; and acknowledgment of the sovereignty, territorial integrity, and political independence of all regional states and of their right to live in peace within secure and recognized boundaries.

As a result of the mediation efforts of then U.S. Secretary of State Henry Kissinger, Syria and Israel concluded a disengagement agreement in May 1974, enabling Syria to recover territory lost in the October war and part of the Golan Heights occupied by Israel since 1967, including Quneitra. The two sides have effectively implemented the agreement, which is monitored by UN forces.

In December 1981, the Israeli Knesset voted to extend Israeli law to the part of the Golan Heights over which Israel retained control. The UN Security Council subsequently passed a resolution calling on Israel to rescind this measure. Syria participated in the Middle East Peace Conference in Madrid in October 1991. Negotiations were conducted intermittently through the 1990s, and came very close to succeeding. However, the parties were unable to come to an agreement over Syria's nonnegotiable demand that Israel withdraw to the positions it held on June 4, 1967. The peace process collapsed following the outbreak of the second Palestinian (Intifada) uprising in September 2000, though Syria continues to call for a comprehensive settlement based on UN Security Council Resolutions 242 and 338, and the land-for-peace formula adopted at the 1991 Madrid conference.

Tensions between Israel and Syria increased as the second Intifada dragged on, primarily as a result of Syria's unwillingness to stop giving sanctuary to Palestinian terrorist groups conducting operations against Israel. In October 2003, following a suicide bombing carried out by a member of Palestinian Islamic Jihad in Haifa that killed 20 Israeli citizens, Israeli Defense Forces attacked a suspected Palestinian terrorist training camp 15 kilometers north of Damascus. This was the first such Israeli attack deep inside Syrian territory since the 1973 war.

During the summer of 2006 tensions again heightened due to Israeli fighter jets buzzing President Asad's summer castle in response to Syria's support for the Palestinian group Hamas, Syria's support of Hizballah during the July-August 2006 conflict in Lebanon, and the rearming of Hizballah in violation of UN Resolution 1701. Rumors of negotiations between the Israeli and Syrian Governments were initially discounted by both Israel and Syria, with spokespersons for both countries indicating that any such talks were not officially sanctioned. However, the rumors were confirmed in early 2008 when it was announced that indirect talks facilitated by Turkey were taking place. The talks continued until December 2008 when Syria withdrew in response to Israel's shelling of the Gaza Strip.

Membership in International Organizations

Syria is a member of the Arab Bank for Economic Development in Africa, Arab Fund for Economic and Social Development, Arab Common Market, Arab League, Arab Monetary Fund, Council of Arab Economic Unity, Customs Cooperation Council, Economic and Social Commission for Western Asia, Food and Agricultural Organization, Group of 24, Group of 77, International Atomic Energy Agency, International Bank for Reconstruction and Development,

International Civil Aviation Organization, International Chamber of Commerce, International Development Association, Islamic Development Bank, International Fund for Agricultural Development, International Finance Corporation, International Labor Organization, International Monetary Fund, International Maritime Organization, INTERPOL, International Olympic Committee, International Organization for Standardization, International Telecommunication Union, International Federation of Red Cross and Red Crescent Societies, Non-Aligned Movement, Organization of Arab Petroleum Exporting Countries, Organization of the Islamic Conference, United Nations, UN Conference on Trade and Development, UN Industrial Development Organization, UN Relief and Works Agency for Palestine Refugees in the Near East, Universal Postal Union, World Federation of Trade Unions, World Health Organization, World Meteorological Organization, and World Tourism Organization.

Syria's 2-year term as a nonpermanent member of the UN Security Council ended in December 2003.

U.S.-SYRIAN RELATIONS

U.S.-SYRIA RELATIONS

The United States established diplomatic relations with Syria in 1944 following U.S. determination that Syria had achieved effective independence from a French-administered mandate. Syria severed diplomatic relations with the United States in 1967 in the wake of the Arab-Israeli War. Relations were reestablished in 1974. Syria has been on the U.S. list of state sponsors of terrorism since the list's inception in 1979. Because of its continuing support and safe haven for terrorist organizations, Syria is subject to legislatively mandated penalties, including export sanctions under the Syrian Accountability Act and ineligibility to receive most forms of U.S. aid or to purchase U.S. military equipment.

During 1990-2001, the United States and Syria cooperated to a degree on some regional issues, but relations worsened from 2003 to early 2009. Issues of U.S. concern included the Syrian Government's failure to prevent Syria from becoming a major transit point for foreign fighters entering Iraq, its refusal to deport from Syria former Saddam Hussein regime elements supporting the insurgency in Iraq, its interference in Lebanese affairs, its protection of the leadership of Palestinian rejectionist groups in Damascus, its human rights record, and its pursuit of weapons of mass destruction. In early 2009, the United States began to review its Syria policy in light of changes in the country and the region, leading to an effort to engage with Syria to find areas of mutual interest, reduce regional tensions, and promote Middle East peace.

In March 2011, a group of Syrian students was arrested in the southern city of Dara'a for writing political graffiti on walls that said, "Down with the regime." The government's brutal response to the Syrian people's call for freedom and dignity sparked nation-wide demonstrations and escalating tensions, which descended into an armed conflict that has lasted three years, taken more than 146,000 lives, and displaced nearly 9 million people within the country and beyond its borders. The U.S. government has repeatedly called for President Bashar al-Assad to step aside and has led the international community's efforts to work towards a negotiated political solution to the conflict.

U.S. Assistance to Syria

The United States remains deeply concerned by the humanitarian crisis caused by the violence in Syria and is providing assistance to help internally displaced persons and refugees fleeing Syria. We also support the Syrian people's aspirations for a democratic, inclusive, and unified Syria and are providing direct, non-lethal support to the moderate Syrian opposition.

Syria–United States relations are currently non-existent. Relations have been suspended since 2012 due to the Syrian Civil War. Priority issues between the two states include the Arab–Israeli conflict, the Golan Heights annexation, and the Iraq War. According to the 2012 U.S. Global Leadership Report, through a poll conducted during the Syrian civil war, 29% of Syrians approve of U.S. leadership, with 40% disapproving and 31% uncertain

On 29 March 2017, during the Presidency of Donald Trump the United States Secretary of State Rex Tillerson expressed that the longer term status of president Bashar al-Assad is to be "decided by the Syrian people". This appears as a policy shift, since under president Barack Obama's administration, the US made the departure of Assad a key policy aim. On March 30, 2017, United States Ambassador to the United Nations Nikki Haley reaffirmed that the priority of the United States policy concerning Bashar Assad is to no longer force him out of power.

On 7 April 2017 US missiles destroyed Shayrat Air Base in Homs Governorate which US military claimed to be the base for the aircraft that carried out the Khan Shaykhun chemical attack three days earlier

Bilateral Economic Relations

Syria has been subject to U.S. economic sanctions since 2004 under the Syria Accountability Act, which prohibits or restricts the export and re-export of most U.S. products to Syria. Sanctions in August 2008 prohibited the export of U.S. services to Syrian and banned U.S. persons from involvement in the Syrian petroleum sector, including a prohibition on importing Syrian petroleum products. In response to regime brutality against peaceful protesters beginning in 2011, the U.S. Government imposed additional sanctions beginning in April 2011, designating those complicit in human rights abuses or supporting the Assad regime.

Syria's Membership in International Organizations

Syria and the United States belong to a number of the same international organizations, including the United Nations, International Monetary Fund, and World Bank. Syria also is an observer to the World Trade Organization.

Bilateral Representation

The U.S. Special Envoy to Syria is Michael Ratney; other principal embassy officials are listed in the Department's **Key Officers List**. The U.S. Embassy in Damascus suspended its operations in February 2012. The Government of the Czech Republic, acting through its Embassy in Damascus, serves as protecting power for U.S. interests in Syria.

Syria maintains an embassy in the United States at 2215 Wyoming Avenue, NW, Washington, DC 20008 (tel. 202-232-6313). On March 18, 2014, the State Department notified the Syrian Embassy that their operations must be suspended immediately and that all personnel at the Embassy who are not U.S. citizens or lawful permanent residents must depart by March 31, 2014. After this date of ordered departure, the United States will no longer regard accredited Embassy personnel as entitled to any of the diplomatic privileges, immunities, or protections. This notification also requires the suspension of operations of Syria's honorary consulates in Troy, Michigan and Houston, Texas.

TRAVEL AND BUSINESS INFORMATION

The U.S. Department of State's Consular Information Program advises Americans traveling and residing abroad through Country Specific Information, Travel Alerts, and Travel Warnings. **Country Specific Information** exists for all countries and includes information on entry and exit requirements, currency regulations, health conditions, safety and security, crime, political disturbances, and the addresses of the U.S. embassies and consulates abroad. **Travel Alerts** are issued to disseminate information quickly about terrorist threats and other relatively short-term conditions overseas that pose significant risks to the security of American travelers. **Travel Warnings** are issued when the State Department recommends that Americans avoid travel to a certain country because the situation is dangerous or unstable.

For the latest security information, Americans living and traveling abroad should regularly monitor the Department's Bureau of Consular Affairs Internet web site at http://www.travel.state.gov, where the current Worldwide Caution, Travel Alerts, and Travel Warnings can be found. Consular Affairs Publications, which contain information on obtaining passports and planning a safe trip abroad, are also available at http://www.travel.state.gov. For additional information on international travel, see http://www.usa.gov/Citizen/Topics/Travel/International.shtml.

The Department of State encourages all U.S. citizens traveling or residing abroad to register via the State Department's travel registration website or at the nearest U.S. embassy or consulate abroad. Registration will make your presence and whereabouts known in case it is necessary to contact you in an emergency and will enable you to receive up-to-date information on security conditions.

Emergency information concerning Americans traveling abroad may be obtained by calling 1-888-407-4747 toll free in the U.S. and Canada or the regular toll line 1-202-501-4444 for callers outside the U.S. and Canada.The National Passport Information Center (NPIC) is the U.S. Department of State's single, centralized public contact center for U.S. passport information. Telephone: 1-877-4-USA-PPT (1-877-487-2778); TDD/TTY: 1-888-874-7793. Passport information is available 24 hours, 7 days a week. You may speak with a representative Monday-Friday, 8 a.m. to 10 p.m., Eastern Time, excluding federal holidays.

STRATEGIC AND PRACTICAL INFORMATION FOR CONDUCTING BUSINESS[1]

DOING BUSINESS IN SYRIA

MARKET OVERVIEW

The Syrian Arab Republic, a country the size of North Dakota, is rich in history, culture, and resources, but has an economy desperately in need of reform following decades of failed state planning and mismanagement. Syria is a lower-middle income developing country, with a population of 20.1 million (including refugees) as of early 2009, according to the Central Bureau of Statistics. According to the IMF, the annual per capita income in 2009 was estimated at $2,590. Proposals to reform the heavily state-controlled and stagnant economy have been only partially implemented, and economic growth has not kept pace with population growth and resulting increases in the labor force. Syria's IMF projected final GDP growth rate for 2009 of 3.9 percent outpaced its estimated 2009 population growth rate of 2.4 percent. Most unofficial sources report that Syria's rate of unemployment exceeded 15 percent, although official government statistics reported a rate of 9.8% percent in 2008. Syria's primary non-Arab trading partners (imports and exports) are Russia ($2.3 billion), Germany ($2 billion), China ($1.9 billion) and Italy ($1.2 billion). Syria's largest trading partners within the Middle East are Iraq ($2.9 billion), Saudi Arabia ($1.7 billion), Lebanon ($0.3 billion), Jordan ($0.1 billion) and Egypt ($0.1 billion). The energy sector continues to attract foreign direct investment (FDI), although FDI has decreased commensurate with the Syria's declining petroleum production. After peaking in the late 1990s at 600,000 b/d, Syrian oil production stood at 379,000 b/d in 2009. In 2007, Syria became a net importer of oil as consumption of refined petroleum by-products finally exceeded production. For years the Syrian government's subsidies for the domestic price of diesel contributed to widespread smuggling to neighboring countries and placed a multi-billion dollar burden on the state's budget. In an effort to combat diesel smuggling and reduce costs, the government cut the diesel subsidy by approximately half in May 2008. The cut resulted in a 257% increase in diesel prices, which was reflected across the spectrum of goods and services. Official government statistics place the rate of inflation at 3% in 2009.

The development of many services, mainly in the banking and tourism sectors, continues to be impeded by the Syrian government's own policies and mismanagement. Therefore, the contribution of these sectors to Syria's economy remains limited. In 2009, the total number of private banks operating in Syria increased to 13, of which two practiced Islamic Banking (Cham Bank and Syria International Islamic Bank). A third Islamic Bank (Al-Barakah Bank) is set to take off in the first quarter of 2010. However,

due to Syria's unfavorable regulatory environment, the level of FDI remains low compared to other countries in the region. In an effort to modernize Syria's economy, President Asad issued a new commercial law in late 2007 to update the regulations for appraising, selling and obtaining a mortgage on commercial real estate. Additionally, the new law authorizes the maintenance of business accounts in electronic format, and declares documents sent by either fax or telex to be legal. In March 2008, the Companies Law was issued by Decree No. 3. The new law provides for new types of companies such as holding companies and offshore companies, (companies whose main activity is contracting for projects outside Syria, but are not entitled to practice business in Syria.) It also provides new details on procedures, including transforming companies from one form to another. Subsequent to the Companies Law, the Arbitration Law (Decree No.4/2008) was

---

[1] The information in this chapter reflects mostly the situation before the war.

For additional analytical, business and investment opportunities information, please contact Global Investment & Business Center, USA at (703) 370-8082. Fax: (703) 370-8083. E-mail: ibpusa3@gmail.com Global Business and Investment Info Databank - www.ibpus.com

issued which allowed the establishment of arbitration centers in Syria, to be registered with the Ministry of Justice. The law entitled public-sector companies to use arbitration to settle disputes. The Syrian government announced its intention to enact a Value Added Tax (VAT) in 2009 as one means of increasing revenues, but has yet to solve the myriad of details associated with implementation. President Asad issued Decree No. 60 in 2007, authorizing the Central Bank to issue Treasury Bills. Recently, the Governor of the Central Bank announced that T-Bills would be issued in 2010. In theory, the Syrian government would use T-bills to help finance public debt and the instruments would be tradable on the Damascus Stock Exchange, which started operation in 2009. The United States Government maintains a range of economic sanctions against the Syrian government that makes participation in the Syrian economy by U.S. companies extremely difficult. Since 1979, when Syria was added to the State Department's list of State Sponsors of Terrorism, U.S. businesses investing in Syria have not been allowed to utilize OPIC or other U.S. government investment insurance programs, or access financing from the Export-Import Bank, the Small Business Administration, the Commodity Credit Corporation or the Trade Development Agency. On May 11, 2004 the President signed an executive order implementing the Syria Accountability and Lebanese Sovereignty Act (SAA), which prohibits the export to Syria of all U.S. products, with the exception of foods and medicines and a few categories of goods that the U.S. Department of Commerce may license on a case-by-case basis. The definition of a U.S. product includes any good produced in or shipped from the U.S., in addition to any good with more than 10 percent de minimus U.S. origin content. In addition to U.S. sanctions, Syria has been under international pressure since the United Nations Security Council began its investigation into the February 14, 2005 assassination of former Lebanese Prime Minister Rafik Harriri.

In 2009, the volume of sanctions-compliant trade between the U.S. and Syria (from January through November) amounted to 565.5 million. A breakdown of U.S. trade with Syria is available at: http://www.census.gov/foreign-trade/balance/c5020.html#2008

MARKET CHALLENGES

In addition to the obstacles posed by U.S. economic sanctions, U.S. businesses find the current business environment difficult to navigate and a challenging one in which to succeed. U.S. businesses have listed the following challenges as most acute:

  • Antiquated policies and regulations that do not favor free-market mechanisms;

  • The lack of transparency in implementing laws and regulations and in enforcing contractual obligations, and a dysfunctional judicial system;

  • Rampant corruption and cronyism;

  • An inadequate banking system that severely limits foreign exchange and project financing; and

  • Confusing and inconsistent enforcement of tariffs, customs duties, and taxes for goods and services.

MARKET OPPORTUNITIES

U.S. law prohibits the export of most products of the United States, with the exception of foods and medicines that do not require export licenses and a few categories of goods that must be licensed, which are:

  • Medical devices (as defined in Part 772 of the Export Administration Regulations (EAR)

• Safety-of-flight related spare parts and components for civilian aircraft

• Telecommunications equipment and associated computers, software and technology.

In this environment, the U.S. Embassy will not identify any market opportunities for U.S. businesses and will not actively promote U.S. investment in Syria.

MARKET ENTRY STRATEGY

Pursuant to Executive Order 13338 of May 11, 2004 implementing the SAA, the export of all products of the United States is prohibited, with the exception of the aforementioned five categories. Based on the President's exercise of national security waiver authority under the provisions of the SAA, export license applications for medical devices and equipment as defined in Part 772 of the EAR and for telecommunications equipment and associated computers, software, and technology will be accepted and reviewed on a case-by-case basis by the Commerce Department's Bureau of Industry and Security (BIS). U.S. exporters may request an advisory opinion from BIS as to whether or not an export license may be approved by contacting BIS Foreign Policy Division in Washington, DC, at (202) 482-4252. Specific information on export controls, the EAR, and the SNAP-R export license application process is available at: http://www.bis.doc.gov/

U.S. exporters seeking general export information/assistance or country-specific commercial information should consult with their nearest Export Assistance Center or the U.S. Department of Commerce's Trade Information Center at (800) USATRADE, or go to the following website: http://www.export.gov . The U.S. Government considers the information contained in this report to be accurate as of the date published. However, the Department of Commerce does not take responsibility for actions readers may take based on the information contained therein. Readers should always conduct their own due diligence before entering into business ventures or other commercial arrangements. The Department of Commerce can assist companies in these endeavors.

SELLING U.S. PRODUCTS AND SERVICES

USING AN AGENT OR DISTRIBUTOR

In order to register a local agency for a foreign company, an application must be filed with the Ministry of Economy and Trade accompanied by the following documentation:

• The agency contract, which must include:

1. The name and commercial address of the company. 2. The nationality of the company and where it was founded. 3. The full name and address of the company headquarters (as well as the name and addresses of branches, if the agency includes them.) 4. The type of agency (commission, distribution.) 5. The percentage of commission and the method of determining the agent's financial rights. 6. The subject and category of the agency. 7. The duration of the agency license and renewal procedures. 8. The local agent's name, commercial address, telephone and fax. 9. Region of the agency: Syrian Arab Republic .

10. The number of the foreign company's commercial register. 11. The agent's commercial register and where it was registered. 12. The agent's tax number. 13. Any other useful and relevant information. 14. The agency contract must explicitly state that contact with the local agent must be done directly and not through a third-party. 15. The agency contract must clearly

state that the company will not retain any commission due to the Syrian agent abroad and will transfer these commissions through Syrian banking channels.

• The agency documentation should be accompanied by a duly notarized commercial register of the agent.

• The agency documentation and application must be duly notarized by the following organizations:

1. The Chamber of Commerce in the applicant company's home country. 2. The Syrian Embassy in the applicant company's home country. 3. The Ministry of Foreign Affairs in Damascus. All documents must be translated into Arabic by a notarized translator.

ESTABLISHING AN OFFICE

To open a branch office in Syria, a firm must file an application accompanied by the following documentation with the Ministry of Economy and Trade: 1. Home country documentation of incorporation. 2. Documentation outlining the applying firm's internal regulations. 3. Financial statements that verify the applicant's capital, including reserves (provided the capital (including reserves) is at least 25 million Syrian Pounds (SYP) (approximately $500,000).) 4. The company's commercial registration. 5. The type of company. 6. A declaration of the company's decision to open a branch office in Syria, along with a declaration that this branch will be directly affiliated with the company's headquarters. 7. Power of Attorney for the manager of the new Syrian branch granting him/her all managerial, financial, and technical authority in Syria.

8. Copies of the applicant company's latest trade balance sheets. These documents must be certified by the following organizations: 1. A chamber of commerce in the applicant company's home country. 2. The Syrian Embassy in that country. 3. The Syrian Ministry of Foreign Affairs. All documents must be translated into Arabic by a notarized translator. In December 2008, President Asad issued Law No. 34 which regulates the operations of foreign companies in Syria. The law, which is a modernization of Law No. 151 from 1952, includes changes that enable a foreign company to open a temporary office for the supervision of only one contract, with the option of renewal; to open a representational office solely for promotion of the headquarters company; to establish a regional office in Syria for supervising activities outside of Syria; and to authorize a commercial middleman to sign contracts with public entities on behalf of the foreign company. The paid-up capital of foreign companies wishing to be established under any of these forms must be at least SYP 25 million (approximately $500,000.) The Ministry is discussing internally a proposal to reduce the amount further to SYP 15 million. The law also empowered the Ministry of Economy and Trade to supervise agents and branches of foreign companies and gave the Syrian courts the jurisdiction to rule in relevant disputes which must be settled in the Syrian territories. Accordingly, commercial arbitration in Syria is acceptable.

FRANCHISING

While the Syrian Law of Commerce No. 33/2007 did not address the subject of franchising, Decree No. 47/2009 did authorize franchising. In 2009, the French retailer Carrefour opened in a store in Aleppo and KFC has opened many branches throughout the country. However, foreign restaurant franchises face the Syrian government's "general policy" of "encouraging" restaurants to use local food products, although imported food ingredients are not explicitly banned. This is but one example of the inconsistent application of Syrian laws and the difficulty foreign businessmen will encounter when navigating the many gray areas of Syrian government bureaucracy.

DIRECT MARKETING

American companies can use a direct marketing approach to their products to end users in Syria. However, it is recommended to work through a local representative. American companies can find local firms that are capable of organizing marketing campaigns for their products through a wide range of media.

JOINT VENTURES/LICENSING

See Chapter 6: Investment Climate, "Openness to Foreign Investment"

SELLING TO THE GOVERNMENT

The lack of regulatory transparency and specificity, particularly when dealing with government-affiliated entities, leads to a climate of bureaucracy, confusion, intimidation, and corruption. Foreign vendors often are hampered by a lack of awareness throughout the tendering process and complain that winning bids are often based more on contacts and relationships than the actual merits of a proposal. Certain ministers in the government have acknowledged this problem within the last few years and have tried unsuccessfully to address it. Similarly, in the judicial system, judgments are subject to external pressures that make it difficult for businesses to ensure that contracts are binding. The awarding of contracts is often delayed by the lobbying efforts of influential local business interests and groups. Even in cases devoid of external influence, bureaucrats fear accusations of corruption and abuse, and therefore often require additional reviews of investment proposals that are not mandated by law and that inordinately delay projects. The Syrian government has reiterated its commitment to increasing the degree of transparency in the process, but foreign and Syrian firms continue to cite problems. However, a new development took place with the launch of the first arbitration center in Damascus on December 22, 2009. It is anticipated that 11 additional centers will open within a short period once the Ministry of Justice approves the license requests submitted by applicants. Once these centers open, public-sector companies will be able to resort to arbitration. Although government officials had previously stated that no privatization of state enterprises would take place during the current Five-Year Plan that runs through 2010, in 2008 the Syrian government awarded a contract to privatize the operation of its largest container port, in Lattakia. The tendering process was typically opaque and the winning French company may have benefited from having an influential Syrian partner and an improving political relationship between Syria and France. Also in 2008, the Syrian government awarded a license to a private holding company headed by the Syrian President's cousin to construct the first privately-owned power generation plant in Syria. Recently, the Ministry of Industry was "discreetly" directed by the Prime Minister to shut down 17 public companies operating in the industrial sector. To date, no definite decision has been made as to the fate of these companies, but there were attempts to offer them for private investment. The Syrian government is currently preparing legislation on Public-Private Partnerships (PPP) in an attempt to attract foreign investment. The British-Syrian Society, in association with the Syrian government, held a conference on PPP from October 30th through November 1st, 2009 which focused on four key infrastructure sectors that have been identified by the government for PPP: oil & gas, electricity, social housing, and transport & infrastructure.

DISTRIBUTION AND SALES CHANNELS

The majority of goods enter Syria via the Mediterranean ports of Lattakia and Tartous. Bulk commodities are generally shipped to Tartous, while both ports are equipped to receive containers. A freight railway connection was launched in 2009 between the Lattakia and Tartous ports and Umm Qaser, Iraq. Customs officials at the ports wield considerable authority and may expect bribes to expedite administrative processing. An operational, albeit antiquated, railroad is available to transport goods from the port cities to major population centers. Syria and Jordan are planning to build a railway linking the Red sea port of Aqaba with the Syrian border starting in 2010. The $6 billion freight railway could take three years to complete. Imported goods also enter Syria via truck across the land borders with Turkey, Lebanon and Jordan. Foreign trucks report significant delays at the border while awaiting police escort to their ultimate destinations. The Ministry of Transport extended until December 3, 2009 the call for an "expression of interest" for the design, construction, operation and maintenance of two international motorways linking north to south and east to west: a north-south 432-km road running from Bab Al Hawa on the Turkish border to Nassib on the Jordanian border and a 351-km west-east motorway running from Tartous to Al-Tanf on the Iraqi border. About 14 "expressions of interest" have been received so far from regional and international companies, including France's Bouygues. Air freight accounts for a small percentage of total goods entering Syria, primarily fragile technological components or time-sensitive equipment. Damascus International Airport is the main passenger point of entry into Syria, although some regional and European carriers do maintain direct routes to Aleppo.

SELLING FACTORS/TECHNIQUES

Cost, delivery time frame, responsiveness to Requests for Quotation and credit terms are of significant importance in purchasing decisions. Since the majority of Syrians do not speak or read English, from a marketing perspective it is recommended to have catalogues/brochures translated into Arabic.

ELECTRONIC COMMERCE

Electronic commerce within Syria is complicated by an antiquated IT infrastructure, government censorship, and U.S. economic sanctions. With the exception of mobile telephone service, most Syrian IT infrastructure is at least ten years behind that of Syria's regional neighbors. On February 25, 2009, President Asad issued law No. 4 on Electronic Signature (e- Signature); a law addressing e-Commerce is still under consideration by the Prime Ministry. Parallel to that, the Syrian government has concluded a strategy for the implementation of e-Government targeted for 2020. To meet that end, the Ministry of Telecommunication has moved to the second phase of launching a portal and is currently preparing the terms of reference to be distributed to interested companies.

TRADE PROMOTION AND ADVERTISING

The following websites may contain useful information regarding trade fairs, trade promotion exhibitions, and advertising in Syria:

www.arabiangroup.com

www.buildexonline.com

www.simafairs.com

www.alliedexpo.com

www.syrianfairs.com (Arabic only)

PRICING

Local importers base their pricing on the export price, freight costs, applicable import tariffs and taxes, and profit margin. A Value Added Tax (VAT) is expected to be imposed in 2010. It is recommended for U.S. manufacturers and suppliers to coordinate with local representatives before assigning a final price to a product as prices may vary greatly according to the targeted market niche.

SALES SERVICE/CUSTOMER SUPPORT

In a country where technical skills are scarce, companies offering responsive and competent customer services quickly earn a strong reputation which helps to increase sales. Syrians are becoming more aware of the benefits of customer services and after-sales / guarantee services are now available for most products (e.g. air conditioners, computers, cars).

PROTECTING YOUR INTELLECTUAL PROPERTY

Several general principles are important for effective management of intellectual property rights in Syria. First, it is important to have an overall strategy to protect IPR. Second, IPR is protected differently in Syria than in the U.S. Third, rights must be registered and enforced in Syria, under local laws. Companies may wish to seek advice from local attorneys or IP consultants. The U.S. Commercial Service can often provide a list of local lawyers upon request. It is vital that companies understand that intellectual property is primarily a private right and that the U.S. government generally cannot enforce rights for private individuals in Syria. It is the responsibility of the rights holders to register, protect, and enforce their rights where relevant, retaining their own counsel and advisors. While the U.S. Government is willing to assist, there is little it can do if the rights holders have not taken these fundamental steps necessary to securing and enforcing their IPR in a timely fashion. Moreover, in many countries, rights holders who delay enforcing their rights on a mistaken belief that the USG can provide a political resolution to a legal problem may find that their rights have been eroded or abrogated due to doctrines such as statutes of limitations, laches, estoppel, or unreasonable delay in prosecuting a law suit. In no instance should USG advice be seen as a substitute for the obligation of a rights holder to promptly pursue its case.

It is always advisable to conduct due diligence on partners. Negotiate from the position of your partner and give your partner clear incentives to honor the contract. A good partner is an important ally in protecting IP rights. Keep an eye on your cost structure and reduce the margins (and the incentive) of would-be bad actors. Projects and sales in Syria require constant attention. Work with legal counsel familiar with Syrian laws to create a solid contract that includes non-compete clauses, and confidentiality/non-

disclosure provisions. It is also recommended that small and medium-size companies understand the importance of working together with trade associations and organizations to support efforts to protect IPR and stop counterfeiting. There are a number of these organizations, including: - The U.S. Chamber and local American Chambers of Commerce - National Association of Manufacturers (NAM) - International Intellectual Property Alliance (IIPA) - International Trademark Association (INTA) - The Coalition Against Counterfeiting and Piracy - International Anti-Counterfeiting Coalition (IACC) - Pharmaceutical Research and Manufacturers of America (PhRMA) - Biotechnology Industry Organization (BIO) IPR Climate in Syria Although Syria has recently taken legislative measures to comply with international standards regarding Intellectual Property Rights (IPR), foreign businessmen should be aware that the Syrian judicial system is notoriously corrupt and has no experience in prosecuting IPR violations. In the past, IPR registration was carried out according to a deposit system whereby an applicant could register any trademark based on his/her word. In a bid to encourage investment the Ministry of Economy started using a verification system in 2007, whereby the IPR Department assumed the responsibility of verifying any violation and was entitled to terminate any "suspicious" trademark registration within 30 days even if the court was hearing the case. To register a trademark in Syria, it is easier to submit an application with the relevant office in any of the member countries to the Madrid System for International Registration of Trademarks. The application form is available online and is processed once filled out by the applicant and the required fee is wired to the International Bureau of the World Intellectual Property Organization (WIPO) in Geneva, Switzerland. No agent is required if the application is submitted through the Madrid system. Syria has been a member since early 2006, and the Madrid System registration procedures are less tedious and more flexible than those inside Syria. To register a trademark directly with the Syrian government, a foreign company must first appoint a local Syrian agent. The agency agreement must be notarized by the Syrian Ministry of Foreign Affairs and the Syrian Embassy in the country in which the application was submitted. A declaration of compliance with the Arab League General Boycott of Israel was waived in 2009. Foreign companies that are first-time applicants for trademark registration can now file an application without a prior Israel Boycott Declaration. The total cost of registering a trademark in Syria is SYP 23,000 ($500).

In addition to being a member of the World Intellectual Property Organization (WIPO), Syria joined the Geneva Act of the Hague Agreement pertaining to the protection of international designs in September 2007 and the treaty entered into force in January 2008. On March 12, 2007 President Asad issued Law No. 8 of 2007, regulating Trademarks, Geographical Indications, Industrial Models and Designs, Unfair Competition and the Protection of Intellectual Property. This law came into force on April 12, 2007, and was amended in 2009 by Decree No. 47 in order to quickly resolve

disputes pertaining to famous trademarks and to protect the owners by allowing them to submit a request to the Ministry of Economy and Trade to prevent others from registering or using an identical or similar mark even if the trademark is not registered in Syria. IPR Resources A wealth of information on protecting IPR is freely available to U.S. rights holders. Some excellent resources for companies regarding intellectual property include the following:

- For information about patent, trademark, or copyright issues -- including enforcement issues in the US and other countries -- call the STOP! Hotline: 1-866-999-HALT or register at www.StopFakes.gov . - For more information about registering trademarks and patents (both in the U.S. as well as in foreign countries), contact the US Patent and Trademark Office (USPTO) at: 1-800-786-9199. - For more information about registering for copyright protection in the US, contact the US Copyright Office at: 1-202-707-5959.

- For US small and medium-size companies, the Department of Commerce offers a "SME IPR Advisory Program" available through the American Bar Association that provides one hour of free IPR legal advice for companies with concerns in Brazil, China, Egypt, India, Russia, and Thailand. For details and to register, visit: http://www.abanet.org/intlaw/intlproj/iprprogram_consultation.html

- For information on obtaining and enforcing intellectual property rights and market-specific IP Toolkits visit: www.StopFakes.gov . This site is linked to the USPTO website for registering trademarks and patents (both in the U.S. as well as in foreign countries), the U.S. Customs & Border Protection website to record registered trademarks and copyrighted works (to assist customs in blocking imports of IPR-infringing products) and allows you to register for Webinars on protecting IPR. - For an in-depth examination of IPR requirements in specific markets, toolkits are currently available in the following countries/territories: Brazil, Brunei, China, Egypt, European Union, India, Italy, Malaysia, Mexico, Paraguay, Peru, Russia, Taiwan, Thailand, and Vietnam.

- For assistance in developing a strategy for evaluating, protecting, and enforcing IPR, use the free Online IPR Training Module on www.stopfakes.gov .

- The U.S. Commerce Department has positioned IP attachés in key markets around the world. You can get contact information for the IP attaché who covers Syria at: http://www.buyusa.gov/egypt/en/ipradvisoryprogram.html

DUE DILIGENCE

There are practically no government agencies in Syria that can perform due diligence or provide bona fides services on banks, agents, and/or customers. These services are available upon request on a case-by-case basis by private consulting firms. The

Economic/Commercial Section of the U.S. Embassy in Damascus maintains a list of private entities that may be able to perform due diligence for U.S. firms. *Disclaimer of Responsibility: The U.S. Embassy in Damascus assumes no responsibility for the professional ability or integrity of the persons or firms whose names appear in the linked document. (Nevertheless, care and selectivity have been exercised in the preparation of this list.)*

http://damascus.usembassy.gov/media/pdf/econcommercial-pdf/private-consulting-firms-operating-in-syria.pdf

LOCAL PROFESSIONAL SERVICES

Because Syrian law and Arabic language pose significant obstacle to the conduct of U.S. business in Syria, hiring a local attorney is a sensible and often necessary action. A link to a partial list of Syrian attorneys who provide services to foreigners is included below. Area covered by list: This list covers the capital, Damascus, and the major cities of Syria, namely Aleppo, Homs, Hama, and Lattakia. Specialties: While an attempt has been made in the following list to point out the particular branches of legal work, which each attorney generally handles, it should be noted that most attorneys practicing in Syria accept all types of cases. Collection Agencies: There are no firms or individuals operating as collection agencies in Syria; however, most of the attorneys listed handle collection cases. *Disclaimer of Responsibility: The American Embassy at Damascus assumes no responsibility for the professional ability or integrity of the persons or firms whose names appear in the linked document. Nevertheless, care and selectivity have been exercised in its preparation.*

http://damascus.usembassy.gov/media/pdf/cons-acs-pdf/list-of-lawyers-in-syria-09.pdf

WEB RESOURCES

Ministry of Economy and Trade: http:// www.syrecon.org

Ministry of Industry: http:// www.syrianindustry.org

Ministry of Tourism: http://www.syriatourism.org

Ministry of Transport: http://www.mot.gov.sy

Customs Department: www.customs.gov.sy

http://www.syriainvestmentmap.org/Introduction.htm

LEADING SECTORS FOR EXPORT AND INVESTMENT

The Syria Accountability and Lebanese Sovereignty Act (SAA) prohibits the export and re-export of most products to Syria. Products of the United States are defined as not only any good that is produced in and shipped from the U.S., but also any good that contains more than 10% *de minimus* U.S.-origin content regardless of where it is produced. In implementing the SAA, the President specified that certain items are eligible for export under waiver. These items are food and certain medicines, which do not require an export license. The following major categories of items require licenses for export, which are reviewed on a case-by-case basis: (1) controlled pharmaceuticals and medical supplies and devices; (2) telecommunications equipment and associated computers, software and technology; and (3) parts and components intended to ensure the safety of civil aviation and the safe operation of commercial passenger aircraft. For detailed information on all exempted items and a better understanding of the law, U.S. businesses should contact the U.S. Department of Commerce, Bureau of Industry and Security (BIS) Foreign Policy Division at (202) 482-4252. Specific information on export controls, the EAR, and the SNAP-R export license application process is available at: http://www.bis.doc.gov/

U.S. exporters seeking general export information/assistance or country-specific commercial information should consult with their nearest Export Assistance Center or the U.S. Department of Commerce's Trade Information Center at (800) USATRADE, or go to the following website: http://www.export.gov

Even though investments are not currently banned under the law, U.S. businesses considering investment in Syria should contact the Office of Foreign Assets Control at the Department of Treasury at: http://www.ustreas.gov/offices/enforcement/ofac Further details and source documents regarding sanctions are available at the U.S. Embassy Damascus website (Trade and Commerce) at:

http://damascus.usembassy.gov/trade-and-commerce.html It is worth mentioning that the President of the United States retains the authority to enact additional sanctions under the SAA at any time that could prohibit American citizens from investing in Syria above a designated threshold amount.

AGRICULTURAL SECTORS

Corn	2007	2008	2009 (estimated)
Total Market Size	1,550,000 MT	1,600,000 MT	1,800,000 MT
Total Local Production	150,000 MT	150,000 MT	150,000 MT
Total Exports	0	0	0
Total Imports	1,400,000 MT	1,450,000 MT	1,650,000 MT
Imports from the U.S.	1,287,000 MT	663,000 MT	600,000 MT

(Source: U.S. Department of Agriculture, Syrian Statistical Abstract, and Global Trade Atlas) Corn has been the leading imported agricultural commodity from the United States for many years. Due to limited domestic production and increasing demand for both feed and the production of starch and glucose, corn imports are forecast to grow in the foreseeable future. However, the

United States market share was reduced due to competition from the Black Sea countries in 2008 and 2009.

Soybeans	2007	2008	2009 (estimated)
Total Market Size	310,000 MT	370,000 MT	510,000 MT
Total Local Production	10,000 MT	10,000 MT	10,000 MT
Total Exports	0	0	0
Total Imports	300,000 MT	500,000 MT	500,000 MT
Imports from the U.S.	237,000 MT	344,000 MT	400,000 MT

(Source: U.S. Department of Agriculture, Syrian Statistical Abstract, and Global Trade Atlas)
Syrian soybean consumption rates have increased significantly in recent years due to the increase in domestic soybean crushing capacity. Consequently, demand has increased for soybean by-products, particularly soybean meal that is used as a protein ingredient in poultry feed. Soybean oil is also marketable in Syria as a low-cost alternative to olive oil for cooking. In 2009, American soybean exports to Syria are estimated to exceed corn exports in value for the first time since the unit price of soybeans is more than that of corn.

BEST PRODUCTS/SERVICES

Due to the ongoing desertification of Syria's rain-fed agricultural lands and increasing cost of plant production resulting from the increase in the cost of irrigation and fertilization, Syria's reliance upon imported agricultural products is expected to grow. While Syria remains a relatively poor country, the economy's overall growth may

increase the average Syrian's standard of living which would enable greater consumption of animal proteins. Consequently, animal husbandry – particularly poultry production – is expected to increase, with a concomitant increase in demand for imported feed. Soybeans and corn are estimated to remain the main U.S. export items to Syria in the foreseeable future.

RESOURCES

Annual cotton, grain and feed, and tree nut reports are available at the U.S. Embassy Damascus Agricultural Section website: http://damascus.usembassy.gov/agri.html

TRADE REGULATIONS AND STANDARDS

IMPORT TARIFFS

Syria is a partner to two free trade agreements, the Greater Arab Free Trade Area (GAFTA) which took effect on January 1, 2005, and a bilateral Free Trade Agreement (FTA) with Turkey, which entered into force on January 1, 2007. GAFTA eliminated import tariffs on goods from Arab states. The FTA with Turkey will eliminate tariffs on Turkish goods over a 3-to-12 year period. Syria also has initialed an Association Agreement with the European Union (EU), but a final signature on this agreement is still pending. The Syrian government rejected an invitation to a ceremony on October 26, 2009 in Luxembourg to sign the long-delayed EU Association

For additional analytical, business and investment opportunities information,
please contact Global Investment & Business Center, USA
at (703) 370-8082. Fax: (703) 370-8083. E-mail: ibpusa3@gmail.com
Global Business and Investment Info Databank - www.ibpus.com

Agreement. Syrian officials have told the EU that they need more time to study the future impact of the agreement on the Syrian economy. With an eye to eventual WTO membership, the Syrian Ministry of Economy and Trade established in October 2006 an office of administration for WTO membership which is responsible for all trade issues related to accession. In 2007, the Syrian government harmonized its import tariffs and customs duties to bring them into compliance with WTO standards. Most goods from countries with which Syria does not have a free trade agreement are still subject to progressive tariff rates that start at 1 percent and reach a maximum of 60 percent of the value of the good, depending in part on the government's view of the necessity of the product. However, the Ministry of Economy and Trade started the liberalization of import in 2007 and the number of banned goods has been greatly reduced.

TRADE BARRIERS

Syria has a number of non-tariff trade barriers that include a non-convertible currency, an inadequate banking system, and cumbersome and confusing government regulations. For a more comprehensive understanding of non-tariff trade barriers, please refer to Chapter 6: Investment Climate.

IMPORT REQUIREMENTS AND DOCUMENTATION

In order to import goods into Syria from countries other than Turkey and members

of the GAFTA, importers must present the following documents: (1) proof of a clean financial record; (2) a valid import license; (3) a packing list in triplicate; (4) a certificate of origin in triplicate; (5) a letter from the corresponding bank; (6) a commercial invoice in triplicate describing the type of goods imported, price, basic specifications, and method of payment used; (7) Commercial register; (8) a copy of the importer's ID; and (9) a copy of the insurance contract. All documents must be certified by the Syrian Chamber of Commerce (or any Arab/foreign Chamber of Commerce) and the Syrian Embassy in the country of origin, or by another Arab Embassy in that country, in the absence of a Syrian Embassy. Obtaining an import license is required for all imported items. Proof that payment, by means of documentary letter of credit, has been implemented for commercial transactions is required. The exporter is also required to include a statement on the invoice stating that the exporter has an agent in Syria. Although Syria enforces the Arab League boycott of Israel and goods of Israeli origin may not be imported into Syria, it no longer requires companies to certify compliance with the boycott. . U.S. exporters are advised to obtain competent advice regarding U.S. anti-boycott regulations before proceeding. One excellent source of such information is the U.S. Department of Commerce, Office of Anti-Boycott Compliance, Telephone: 202-482-2381; Fax: 202-482-0913.

U.S. EXPORT CONTROLS

The Syria Accountability and Lebanese Sovereignty Act (SAA), implemented on May 11, 2004, prohibits the export and re-export of most products of the United States to Syria. Products of the United States are defined as not only goods that are produced in and shipped from the U.S., but also goods that contain more than 10 percent *de minimus* U.S.-origin content regardless of where they are produced. In implementing the SAA, the President specified that certain items are eligible for export under waiver. These items are food and certain medicines, which do not require an export license, and the following major category of items, which require a license. The U.S. Department of Commerce may consider licenses for export on a case-by-case basis for: (1) controlled pharmaceuticals and medical supplies and devices; (2) telecommunications equipment and associated computers, software and technology; and (3) parts and components intended to ensure the safety of civil aviation and the safe operation of commercial passenger aircraft. In fiscal year 2009, the Bureau of Industry and Security (BIS) at the U.S. Department of Commerce processed 421 license applications, of which 345 were approved, 68 were returned without action, and 8 were denied. The majority of approved applications with the greatest dollar value were for medical supplies and devices (255). Applications for telecommunications equipment (69) and for parts and components for the safety of flight and the safe operation of commercial passenger aircraft (6) accounted for most of the remainder. Of the applications returned without action, most were returned because the application forms were incomplete. The denials were for applications to export items that did not qualify for approval under any of the six waiver categories pursuant to the Syria Accountability Act (SAA). For detailed information on all exempted items and a better understanding of the law,

U.S. businesses should contact the U.S. Department of Commerce, Bureau of Industry and Security (BIS) Foreign Policy Division at (202) 482-4252.

Specific information on export controls, the EAR, and the SNAP-R export license application process is available at: http://www.bis.doc.gov/ Other useful links include the following:

http://www.bis.doc.gov/forms/rpdform.html -- Advisory Opinion Request

http://www.bis.doc.gov/policiesandregulations/syriaguidance8_07_09.htm -- Syria Web Guidance

http://www.bis.doc.gov/licensing/syriaimplementationmay14_04.htm -- Implementation of the Syria Accountability Act

http://www.bis.doc.gov/licensing/syriafaq_may14_04.htm -- Frequently Asked Questions - Syrian Accountability and Lebanese Sovereignty Restoration Act (SAA)

U.S. exporters seeking general export information/assistance or country-specific commercial information should consult with their nearest Export Assistance Center or the U.S. Department of Commerce's Trade Information Center at (800) USATRADE, or go to the following website: http://www.export.gov Further details and source documents regarding sanctions are available at the U.S. Embassy Damascus website (Trade and Commerce) at:

http://damascus.usembassy.gov/sanctions-syr.html

TEMPORARY ENTRY

The Syrian government grants temporary entry, free of customs duties and taxes, for the following entities and categories: *1.- Foreign Projects:* A foreign company executing a project in Syria is entitled to temporarily import any equipment necessary for the completion of the project. When the work is completed, the company must then re-export all equipment and vehicles. However, companies have experienced difficulties re-exporting equipment, especially computers and vehicles. The private sector's temporary entry request must be approved by the Minister of Finance, while temporary imports for the public sector's must be endorsed by the Prime Minister. *2.- International Organizations:* International organizations are entitled to import vehicles, furniture, and other necessary equipment, duty-free, on the condition that all imported goods be re-exported. For joint projects with the Syrian government, the international organization must transfer ownership of the vehicles, furniture and equipment used in that project to the public entity in charge of the project, or dispose of the items in accordance with the contract signed with the Syrian government. *3.- Tourists:* Tourists are entitled to bring in passenger vehicles for personal travel for a period of three months, subject to a one-month extension.

4.- Trade Shows: Trade show participants may temporarily import goods for display, but must re-export them at the conclusion of the event. Occasionally, the Syrian authorities permit the permanent importation of goods that are displayed during the government-organized annual Damascus International Fair. *5.- Export manufacturers:* Under a special procedure, local manufacturers are granted temporary entry permit for raw materials duty-free if the resulting manufactured products are wholly intended for export. *6.- Projects under Investment Law No. 10:* Investment Law No. 10 permits investors duty-free import of machinery, capital equipment, and supplies needed for special projects. Customs duties are imposed on all raw materials for manufacturing. However, in late 2005 the government reduced the duties imposed on certain raw materials to 1 percent. Custom duties for the import of production components do not exceed 5%.

LABELING AND MARKING REQUIREMENTS

Medicines, food, dairy, garments, and other consumer products must be labeled. The labeling should include: name of producer/exporter, ingredients, date of manufacturing, date of expiration, as well as the country of origin. Medications also require a batch number. The Ministry of Economy and Trade has enforced the labeling for products designed for local consumption, according to the international standards. In accordance with pending and completed Free Trade Agreements, Syria is working to implement more updated labeling and marking requirements on both imported and exported goods, to bring its requirements in line with WTO standards.

PROHIBITED AND RESTRICTED IMPORTS

On June 1, 2006, the Ministry of Economy and Trade issued a document, called the "negative list", which includes all prohibited imports. In keeping with the government's intention to liberalize trade, some goods were taken off the negative list in early 2007 as the Ministry of Economy and Trade issued new lists of liberalized imports on almost a bi-weekly basis. The previous 73-page "negative list" was reduced to just seven pages dealing with items that pertain to security, health, ethics and religion. In past years, only the government was permitted to import alcoholic beverages and cigarettes for sale on the local market. However, on November 21, 2007, the Ministry authorized the private import of the following alcoholic beverages as shown below with their Harmonized System code: 2204: wine of fresh grapes 2205: vermouth & other wine of fresh flavored grapes 2206: fermented beverages (cider, mead, etc.) 2208: ethyl alcohol, whose alcohol rate is below 80%, spirits and alcohol beverages, etc. In May 2008, the Ministry of Economy and Trade announced that it had completed the liberalization of the country's import trade. Trade liberalization has reduced the list of prohibited imports for members of GAFTA. For more information on the items prohibited from being imported, please check the (Arabic language only) provided website for the negative list at:

http://www.syrecon.gov.sy/servers/media/20080505-043418.pdf

CUSTOMS REGULATIONS AND CONTACT INFORMATION

Mr. Mustafa al-Bukaei Director General Baramkeh, Damascus, Syria Telephone: ☐ 11 – 2127900, 2125751, 2126901, 2129137, 2123937, 2127902/3 Fax: ☐ 11 – 2132577, 2126921 For additional information, please check the website for Syrian

Customs: http://www.customs.gov.sy

STANDARDS

· Overview

· Standards Organizations

· Conformity Assessment

· Product Certification

· Accreditation

· Publication of Technical Regulations

· Labeling and Marking

· Contacts

Syria has a complex bureaucratic standards system that involves ten different agencies (depending on the nature of the product) and seven ministries, supervised by the Commission for Standards and Measurement under the Ministry of Industry. As a member of the International Organization for Standardization (ISO), Syria incorporates many of the international norms within the local system. While the regulations are well developed, enforcement is not as consistent, with some products and producers enjoying looser enforcement than others.

STANDARDS ORGANIZATIONS

The primary responsibility for drafting and enforcing standards falls to the Commission for Standards and Measurements under the Ministry of Industry. However, many other agencies and ministries are involved, depending on the commodity in question. Syria officially agreed to host the regional headquarters of the Arab Standardization and Measurement Union, which is affiliated with the Arab League. This approval came upon a decree issued by Syrian President Asad on December 30, 2009. The decree allows the Arab Union to set up its regional office in Syria with Damascus as its base, provided the office works in accordance with the rules of the Arab Standardization and Measurement Union.

NIST NOTIFY U.S. SERVICE

Member countries of the World Trade Organization (WTO) are required under the Agreement on Technical Barriers to Trade (TBT Agreement) to report to the WTO all proposed technical regulations that could affect trade with other Member

countries. Notify U.S. is a free, web-based e-mail subscription service that offers an opportunity to review and comment on proposed foreign technical regulations that can affect your access to international markets. Register online at Internet URL: http://www.nist.gov/notifyus/

Although Syria is preparing to re-submit its application for admission to the WTO, as of the end of 2009 it was not a member.

CONFORMITY ASSESSMENT

Companies interested in obtaining conformity certificates for their products can send their request directly to the Syrian Arab Standards & Metrology Organization (SASMO), affiliated with the Ministry of Industry: http://www.sasmo.net/en/index.php .

PRODUCT CERTIFICATION

Locally produced goods, both for the domestic and export market, are required to certify compliance with local standards. Imports can be subject to government testing to check for compliance.

ACCREDITATION

Imported goods subject to mandatory standards require verification through laboratory testing in Syria. Testing varies according to products. For instance, the labs affiliated with the Ministry of Agriculture at the ports of entries undertake the responsibilities of testing grain imports. As for other food products, the Ministry of Health has the final say. The Customs Department also maintains their own labs inside the Syrian ports. The Syrian Arab Standards & Metrology Organization (SASMO) have food, chemical, textile and engineering testing labs, all of which perform the inspection and testing of samples delivered from the control department..

PUBLICATION OF TECHNICAL REGULATIONS

Technical standards are published by the Syrian Arab Standards & Metrology Organization (SASMO).

LABELING AND MARKING

All products must be properly labeled, including information on the producer, the Ingredients/components, the weight/size, the production license number, the country of origin, and production and expiry dates in Arabic. Specific labeling requirements differ according to the product in question. For measurements, Syria uses the metric system.

CONTACTS

Syrian Arab Standards & Metrology Organization: http://www.sasmo.net/en/index.php

Ministry of Industry: www.syrianindustry.org

TRADE AGREEMENTS

As of January 1, 2005, the Greater Arab Free Trade Agreement (GAFTA) came into effect and customs duties have been eliminated between Arab states. In addition, Syria has signed a free trade agreement with Turkey, which entered into force on January 1, 2007. Although Syria has begun to take measures to meet the requirements of an association agreement with the EU, initialed in October 2004 and again in December 2008, the EU agreement remains unratified despite the EU's invitation to sign it because Syria asked for more time to study its effect on the Syrian economy. Syria also applied in 2001 for membership in the WTO but its application has not yet been processed. In spite of that, the Syrian government has begun the process of bringing its customs system into compliance with WTO standards. Towards that end, the Prime Minister issued Decision No. 1006 in 2007 to establish the formation of four committees to prepare for WTO acceptance: the general preparation committee, the trade committee for merchandise, the trade committee for services, and the committee for the protection of intellectual rights. Also, there is a WTO directorate in the Ministry of Economy and Trade. In anticipation of WTO membership, the four committees finalized an internal Memo of Foreign Trade Regime (MFTR) in May 2007 and are still updating it with the relevant ministries.

MAJOR MINISTRIES

The following is a list of selected ministries and government institutions which foreign businessmen may come into contact with.

OFFICE OF THE PRIME MINISTER
Shahbander Street, Damascus
Tel. 2226000/1/2; Tel. 2210212

INVESTMENT OFFICE

Baghdad Street, Damascus
Tel. 4410448; Tel. 4412039

MINISTRY OF AGRICULTURE AND AGRARIAN REFORM

Jabri Street, Hejaz Square, Damascus
Tel. 2213613/4; Tel. 2219874

MINISTRY OF COMMUNICATIONS

Parliament Street, Damascus
Tel. 2227033/4; Tel. 2221133/4/5

MINISTRY OF ECONOMY AND FOREIGN TRADE

Maysaloun Street, Damascus
Tel. 2213513/4/5; Tel. 2224932

MINISTRY OF EDUCATION

Shahbander Street, Damascus
Tel. 2227033/4; Tel. 2221133/4/5

MINISTRY OF ELECTRICITY

Kouwatly Street, P.O. Box 4900, Damascus
Tel. 2223086; Tel. 2229654; Tel. 2228334; Tel. 2228915

MINISTRY OF FINANCE

Tajreeda Square, P.O. Box 13136, Damascus
Tel. 2219603; Tel. 2216300/1/2/3

GENERAL DIRECTORATE FOR CUSTOMS

Palestine Street, P.O. Box 329, Damascus
Tel. 2215900/1; Tel. 2217900; Tel. 2215751

MINISTRY OF FOREIGN AFFAIRS

Shora, Muhajireen, Damascus
Tel. 3331200/1/2/3

MINISTRY OF HOUSING AND UTILITIES

Yousef Azmeh Square, Damascus
Tel. 2224194/5/6/7; Tel2217570/1/2

MINISTRY OF INDUSTRY

Maysaloun Street, P.O. Box 12835, Damascus
Tel. 2231845; Tel. 2231834; Tel. 3720959

MINISTRY OF INFORMATION

Dar Al-Baath, Mezzeh Autostrad, Damascus
Tel. 6622141/2/3/4; Tel. 6617616/94/24

ARAB ADVERTISING ORGANIZATION

Moutanabbi Street, P.O. Box 2842Damascus
Tel. 2225219/20/21

MINISTRY OF INTERIOR
Al-Marjeh, Damascus
Tel2211001; Tel. 2220100

MINISTRY OF OIL AND MINERAL RESOURCES
P.O. Box 40, Al-Adawi, Damascus
Tel. 4455972; Tel. 4445610

SYRIAN PETROLEUM COMPANY
Moutanabbi Street, P.O. Box 2849 Damascus
Tel. 3120044

MINISTRY OF SOCIAL AFFAIRS AND LABOUR
Yousef Al-Azmeh Square, Damascus

MINISTRY OF SUPPLY AND INTERNAL TRADE
Salhiyeh, Damascus
Tel. 2219044; Tel. 3720599; Tel. 2219241

MINISTRY OF TOURISM
Kouwatly Street, Damascus
Tel. 2210122; Tel. 2215916

MINISTRY OF TRANSPORT
Abou Roumaneh, Damascus
Tel. 3336801/2/3

MINISTRY OF ECONOMY AND FOREIGN TRADE

TASKS OF MINISTRY OF ECONOMY AND FOREIGN TRADE

The tasks assigned to the Ministry of Economy and Foreign Trade since it was created by Legislative Decree No. 82 of 30.06.1947 have experienced some changes enacted over the following years through various legislative instruments.

When decree No. 2804 was issued on 17.12.1969 , those tasks acquired more clarity and became better defined in terms of specialization, highlighting as it does the basic and fundamental role of the Ministry in the following domains:

1. Taking part in the drawing out of the state's economic policy .

2. Preparing the required legislation relevant to foreign trade and granting the necessary permits and licenses.

3. Concluding trade and economic cooperation agreements with Arab and foreign states.

4. Drawing out the country's monetary and banking policies as well as policies of savings, loaning and insurance and following up their implementation.

5. Overseeing the banking system, the system of the insurance establishment as well as foreign trade establishments.

6. Supervising the works of the General Establishment for Cotton Ginning and Marketing, the activities of the General Organization of Tobacco, the General Organization of Free Zones, and the General Establishment for the Damascus International Fair.

7. Looking after investment issues, encouraging, promoting and developing investment regulations.

8. Completing all procedures of importation and exportation for the public, private and mixed sectors.

9. Supervising the organization of exhibitions locally and abroad.

10. Establishing trade centers and commercial representation offices that promote Syrian products in external markets.

The Ministry of Economy and Foreign Trade accomplishes the afore-said tasks in addition to various other tasks connected with its special and significant position in the management of the economy and foreign trade through a number of directorates and offices which form in their combination the backbone of the central administration to which is linked a vast network of directorates existing in the governorates of the Syrian Arab Republic besides a number of establishments and banks affiliated with the Ministry but having their financial and administrative independence supported by their own by-laws.

However, in order to give a clear view of the administrative and organization structure that enables the Ministry of Economy and Foreign Trade to perform its active role and accomplish the tasks assigned to it , we find it useful to outline the following:

THE CENTRAL ADMINISTRATION

Directorate of:

1. The minister's own office.

2. Administration and finance.

3. Arab relations.

4. International relations and organizations.

5. Monetary and banking business, Insurance and savings.

6. Planning, statistics and follow up.

7. Foreign Trade.

8. Internal control.

9. Organizations of productive nature affairs.

10. Organizations of commercial nature affairs.

11. International fairs and exhibitions.

12. Economic affairs.

13. Commercial representation and export promotion.

14. Secretariat of export committee.

15. Export bureau.

16. Investment affairs.

ECONOMIC DIRECTORATES IN THE GOVERNORATES

Damascus- Damascus Country Side- Aleppo- Homs- Hama- Lattakia- Tartous- Hasakeh- Dara'a- Al-Sweida- Al-Rakka- Idleb- Al-Kunaitra- Deir Ez-Zor.

ORGANIZATIONS

1. General Organization of Free Zones.

2. General organization of Tabacoo.

3. Public organization for cotton ginning and marketing.

4. General organization of Damascus International Fair.

5. Geza.

6. Sayarat (vehicles).

7. Maaden (metals).

8. Gota.

9. Saydaliah (pharmacy).

10. Naseej (textiles).

BANKS

1. Central Bank Of Syria.
2. Commercial Bank Of Syria.
3. Real Estate Bank.
4. Public Loaning Bank.
5. Industrial Bank.
6. Agricultural Bank.
7. Syrian General Establishment for insurance.

COMPANIES

1. George and Anton Ginajeh
2. Machines, Electricity and agriculture (Mercedes)
3. Al-Niser for industry and commerce

4. Industrial and Agricultural Production Market in Aleppo: minister of economy and foreign trade was designated, by decree no. 2563 of 1962, as a trustee of the market's fund.

AGREEMENTS SIGNED WITH FOREIGN STATES ON PROTECTION AND GUARANTEE OF INVESTMENT

State	Type of Agreement	Date of Signing	Instrument of Ratification and Date	Remarks
United States of America	Exchanged Notes on Manner of Guaranteeing American Investments in Syria	09.08.1976	Legislative Decree No.33 dated 01.08.1977	
Swiss Federation	Accord on Encouraging and protecting Investments	22.06.1977	Legislative Decree No.24 dated 12.07.1978	Most Favoured Nation
France	Agreement on Reciprocal Encouragement and Protection of Investments	28.11.1977	Legislative Decree No.30 dated 31.07.1978	Most Favoured Nation
Federal Germany	Agreement on Reciprocal Encouragement and Protection of Investments	02.08.1977	Legislative Decree No.34 dated 11.09.1978	Most Favoured Nation
Pakistan	Accord on Reciprocal Encouragement and Protection of Investments	25.04.1996	Law No. 5 dated 02.07.1997	
People's Republic of China	Accord on Reciprocal Encouragement and Protection of Investments and Appended Protocol	09.12.1996	Law No. 11 dated 04.08.1998	Protocol treats investment formalities and the transfers resulting from investment
Indonesia	Accord on Reciprocal Encouragement and Protecting Investments and Appended protocol	27.06.1997	Law No. 19 dated 31.12.1996	Most Favoured Nation. Protocol regulates transfers resulting from investment
Iran	Accord on Reciprocal Encouragement and Protection of Investments	05.02.1998	Legislative Decree No.3 dated 11.02.1998	Most Favoured Nation
Belorussia	Accord on Reciprocal Encouragement and	11.03.1998	Legislative Decree No.8 dated	

	Protection of Investments	04.08.1998		

TRADE AGREEMENTS SIGNED WITH FOREIGN STATES

State	Type of Agreement	Date of Signing	Instrument of Ratification and Date	Remarks
Russian Federation	Technical, Economic and Commercial Cooperation	15.04.1993	Law No. 11 dated 22.06.1993	
Bulgaria	Trade	02.05.1974	Legislative Decree No.54 dated 24.07.1974	New trade agreement was initialed by the two states on 13.03.1996
Hungary	Syrian side notified Hungarian side of its decision to nullify the trade agreement of 1974			New trade agreement has been initialed by the two sides
Albania	Trade	17.06.1979	Decree No.1252 dated 08.02.1980	
Cuba	Trade	27.03.1974	Decree No.167 dated 24.07.1974	It provides for exemption from Consular legalization. New trade agreement was initialed on .03.1998
Poland	Trade	20.08.1974	Decree No.303 dated 04.12.1974	
Czech	Syrian side nullified the trade agreement of 1975 signed with Czechoslovakia when the latter broke up as of 01.01.1993			The two sides have not agreed to signing new trade agreement
Slovak	Long term trade agreement	29.08.1995	Law No. 7 dated 03.07.1996	
Romania	Trade	13.04.1993		
Korea	Trade	28.06.1982	Law No.5 dated 08.02.1983	It provides for exemption from Consular Legalization
Vietnam	Trade	12.05.1994	Legislative Decree No.12 dated 27.06.1994	

For additional analytical, business and investment opportunities information,
please contact Global Investment & Business Center, USA
at (703) 370-8082. Fax: (703) 370-8083. E-mail: ibpusa3@gmail.com
Global Business and Investment Info Databank - www.ibpus.com

People's Republic of China	Trade	16.03.1982	Law No. 23 of 1982	
Byelorussia	Technical, Economic and Commercial	11.03.1998	Legislative Decree No.9 dated 04.08.1998	
Armenia	Trade	30.03.1992	Legislative Decree No.7 dated 11.07.1992	
Turkmenistan	Trade	26.03.1992	Legislative Decree No.8 dated 11.07.1992	
Kazakhstan	Trade	27.03.1992	Legislative Decree No.9 dated 11.07.1992	
Azerbaijan	Trade	28.03.1992	Legislative Decree No.10 dated 11.07.1992	
Tajikistan	Trade	19.03.1992	Legislative Decree No.11 dated 11.07.1992	
Republic of Tanzania	Trade	15.02.1974	Decree No.166 dated 15.03.1974	
Republic of Niger	Trade	26.06.1980	Decree No.2661 dated 22.12.1980	
Republic of Nigeria	Trade	17.09.1969	Decree No.242 dated 23.12.1969	
Republic of Guinea	Trade	22.01.1979	Decree No.1209 dated 23.01.1979	
Republic of Senegal	Economic, Commercial, Cultural, and Technological	04.11.1975	Decree No.589 dated 03.03.1976	
Cyprus	Long term trade agreement	23.02.1982		
Pakistan	Trade Annex to trade agreement	11.08.1969 25.04.1996	Legislative Decree No.342 dated 23.11.1969	
Sri Lanka	Trade and Payments	09.10.1966	Legislative Decree No.29 dated 09.04.1966	
Turkey	Trade	17.09.1974	Decree No.31 dated 02.12.1974	
India	Trade	09.10.1969	Decree No.345 dated 23.12.1969	
Indonesia	Trade	18.03.1976	Decree No.1220 dated 09.07.1977	
Argentina	Trade	06.09.1989		

For additional analytical, business and investment opportunities information, please contact Global Investment & Business Center, USA at (703) 370-8082. Fax: (703) 370-8083. E-mail: ibpusa3@gmail.com Global Business and Investment Info Databank - www.ibpus.com

Grenada	Trade	22.01.1980	Decree No.1144 dated 27.05.1980	
Chile	Trade	27.02.1990	Legislative Decree No.12 dated 24.05.1990	
Iran	Trade	21.08.1996	Decree No.241 dated 10.11.1997	
European Union	Cooperation	18.01.1977	Legislative Decree No.14 dated 05.07.1977	

INVESTMENT CLIMATE

OPENNESS TO FOREIGN INVESTMENT

The Syrian government has adopted a hesitantly positive attitude toward foreign investment in recent years. However, most representatives of foreign firms find Syria's business environment a difficult one.

The government has passed three key pieces of legislation since1985 to encourage foreign investment. In 1985, the SARG issued" Decision 186" to encourage investment in tourism. In1986, the government issued "Decree 10" to encourage the establishment of joint-venture agricultural companies.

In June 1991, as part of its overall reform program to encourage the private sector, the government passed a new investment law--"Law Number 10"-- to promote investment in all sectors of the economy. The new law offers the same incentives to local and foreign investors. Specifically, companies that receive licenses under the new law are accorded duty free privileges for the import of capital goods and materials necessary for a project, including vehicles, and a tax holiday for the first five years of operation. Companies that export over 50 percent of their products enjoy seven year tax holiday.

All applications for investment under the law must be screened and vetted through the Higher Council for Investment. The council meets at least once every two months. Membership includes the Prime Minister, and the Ministers of Economy, Agriculture, Transportation, Supply, Industry, Planning, Finance, and the Director of the Investment Bureau. No definitive criteria for approving investment is made explicit under the new law, but the council is more likely to approve a project if it:

- Maximizes the use of local resources
- Utilizes advanced technologies
- Boosts exports
- Creates jobs
- Advances the government's development plans

Most foreign investment in Syria is in the energy sector. Beginning in the late 1980s, the government actively courted international oil companies to sign concession agreements to explore for oil. In 1990, twelve foreign firms had operations in Syria, but today, only three remain.

Western firms departed because of disappointments over dry wells, rising costs, and friction with the Syrian government over contractual terms.

Foreign oil company representatives have mentioned several difficult aspects of doing business in Syria, citing both Syrian and U.S. government policies and restrictions.

- In past exploration and production contracts, the SARG required foreign oil companies to use the unfavorable official rate of11.2 Syrian pounds (SP)/USD versus the neighboring country rate of 43.5 SP/USD and the offshore rate of 49-52 SP/USD for all business transactions with Syrian individuals and companies. Recently however, faced with the departure of most exploration companies, the SARG decided that all new contracts be at the neighboring country rate.

- The SARG requires that export and import licenses be obtained for every single item imported and then re-exported, regardless of value. Several company representatives recalled that documentation for even minor items, such as paint cans and used spark plugs, had to be kept to prove to customs officials that they had not been illegally re-exported or sold locally. Likewise, foreign companies must acquire temporary permits for each item of equipment intended for temporary use and subsequent re-export (i.e. drilling rigs) to avoid paying import duties. These permits can be difficult to extend if the company's service contract has expired, and fit wants to keep the equipment in-country for stand-by usage. Delays in the re-export of equipment after a temporary permit expires has drawn heavy fines.

- In the absence of an adequate infrastructure in Syria, such as telecommunications, maintaining contact with field crews became costly as companies leased expensive, dedicated lines from the Syrian Telecommunications Establishment at the official exchange rate. However, as of August 1, 1996, the government began to apply the neighboring country rate, thereby reducing costs.

- USG foreign policy sanctions and individual validated licensing requirements imposed on "dual use items" such as computer equipment and oil exploration technology, including global positioning indicators, make work difficult. Also mentioned was the "Grassley Amendment ," another USG sanction on Syria, that prevents U.S. companies from taking advantage of foreign tax credits on loyalties paid to the SARG.

- In April 1996, Congress enacted new Antiterrorism legislation affecting financial transactions with Syria.

According to the final regulations, all financial transactions between U.S. persons or entities and the Government of the Syrian Arab Republic are authorized unless the transaction constitutes a donation to the U.S. person or entity, or the U.S. person or entity recipient knows or has reasons to know that the transfer poses a risk of furthering terrorist acts in the United States. Additional information is available from the Department of Treasury's Office of Foreign Assets Control, at (202) 622-2520.

RIGHT TO PRIVATE OWNERSHIP

All major private investment projects must be licensed. Over the past few years, the Syrian government has steadily opened sectors, formerly reserved to government monopolies, to private sector investment. Key sectors opened since 1994 included flour milling, sugar refining, and cement manufacturing. The Prime Minister has stated publicly that the Higher Council of Investment, which he chairs, is open to any and all proposals for investment, in any industry and on any scale. Nevertheless, state enterprises withal competing interest in a proposed project are routinely consulted by the Investment Council.

For additional analytical, business and investment opportunities information,
please contact Global Investment & Business Center, USA
at (703) 370-8082. Fax: (703) 370-8083. E-mail: ibpusa3@gmail.com
Global Business and Investment Info Databank - www.ibpus.com

The standard of competitive equality is not applied to private enterprises competing with state enterprises in a number of important areas. For example, although a number of state banks, such as the Real Estate and Industrial Bank, are authorized to loan local currency to help finance private sector projects, state enterprises continue to have privileged access to local credit and exclusive access to official foreign exchange loans from the Commercial Bank of Syria. However, private companies can sometimes access offshore financing. Likewise, according to local business sources, state enterprises have priority in the allocations of commodities and material produced by other state enterprises. Public sector firms also appear to have greater access to public services, such as telecommunications and electricity.

The government has rejected "privatization" of state enterprises as a viable strategy because of the unmarketability of most state enterprises and the continued dependence of the national workforce on public sector employment.

PROTECTION OF PROPERTY RIGHTS

Syria's legal system recognizes and facilitates the transfer of property rights, including intellectual property rights. Under its own law, the Syrian government has raided shops known to pirate computer software. In April 1995, the Syrian government announced its intention, in principle, to join the Paris Union for the International Protection of Industrial Property. The government also stated that it is considering joining the 1967 Stockholm Intellectual Property Rights Agreement.

The following information details the specific legal protections for patents, copyrights, and trademarks:

Patents: These are issued for fifteen year periods, provided the invention has been utilized within two years after the patent was granted.

Copyrights: Most books printed in Syria are in Arabic and by Arab authors. However, instances of copyright infringement especially of Arabic translations of English texts, have occurred. Pirated records, cassettes, and videos are widely available.

Despite government efforts, pirated computer software is also readily available. The amount of lost revenue is probably minimal. In any event, enforcement and the associated litigation would-be, if not impossible, extremely costly compared to any positive benefits that may result.

The motion picture industry estimates the home video market in Syria is 100 percent pirated, and is also concerned with unauthorized hotel video performances, which are said to be common. However, only a few hotels have internal video systems.

Additionally, 100 percent of both Arab and non-Arab commercial music products are pirated. Given the lack of technical sophistication of Syrian industry and strict government control of communications and data processing, infringements on new technologies are note problem.

Trademarks: These may be registered for ten-year periods. The first applicant is always entitled to registration.

PERFORMANCE REQUIREMENTS AND INCENTIVES

Apart from specifying a minimum investment of ten million Syrian pounds, the new investment law has no formal performance requirements. For example, foreign investors are not required to employ a fixed proportion of local labor, although there are reports that informal guidelines are negotiated on a case-by-case basis during the licensing process. Investors' access to foreign exchange is limited as it's a function of the value of a company's exports.

Proprietary information may also have to be disclosed for project approval. The Ministry of Supply has the authority to set prices and/or profit margins for products destined for the local market, buts far, foreign investors have not encountered problems as a result of this practice. Under Investment Law 10, there are additional incentives for investment in rural areas and for those companies that use local raw materials.

Prior to coming to Syria, all U.S. citizens must obtain an entry visa which may be procured from the Syrian embassy in Washington. Although there are no discriminatory or excessive visa, residence, or work permit requirements, if an individual wishes to remaining Syria longer than 14 days, that person must register with the government and acquire a temporary residence permit (in addition to the entry visa). The Syrian government will not grant entry to persons with passports bearing an Israeli visa or entry/exit stamp, or to persons born in the Gaza region or of Gazan descent.

REGULATORY SYSTEM

The Syrian regulatory system is not oriented toward promoting competition either among private firms or between private and state enterprises. Regulations enforced by the Ministry of Supply are aimed at promoting consumer protection by preventing hoarding and price gouging.

Nevertheless, to foster competition, the government has put public sector enterprises on notice that they will no longer be permitted to monopolize whole sectors, particularly if private capital, whether foreign or domestic, can be attracted to finance needed projects. As for fiscal and welfare regulations, such as tax, labor, safety, and health laws, these appear to been forced without discrimination. Bureaucratic procedures for licensing and necessary documentation move slowly and require official approval from many levels within the government. In this regard, under-the-table payments are often required as corruption is endemic at nearly all levels of government.

The absence of organized capital, foreign exchange, and financial markets continues to be an important impediment to private investment, both domestic and foreign. In 1994, the parliament approved legislation authorizing the re-opening of the Damascus stock market; however, it still awaits the President's approval. The government continues to impose strict foreign exchange controls on private sector operations outside the specific concessions granted under the new investment law to operate self-funding foreign exchange accounts at the Commercial Bank of Syria.

CORRUPTION

Syrian laws prohibit corruption and accepting money donations. The Central Commission for Control and Inspection is responsible for criminalizing such actions. Both the briber and the recipient will be subject to imprisonment and/or confiscation of property. Occasionally, newspapers publish lists of government employees who were fired for "reasons related to integrity". However, incomes are so low in the public sector that some fringe benefits are unofficially accepted as means of direct compensation, especially in government procurement, investment licensing, and obtaining importation approval.

LABOR

The private sector has been able to recruit both skilled and professional labor. On the other hand, state enterprises have difficulty attracting qualified personnel, due to low salaries. To resign their positions, public sector employees must obtain permission, which is often difficult.

The government-controlled Syrian General Federation of Trade Unions(GFTU) oversees all aspects of union activity. The GFTU is affiliated with the International Confederation of Arab Trade Unions. In the public sector, unions do not normally bargain collectively on wage issues, but there is some evidence that union representatives participate with the representatives of the employer and Ministry of Labor in establishing sect oral minimum wages.

In a country whose major industries are state-owned, workers make up the majority of each board of directors and union representatives are always included on those boards. They also monitor and enforce compliance with the labor law. In the private sector, unions are active in monitoring compliance with the laws and ensuring workers' health and safety. The unions, under the law, can undertake negotiations for collective contracts with employers, but there is no information available on whether such contracts envision that unions can also sue and be represented in court. The government has continued to resist the abolition of the Minister of Labor's power over collective contracts. Organized unions do not seem to have a role in the receptivity of foreign investment.

EFFICIENT CAPITAL MARKETS AND PORTFOLIO INVESTMENT

Policies do not facilitate the free flow of financial resources. Capital can be brought into the country, but must be exchanged at the unfavorable exchange rate which is about 20% less than the free market rate. On the other hand, repatriation of capital remains a problem because foreign investors do not have access to foreign exchange. Investors wishing to repatriate their funds are expected to generate foreign currencies from their exports.

There are no foreign banks operating in Syria. Furthermore, all Syrian banks are government-owned and offer only basic banking services. Local and foreign investors may acquire small loans from local banks through very complicated and impractical procedures.

Legal, regulatory, and accounting systems are consistent with international norms in theory. In reality, however, local businesses do not comply with these regulations in order to avoid confiscator tax rates.

There are no stock or bond markets in Syria.

CONVERSION AND TRANSFER POLICIES

The new investment law sets no limits on the inflow of funds. Beneficiaries under the law are permitted to open foreign exchange accounts with the Commercial Bank of Syria. An investor must deposit100 percent of all foreign exchange capital and hard currency loans secured by the project, and 75 percent of export earnings. Outward capital transfers and profit remittances are prohibited, unless approved by the Prime Minister or sanctioned under the new investment law or a specific arrangement, as in the case of production sharing agreements concluded with oil exploration companies.

Under Law 10/1991, invested capital may be repatriated after five years from the project completion date (six months, if the project fails due to events beyond the control of the investor), and profits remitted on an annual basis.

Expatriate employees are permitted to transfer abroad 50 percent of their salaries, and 100 percent of severance pay. In the case of foreign oil companies, "cost recovery" of exploration and development expenditures misgoverned by formulas specifically negotiated in the applicable concession agreement.

For additional analytical, business and investment opportunities information, please contact Global Investment & Business Center, USA at (703) 370-8082. Fax: (703) 370-8083. E-mail: ibpusa3@gmail.com Global Business and Investment Info Databank - www.ibpus.com

Foreign oil partners in production sharing joint-ventures with the state oil company report delays in the recognition of "cost recovery" claims, although such payments are eventually approved.

The private sector has had no access to official foreign reserves since 1984. Under the new investment law, all foreign exchange operations must be generated from company operations and transacted through the investor's foreign exchange account at the Commercial Bank of Syria. No mechanism exists in the parallel "gray" foreign exchange market, funded from permitted private sector retained export earnings, for the repatriation of capital and profits.

Strict foreign exchange restrictions are enforced outside the concessions granted under law 10/1991. The export of capital requires the approval of the Central Bank, as does overseas borrowing. Foreign companies operating outside the new investment law may transfer capital only in accordance with the special agreements, usually in the form of a presidential decree, which allow their operation in Syria.

EXPROPRIATION AND COMPENSATION

There have been no expropriations of private property for public use since the 1960s. Although protection against expropriations not explicitly stated in the new investment law, older investment laws include such clauses, which presumably remain valid and applicable under the new investment law.

DISPUTE SETTLEMENT

Few investment disputes have occurred during the past several years. The few that have transpired have typically been settled(often with long delays) through negotiations or via arbitration clauses in contracts. While a number of U.S. suppliers have asserted claims against state enterprises for non-payment on goods and services delivered, the Syrian government, working closely with the Commercial Bank of Syria, has taken steps since early 1995to settle some of these debts on a case by case basis.

Property and contractual rights are protected by the constitution and enforced by law. However, there is considerable government interference in the court system and judgments by foreign courts are generally accepted only if the verdict favors the Syrian government. Although a written bankruptcy law exists, it is not applied fairlyland creditors may or may not salvage their investment. Monetary judgments in such cases are made in the local currency which can not be converted to a hard currency.

The government accepts binding international arbitration of investment disputes between foreign investors and the state in cases where the investment agreement or contract includes such a clause. Otherwise, local courts have jurisdiction. Syria is neither a member of the International Center for the Settlement of Investment Disputes nor of the New York Convention of 1958 on the recognition and enforcement of foreign arbitral awards.

BILATERAL INVESTMENT AGREEMENTS

Syria is a safe environment for personal security, and the country has enjoyed over 25 years of political stability. However, with the economy and progress in the Middle East peace process stalled, and uncertainty over succession of the aging President Asad, future stability is an area of concern.

Syria and the U.S. signed an investment guarantee agreement on August 9, 1976 that protects investments from nationalization and confiscation. Similar agreements were also signed with

Germany, France, and Switzerland. In addition, since the Gulf War, a number of bi-national committees have been established with Gulf Arab countries to explore private and mixed joint-ventures.

U.S. investment is not eligible for OPIC and other types of insurance programs due to Syria's inclusion on the list of state supporters of terrorism. For the same reason EXIM Bank, small business administration, and commodity corporation financing is not available for U.S.exports to Syria. USAID assistance to Syria was terminated in1983.

FOREIGN DIRECT INVESTMENT STATISTICS

Official foreign investment statistics by country are not available. According to press stories, some 1476 projects valued at about326 billion Syrian pounds (approximately USD 6.5 billion at the offshore rate centered in Beirut) have been approved under the new investment law since its issuance in 1991 and through May1996. However, only a small percentage of approved projects have even begun construction much less operation.

TRADE AND PROJECT FINANCING

BANKING SYSTEM

Syria's government-controlled banking system consists of five banks: The Commercial Bank of Syria, the Agricultural Cooperative Bank, the Industrial Bank, the Real Estate Bank, and the People's Credit Bank. The Central Bank of Syria oversees banking operations and manages the money supply. According to Syrian bank regulations, only the Central Bank and the Commercial Bank may engage in international transactions and hold foreign exchange deposits outside Syria. Within Syria, only the Commercial Bank may sell Syrian pounds for foreign currencies. Except for a few exemptions, unused Syrian pounds cannot be sold back to the Commercial Bank. Moreover, Law24 of 1986 criminalizes the private exchange of foreign currencies and Syrian pounds.

Besides monopolizing the exchange of foreign currencies, the Syrian government maintains one of the last remaining fixed, multiple exchange rate systems in the world. At present the government exchanges money at four different rates, ranging from the "official" rate of 11.2 SP/USD, to the "neighboring country" rate of 43.5 SP/USD. However, virtually all transactions occur at either the "neighboring country" rate, the "offshore" rate, negotiated in the free markets of Amman or Beirut, which ranges between 49 and 52 SP/USD, or the "export dollar" rate, which ranges between 52 and 57 SP/USD.

HOW TO FINANCE EXPORTS/METHODS OF PAYMENT

In general, private Syrian traders finance imports from their own resources or through their own credit. Contracts with the private sector are negotiated on an individual basis with little or no interference from the government. All documentary transactions for imports must be by a letter of credit opened at the Commercial Bank of Syria. Typically, the Bank requires the importer to cover100 percent of the transaction from his own resources offshore or from funds generated by exports. Syrian importers often require that one of the following two clauses be added to the preformed invoices and bills of lading as payment conditions, "free of payment" or "180-day credit facilities."

In this case, the importer pays through his offshore bank, either cash in advance, or via L/C, and the bill of lading is then sent to the Commercial Bank of Syria. In such instances, U.S. exporters are well advised to avoid delayed payment or the "cash against documents" mechanism, since the U.S. exporter has no protection under such a transaction and the Commercial Bank of Syria has no authority to release funds under such a clause.

Moreover, the importer could simply walk away from the contract even after the goods are shipped.

Alternatively, an importer may use foreign exchange earned from exports (export dollars) and deposit it in the Commercial Bank of Syria. The foreign exchange used to cover an L/C opened at the Commercial Bank may be his own, or purchased in an informal secondary market.

In March 1994, the Syrian government transferred several importable goods from the list of items that can be financed from offshore accounts to the list of items that must be purchased with export dollars. Whatever the source of funding, it is strongly recommended that U.S. exporters sell their goods to Syrians under" cash in advance" or "confirmed irrevocable letters of credit" until a satisfactory relationship with the Syrian importer has been established.

For its contracts, the government will open an L/C only after the contractor has posted a ten percent performance bond to ensure that goods will be delivered within the stated time of delivery, free of defects, and identical to the offer in both quality and quantity.

Posting these bank guarantees has been a constraint for U.S. firms wishing to do business in Syria because suppliers' banks often lack correspondence arrangements with the Commercial Bank of Syria. Again, U.S. commercial financing is not a practical way to do business with Syrian firms because foreign exchange impediments make it impossible to guarantee a loan or credit facility for a Syrian beneficiary.

TYPES OF AVAILABLE FINANCING AND INSURANCE

Because Syria remains on the list of state supporters of terrorism, Eximbank financing and insurance is unavailable to U.S. exporters. For the same reason, USAID is not present in Syria.

Moreover, the World Bank will not fund projects in Syria because of unpaid arrears on Syria's debt to that institution. However, Syria has received some project financing from Japan, the EU, and various Arab national and multinational institutions. Projects financed include upgrading the national telephone system, construction of several electrical power plants, and the purchase of earthmoving equipment.

Syrian Banks with correspondent U.S. banking arrangements:

- Central Bank of Syria

- Commercial Bank of Syria

U.S. Banks in New York with known correspondent Syrian banking arrangements:

- Arab American Bank, New York

- Bank of New York, New York

- Morgan Guarantee Trust Company, New York

- Credit Lyonnais, New York

- Citibank, New York

USEFUL ADDRESSES

- ## General company for fruits and vegetables

Damascus P.O.Box: 5603
Tel 5422926-5422824-5422928
Fax 5423001
Tlx: 411914,412734
Cable :KHODAR
Products: Vegetables, Fruits, Fresh, Fruits, and Dehydrated

- ## General Establishment For Food Industries

Damascus P.O.Box :105
Tel :2225290-2234426-2234428
Fax :224537
Products: Soda , Conservatives, Jams, Arak, Oil, and Biscuits

- ## General Establishment For Tobacco

Damascus P.O.Box :616
Tel :2323125-2323126
Fax : 2233805
Tlx :411301   Cable :MONTAB
Products :Tobacco Tobacco Wholly , (Tombac)

- ## General Company Leather Industries

Damascus   P.O.Box :2994
Tel 5121808-5121809-5121810
Tlx :411628
Cable :AHZEAH
Products :Leather Footwear for men & women

- ## General organization for fish

Jableh
Tel :821677-833112-831367
Fax :831367
Tlx :451025
Products :FISH , CARP, FISH ,TILAPIA

- ## General Establishment For Cows

Hama, P.O.Box :48
Tel :410985
Fax :422984
Products: Meat frish, (Frezian,Holoshtin)

- **General Company For Matches ,Chipbord**

Damascus   P.O.Box :2672
Tel :5435734
Fax : 5437337
Tlx :41526 KEBRET SY
Cable :KEBRET-Damascus
Products :Matches ,Playwood, Chipboard ,Pencils (Graphite & Color)

- **General Establishment For Foreign Trade Of Food & Chemical Materials**

Damascus ,Jumhuryah St.
P.O.Box :893
Tel: 2218919-2225421
Fax:2226927
Productes: Cotton Linters,Onion (dried)

- **General Organization For Sugar**

Homs   P.O.Box :4290
Tel :227600-227602- Damascus 2212329
Fax :237899
Tlx :441123-441006 GOFS Cable :GOFS
PRODUCTS :MOLASSES,YEST DRY ,AL-COHOL, MEDICAL

- **"Orient" Company For Underwear**

Damascus   P.O.Box :1100
Tel :5436001-5436003
Fax :5436000
Tlx :412436 O.U.M.C.SY
Products :Ccoton Underwear

- **General Establishment For Cereal Processing And Trade**

Damascus   P.O.Box :4106
Tel :2238364-2238397-2237818
Fax :2232368
Tlx :412511-411027-411391
Cable :HOBOB-Damascus
Products: :Seed Of Lentils ,Lentils, Chick-Peas ,Barley

- **CARPET MANUFACTURING GENERAL CORPORATION**

Damascus   P.O.Box :1400
Tel :8880100 –8816973
Fax :8887002
Tlx :412514 CARP
Cable :CARPETCO
Products :Carpets , Woolen

For additional analytical, business and investment opportunities information,
please contact Global Investment & Business Center, USA
at (703) 370-8082. Fax: (703) 370-8083. E-mail: ibpusa3@gmail.com
Global Business and Investment Info Databank - www.ibpus.com

- **HAMA COTTON YARN COMPANY**

Hama   P.O.Box :11
Tel :511092-551093-511091
Fax :511096
Tlx :431037 HAYC
Cable :GHAZEL Hama
Products :Cotton Carded Or Combed

- **Dry Battery Fabric**

Damascus   P.O.Box :3120
Tel: 6311643-8880789
Fax:2123375
Products: Dried battery

- **GENERAL ESTABLISHMENT FOR TIRES PRODUCTIONS**

Damascus   P.O.Box :12175
Tel :2210355 -2778808
Fax :2247499
 Poducts :Carpets, hand-made rug , carpets, hand made woolen , knit Faber. wool/fine hair

- **GENERAL ESTABLISHMENT FOR TIRES PRODUCTIONS**

Hama, Salamyah rood
Tel:424533-424532
Fax:424531
Tlx:431039
Products:Tires (different kinds)

- **General Company For Asphalt**

Lataquia   P.O.Box :6
Tle: 473121-475826
Fax : 475674
Tlx :451150
Cable :ASPEL
Products :,Nat. Asphalt Bituminous Mixtures Raw Stones

- **General Establishment For Porcelain**

Syria,Hama
P.O.Box : 161
Tel :510896-510996
Fax :511707
PRODUCTS : Porcelain , SANITARY WARE

For additional analytical, business and investment opportunities information,
please contact Global Investment & Business Center, USA
at (703) 370-8082. Fax: (703) 370-8083. E-mail: ibpusa3@gmail.com
Global Business and Investment Info Databank - www.ibpus.com

- **General Organization For Poultry**

Damascus   P.O.Box :5597
Tel :2211968 -2212876
Fax :2217473
Tlx :412423 G.O.P. SYR
Cable :G.O.P. Damascus
Products :POULTRY LIVE, POULTRY FRESH
,EGGS BIRDS IN SHELL (HATCHING) ,EGGS BIRDS IN SHELL (TABLE)

- **Productive Projects Administration**

Damascus   P.O.Box :4703
Tel :2131499-212990-3314790
Fax :2205210
Tlx :412914 SY PRODUC
Products :, ,HONEY (flowred),HONEY (zalloo) ,MEDICAL PLANETS

- **General Establishment For Panting & Chemical Industries**

P.O.Box:1276
Tle : 5435511-5435512
Fax:5431088
Tlx:411299
Products Paints (deferent)

- **General Establishment For Chemical Industries**

Damascus
Tle:2127654-2123363
Fax :2128289
Products :Sport & leather shoes,Plastic houses, Chinaware

- **General Establishment For Engineering Industries**

Damascus
P.O.Box: 3120
Tle :212825-2122650
Fax :2123375
Products: Refrigerators, Household, Appliances, color TV Telephone sets, Cables

- **General Establishment For Textile Industries**

Fardous St.,Damascus
P.O.Box : 620
Tel :2216200-2215624-2215262
Fax :2216021
Tlx:411011
Products :Cotton yarns, Cotton Fabric, Socks , wool Carpets

For additional analytical, business and investment opportunities information,
please contact Global Investment & Business Center, USA
at (703) 370-8082. Fax: (703) 370-8083. E-mail: ibpusa3@gmail.com
Global Business and Investment Info Databank - www.ibpus.com

- **General Establishment For Cleaners chemical Industry**

Damascus, Adra
P.O.Box: 682
Tel : 5810163- 5810164
Fax : 581062
Tlx : 412694 jecoda
PRODUCTS: Cleaners (Powders & Liquid), selphonic aside

- **General Electric Motors Manufacturing Company**

Lataquia   P.O.Box :190
Tel :421850 -421533
Fax :410761
Tlx :451090
Cable :MOTORS
Products :ELICTRICAL CABLE,TRANSFORMER (FLORESANT)

- **GENERAL COMPANY FOR Tanning**

Damascus ,Zablatani road
P.O.Box : 2019
Tel: 457840-454863
Fax : 4424935
Products :Raw & processed leather,leather jacets.

- **General Company For Transformation Industry**

Damascus P.O.Box :2803
Tel :6714574
Fax :6714572
Products :Sanitary Paper (For Baby & Women

For additional analytical, business and investment opportunities information,
please contact Global Investment & Business Center, USA
at (703) 370-8082. Fax: (703) 370-8083. E-mail: ibpusa3@gmail.com
Global Business and Investment Info Databank - www.ibpus.com

SYRIA, MINERALS, OIL AND GAS SECTOR: STRATEGIC INFORMATION AND DEVELOPMENTS

THE MINERAL INDUSTRY OF SYRIA

SYRIA

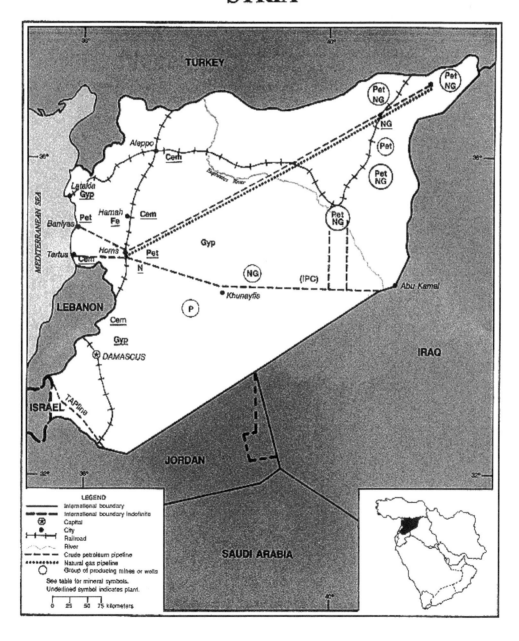

In May 2010, Syria was granted observer status at the World Trade Organization (WTO) after the United States lifted its opposition to Syria's application to join the WTO. The Government announced that it expects to sign a partnership agreement with the European Union by the end of 2010. The Government, based on the assumption that the country's crude oil reserves are sufficient to supply 300,000 bbl/d for the next 40 years, was focusing on developing other sources of energy, such as natural gas and shale oil and promoting private sector involvement in power generation activity in the country through financing and operating the first independent powerplant company.

Private investment in the cement and steel sectors is expected to address the chronic shortages of cement and rebar commodities in the local markets. Phosphate rock and phosphate fertilizer production is likely to increase significantly following the entry of Indian fertilizer production companies to the phosphate production market of Syria (Alexander's Gas & Oil Connections, 2009; Ministry of Petroleum and Mineral Resources, 2010a, b).

Crude oil and phosphate rock were Syria's main contributions to the world supply of minerals in 2009. Syria produced about 1.9% of the world's phosphate rock output and was the world's ninth ranked producer of phosphate rock. Other raw and processed mineral commodities produced in Syria included cement, gypsum, industrial sand (silica), marble, natural crude asphalt, nitrogen fertilizer, phosphate fertilizer, salt, steel, and volcanic tuff (Jasinski, 2010).

MINERALS IN THE NATIONAL ECONOMY

The global economic downturn of 2009 had affected the Syrian economy and caused a 28% decrease in the value of exports because of the decrease of the volume of international trade and a 2.7% decrease in remittances of Syrian expatriates because of the slowdown of the regional economies in 2009. Nevertheless, Syria's real gross domestic product (GDP) grew at a rate of 4.0% in 2009 compared with 5.2% in 2008. Crude oil production was decreased by about 3.6% to 376,000 barrels per day (bbl/d) from 390,000 bbl/d in 2008.

The volume of gross crude oil exports, however, which averaged 250,200 bbl/d in 2009, was a decrease of 16% compared with the export volume in 2005. Net petroleum exports averaged 148,000 bbl/d and were marketed exclusively by the state-owned marketing company Sytrol mainly to European countries, including France, Germany, and Italy. Revenue from the hydrocarbon sector accounted for 4.6% of the GDP compared with 5.2% of the GDP in 2008. The value of crude oil exports decreased by 36% to about $3.5 billion from $5.5 billion in 2008. The value of crude oil and refined oil products decreased by 43% to $3.2 billion from about $5.6 billion in 2008. The decrease in the value and volume of crude oil exports was attributable to increased local consumption of petroleum products and to a decrease in international oil prices (Bank Audi S.A.L., 2010, p. 1, 12; International Monetary Fund, 2010, p. 17-18; Organization of Arab Petroleum Exporting Countries, 2010, p. 19, 57; U.S. Energy Information Administration, 2010).

GOVERNMENT POLICIES AND PROGRAMS

On February 14, 2009, the Government passed law Nos. 14 and 15, which reorganized the state-owned petroleum companies. Law No. 14 created the General Corporation for Refining and Distribution of Petroleum Products. The new agency included Banias Refinery Co., Homs Refinery Co., Syrian Company for Distribution and Storage of Petroleum Products, and Syrian Company for Gas Distribution. Law No. 15 created the General Petroleum Corp. (GPC), which included Syrian Gas Co., Syrian Petroleum Co. (SPC), and Syrian Petroleum Transportation Co. The mission of the GPC was to establish policies related to the development, exploration, and investment in the hydrocarbon sector and to monitor international oil companies' projects in the country (Ministry of Petroleum and Mineral Resources, 2009a, b).

In 2009, the General Establishment of Geology and Mineral Resources (GEGMR) mapped an area of 3,410 square kilometers, drilled 12,718 meters, and analyzed 6,611 samples. The GEGMR had been promoting the development of the country's mining sector by focusing on upgrading rock phosphate production at the As-Sharqiyah and the Khunayfis Mines; building phosphate-based fertilizer plants and phosphate washing and drying units; developing natural crude asphalt mining at the Al-Bishri and the Kafrayya Mines; rehabilitating the marble plants in Damascus and Latakia; increasing the production of volcanic tuff; and starting a bentonite and zeolite mining industry (General Establishment of Geology and Mineral Resources, 2010, p. 11).

In 2009, GEGMR issued 944 licenses for quarrying for building material throughout the country; 17 of these licenses were for cement production. GEGMR invited international companies to invest in the mining of natural crude asphalt from the Al-Bishri deposit to produce petroleum products, generate electricity, and make asphalt mixes for road pavement. The General Company for Phosphate and Mines (GCPM) called on consulting companies to provide technical, feasibility, and environmental studies for the treatment and beneficiation of phosphate rock tailings at the Khunayifis and the As-Sharquiah Mines. In 2010, GPC invited bids for crude oil and natural gas exploration on eight onshore blocks and eight offshore blocks as well as a bid round to develop seven oilfields in the country.

Damascus Securities Exchange (DSE) was reopened in 2009 after 40 years of closure, which was the period when the country was experimenting with a socialist economy. As of yearend 2009, the majority of companies listed on the DSE were financial institutions (Roscoe, 2010, p. 39).

PRODUCTION

In 2009, production of asphalt increased by 57% and gross natural gas output increased by 5% compared with that of 2008. Notable decreases in the output of minerals in 2009 compared with 2008 included gypsum output, which decreased by 30%; rock phosphate, by 23%; marble slabs, by 25%; industrial sand (silica), by 15%; and salt, by 12% (table 1).

STRUCTURE OF THE MINERAL INDUSTRY

State-owned companies that were administrated by the Ministry of Industry or the Ministry of Petroleum and Mineral Resources (MoPMR) carried out the majority of mining activity in Syria. These companies included the General Company for Marble and Asphalt (GEMA), the General Company for Phosphate and Mines, the GPC, the General Organization for Cement and Building Materials (GOCBM), General Fertilizers Co., and the General Company for Iron and Steel Products (Hadeed Hama). Several private local and international investors were involved in the process of building new greenfield cement plants, including Al-Badia Cement Co. J.S.C., Al Rajhi Cement, and Lafarge Cement Syria S.A. Private finished steel producers included Al Wahib Group, Arabian Steel Co. (ASCO), Hmisho International Steel S.A., International Company for Steel Rolling (ICSR), Joudco Steel Ltd., and Syria Steel and Iron Co. (SALB) (table 2).

COMMODITY REVIEW

METALS

Iron and Steel.—Syria's imports of steel products, which included crude, semifinished, and finished steel, had been increasing in recent years because of the inability of the existing plants to meet the increased demand of the construction sector for reinforcement bar (rebar). The country imported 2.2 million metric tons per year (Mt/yr) of steel products in 2009 compared with 2.0 Mt/yr in 2008 and 2.8 Mt/yr in 2007. Steel products were mainly imported from Ukraine, which accounted for 44% of Syria's steel imports, by volume, followed by Russia, which accounted for 13% of the total steel imports, by volume (Arab Steel, 2010).

Apollo Metalex Pvt. Ltd. of India moved forward with upgrading Hadeed Hamas's scrap melting plant. The $34 million project was expected to increase the plant's capacity to 288,000 metric tons per year (t/yr) of billet from 70,000 t/yr by 2010 (Arab Steel, 2009).

Joudco Steel produced 132,000 metric tons (t) of rebar at its plant in Latakia compared with 133,000 t in 2008. All but 575 t of the company's output was sold on the local market. The company was building a new 75,000-t/yr-capacity plant in Adra Industrial City northeast of Damascus for the production of hot-rolled billets. The new billet plant, which was a joint venture with an unnamed foreign investor, was expected to be completed by yearend 2010 (Arab Steel, 2010).

In 2009, Hmisho Steel, produced low-and medium-carbon-content rebar from its newly built mill in Latakia. The company built a new billet plant with an electric arc furnace (EAF), a ladle furnace, and a four-strand billet continuous-casting machine at Adra Industrial City. The capacity to produce 500,000 t/yr of steel was supplied by Daniel Centro Metal Co. of Italy. In October, International Company for Steel Rolling commissioned production of its rolling mill plant, which is located in Hisyah Industrial Zone near Homs. The plant had the capacity to produce 300,000 t/yr of rebar (Hmisho Steel S.A., 2010; International Company for Steel Rolling, 2010).

INDUSTRIAL MINERALS

Cement.—Cement production in Syria, which totaled about 5.5 million metric tons (Mt) in 2009, was expected to double following the completion of projects currently under construction. The country's cement consumption in 2010 was expected to exceed 8 Mt. Lafarge Cement Syria, which was owned by Lafarge S.A. of France (85%) and Mas Economic Group (15%), continued building a new greenfield plant at Manbej, which is located 160 kilometers (km) northeast of Aleppo and 25 km south of the border with Turkey. The 3-Mt/yr-capacity plant was expected to be completed by June 2010. Lafarge had a plan to build a second cement plant near Damascus (Lafarge Cement Syria S.A., 2010).

Al-Badia Cement Co. JSC, which was a joint venture of Muhaidib & Sons Group of Saudi Arabia, Ciment Francais (a subsidiary of Italcementi Group of Italy), and other investors, moved forward with the construction of a new 3.2-Mt/yr-capacity plant at Abu Ash-Shamat, which is located 80 km northeast of Damascus. The plant was being built by CBMI Construction Co. Ltd. of China and was expected to commence first-phase production of 1.6 Mt/yr in late 2010.

Rajhi Cement (a subsidiary of Al Rajhi Group of Saudi Arabia) signed a contract with Chengdu Design and Research Institute of Building Materials Industry Co. Ltd. of China to build a 1-Mt/yr cement plant in Syria (AME Info, 2008; China Cement Net, 2009).

In 2009, GOCBM, which operated eight state-owned cement plants in Syria, produced more than 5 Mt of clinker, which was 125,000 t more than output of 4.9 Mt in 2008, or an increase of 3%. Tartus Cement and Building Material Co. produced about 1.4 Mt of clinker; the Syrian Cement Manufacturing and Building Material Co. in Hama, 1.3 Mt; Arabian Cement Co., 824,000 t; Al Shahaba Cement and Building Material Co., 685,000 t; Adra Cement and Building Material Co., 657,000 t; and Rastan Cement and Building Material Co., 114,000 t. A cement plant that was operated by the Military Housing Establishment of the Ministry of Defense produced 293,000 t of cement. GOCBM was in the process of upgrading and expanding the capacity of the Tartus plant to 1.85 Mt/yr from 1.23 Mt. Pharon Commercial Investment Group of Saudi Arabia financed the

$50 million expansion plan in return for 400,000 t/yr of the plant's future production. Pharon Group was expected to upgrade the Adra cement plant to increase its capacity to about 1.5 Mt/yr from 845,000 t/yr in return for 461,000 t/yr of post-expansion production. Ehdas Sanat Co. of Iran completed building a new cement plant in Hama for GOCBM; the plant, which was initially scheduled for completion in 2007, had a capacity of 1.1 Mt/yr of cement (Syrian Arab News Agency, 2010).

In 2009, Guris Raqqa Cement Co., which was a subsidiary of Guris Construction and Engineering Co. Inc. of Turkey, completed the construction of a 1.5-Mt/yr-capacity clinker mill in Raqqa in northeastern Syria at a cost of $50 million. Guris also owned Al- Hasakeh Cement L.L.C. in the Yurubbiya Free Zone in northeastern Syria. Al-Hasakeh Cement was established in 2007 as a clinker production and milling plant as well as a cement sales outlet (Guris Construction and Engineering Co. Inc., 2010).

Phosphate Rock.—About 2.4 Mt of washed and unwashed phosphate rock was sold mainly to foreign fertilizer manufacturers in 2009. Phosphate rock production in the country decreased significantly for the second year in a row by 0.76 Mt in 2009 compared with that of 2008, which in turn was a decrease of about 0.5 Mt compared with that of 2007. Phosphate rock production was 35% less than the GCPM's production target for 2009. The company attributed the the significant decrease in production to reduced demand by international markets, insufficient mining equipment, and technical difficulties (General Establishment of Geology and Mineral Resources, 2010, p. 17).

In May 2010, the Governments of India and Syria signed a memorandum of understanding to establish a joint-venture company to develop phosphate rock production facilities in Syria, which would increase production to 10 Mt/yr from the current production of 2.2 Mt/yr. The new company would upgrade the phosphate rock mines in Alsharqiya and Kunayfis, transportation equipment, and the phosphate rock export terminal at Tartus Port. The joint venture would also build a phosphoric acid plant at a phosphate rock mine site. India was expected to import most of the phosphate rock, phosphoric acid, and phosphate fertilizer produced by the new company (Ministry of Petroleum and Mineral Resources, 2010a).

Stone, Dimension.—The General Institute for Geology of the MoPMR estimated that the country's dimension stones reserves were more than 50 Mt. In 2009, there were 32 active dimension stone quarries in the country. The GEMA operated 5 quarries directly and contracted 11 quarries; the remaining quarries were operated by private companies. A sector study conducted by the Syrian Enterprise Business Center and funded by the European Union identified 25 types of dimension stones in Syria, 5 of which were chosen for promotion at international markets. These designated types were the Bedrousi, the Rhaibani Light Biege, the Mussyaf, the Palmyra White, and the Palmyra Yellow (Damiani and Giovannangeli, 2008, p. 8).

MINERAL FUELS

Natural Gas.—Syria's natural gas reserves were estimated to be about 280 billion cubic meters. The country's gas production totaled 6.0 billion cubic meters, which was unchanged from the production level in 2008. The Government imported 728 million cubic meters of natural gas from Egypt by way of the Arab Gas Co. in 2009 (BP p.l.c., 2010, p. 24; Ministry of Petroleum and Mineral Resources, 2010b).

In November, the Syrian Gas Co. commenced production at the South Central Area gas treatment plant. The plant processed natural gas produced at the Abu Rabah, the Al Fayed, and the Qumqum gasfields. The plant, which was built by Stroytransgaz of Russia, was expected to produce about 2.5 billion cubic meters per year. Natural gas from the South Central Area plant would be used by the Adra cement plant, power stations, and fertilizer plant. Petrofac Ltd. of the

United Kingdom moved forward with the construction of 1.4-billion-cubic-meter-per-year natural gas processing plant in central Syria. The plant would begin processing natural gas from the Hayan gasfield in the fourth quarter of 2010. In August, the Governments of Syria and Turkey signed a memorandum of understanding to connect the gas networks of both countries, which would enable Syria to buy between 0.5 billion cubic meter and 1.0 billion cubic meters of natural gas per year from Turkey for 5 years beginning in 2011. In July, the GPC signed an agreement with Total S.A. of France to develop the Al-Tabia gasfield, which was located in the Dayr az Zawr Province in northeastern Syria (U.S. Energy Information Administration, 2010).

Petroleum.—In 2009, production of crude oil and condensates in Syria averaged about 376,000 barrels per day (bbl/d), which was about the same level of output achieved in the previous 3 years. Syria's proved petroleum reserves as of yearend 2009 were estimated to be 2.5 billion barrels. State-owned SPC produced more than 191,000 bbl/d of crude oil and condensates, and the international companies working in Syria, including Al-Furat Petroleum Co., Dier Ezour Petroleum Co., Dijla Petroleum Co., Hayan Petroleum Co., Oudeh Oil Co., and Sino Syrian Al Kawkab Oil Co., produced about 180,000 bb/d combined. The country's two petroleum refineries had the capacity to refine 240,000 bbl/d of crude oil. The Banias refinery had the capacity to refine 133,000 bbl/d of petroleum products. and the Homs refinery had the capacity to refine 107,000 bbl/d (Ministry of Petroleum and Mineral Resources, 2010b; U.S. Energy Information Administration, 2010).

The GPC was working with a number of international companies on crude oil and natural gas exploration to halt the downward trend in the country's crude oil production. These companies included Gulfsands Petroleum p.l.c. of the United Kingdom (Block 26), HBS International Egypt Ltd. (Block 22), INA Industrija Nafte of Croatia (Block 10), IPR Mediterranean Exploration Ltd. of the United States (Block 24), Loon Energy Corp. of Canada (Block 9), Morrell Broom Co. (Block 11), Royal Dutch Shell plc of the Netherlands (Blocks 57 and 58), Sayuz Co. of Ukraine (Block 12), Stratic Energy Corp. of Canada (Block 17), and Suncor Energy Inc. of Canada (Al Shaer and Al Sharefea gasfields, and Block 2) (General Petroleum Corp., 2010; Gulfsands Petroleum p.l.c., 2010).

The Government planned to upgrade the country's two refineries at Banias and Homs and to build two new greenfield refineries (one at Al-Furqlus east of Homs and another at Abu Khashab in Dayr az Zawr Province) to satisfy the increase in local demand for refined petroleum products, which was projected to increase by 5% annually for the next 20 years. The Al-Furqlus refinery project was a joint venture of the Governments of Iran, Syria, and Venezuela, and Al-Bukhari Group of Malaysia. It would have the capacity to refine 140,000 bbl/d of petroleum products and would cost about $3 billion to build. A second new greenfield petroleum refinery was planned at Dayr az Zawr in northeastern Syria. It would be built and financed by China National Petroleum Co. (CNPC) and would have a 100,000 bbl/d refining capacity and cost $2 billion to build. An economic feasibility study for the Dayr az Zawr refinery was expected to be completed in 2010.

OIL AND GAS SECTOR: BASIC INFORMATION

ENERGY OVERVIEW

Proven Oil Reserves (January 1, 2010E)	2.5 billion barrels
Total Oil Production	400 thousand barrels per day
Crude Oil Production	368 thousand barrels per day
Oil Consumption	252 thousand barrels per day
Net Petroleum Exports	192 thousand barrels per day
Crude Oil Distillation Capacity	240 thousand barrels per day

Proven Natural Gas Reserves	8.5 trillion cubic feet
Natural Gas Production	208 billion cubic feet
Natural Gas Consumption	213 billion cubic feet
Natural Gas Imports	5 billion cubic feet
Total Energy Consumption	0.8 quadrillion Btu*, of which Oil (69%), Natural Gas (27%), Hydroelectricity (4%)
Total Per Capita Energy Consumption	38.8 million Btu
Energy Intensity	9,388 Btu per $2000-PPP**

OIL AND GAS INDUSTRY

Organization	Upstream and downstream oil and gas sectors controlled by the state-owned Syrian Petroleum Company (SPC) and the Syrian Gas Company (SGC), both part of the Ministry of Petroleum and Mineral Resources. Since 2001, Syria has re-opened upstream oil and gas exploration to international oil companies through production sharing agreements. Investments in downstream infrastructure are also increasingly open to foreign investment.
Major Oil/Gas Ports	Baniyas, Tartous and Latakia
Foreign Company Involvement	Shell Oil, Total, Stroytransgaz, Gulfsands, Soyuzneftegaz, ONGC, CNPC, Petro-Canada, Petrofac, Sinochem, Sinopec, Tatneft.
Major Oil and Natural Gas Basins	Palmyra, Suweidiya, Deir Ez-Zour, Jbessa
Major Pipelines (capacity)	Arab Gas Pipeline (970 MMcf/d when completed to Turkey)
Major Refineries (capacity, bbl/d)	Baniyas (132,725), Homs (107,140)

Syria produces relatively modest quantities of oil and gas but the country's location is strategic in terms of energy transit.

Syria is the only significant crude oil producing country in the Eastern Mediterranean region, which includes Jordan, Lebanon, Israel, the West Bank, and Gaza. In 2009, Syria produced about 400,000 barrels per day (bbl/d) of crude and other petroleum liquids. Oil production has stabilized after falling for a number of years, and is poised to turn around as new fields come on line. In 2008, Syria produced 213 billion cubic feet (Bcf) of natural gas, and is expected to double its gas production by the end of 2010. While much of its oil is exported to Europe, Syria's natural gas is used in reinjection for enhanced oil recovery (EOR) and for domestic electricity generation.

Although Syria produces relatively modest quantities of oil and gas, its location is strategic in terms of regional security and prospective energy transit routes. Regional integration in the energy sector is expected to increase as a result of the 2008 opening of the Syrian link of the Arab Gas Pipeline and ongoing plans for the expansion of the pipeline network to include neighboring countries Turkey, Iraq, and Iran.

OIL

Syrian crude oil production has been in decline since the mid-1990s, but efforts are underway to turn it around in 2010.

According to *The Oil and Gas Journal*, Syria had 2.5 billion barrels of petroleum reserves as of January 1, 2010. Syria's known oil reserves are mainly in the eastern part of the country near its border with Iraq and along the Euphrates River; a number of smaller fields are located in the center of the country.

Organization

Syria's upstream oil production and development has traditionally been the mandate of the Syrian Petroleum Company (SPC), an arm of the Ministry of Petroleum and Mineral Resources. The SPC has undertaken efforts to reverse the trend toward declining oil production and exports by increasing oil exploration and production in partnership with foreign oil companies. The SPC directly controls about half of the country's oil production and takes a 50 percent stake in development work with foreign partners.

Foreign investment is vital for improving production levels. The main foreign producing consortium is the Al-Furat Petroleum Company, a joint venture established in 1985, which currently includes the SPC at 50 percent ownership, Shell Oil at 32 percent, and others, including China's CNPC. Asian national oil companies and smaller independents have been the most active in recent exploration tenders, including Gulfsands, led by Sinochem.

Production

Since peaking at 583,000 barrels per day (bbl/d) in 1996, Syrian crude oil production declined to an estimated 368,000 bbl/d in 2009, down from 390,000 bbl/d in 2008. Total oil liquids production, which includes crude and natural gas liquids (NGL), is estimated at about 400,000 bbl/d in 2009. Syrian oil minister Suffian Alao announced in April 2010 that the government expects oil production to increase in 2010 following 13 years of steady decline. Syria consumed 252,000 bbl/d of petroleum liquids in 2009.

The largest and most mature fields are Al-Furat's Omar and SPC's Jbessa fields, which reportedly had production capacity of 100,000 and 200,000 barrels per day, respectively, at the start of 2010. Other smaller mature fields, such as Oudeh, Gbeibe, and Tishrine, are under field rehabilitation contracts to CNPC and Sinopec, and their production capacity is on the rise. Contracts have been awarded to Shell and Total in 2008 and 2010 for exploration at greater depths in existing mature fields in the Euphrates and central areas. Gulfsands' Khurbet East field came onstream in 2008 with initial production of 10,000 bbl/d rising to 18,000 by the end of 2009.

Khurbet East capacity is currently expected to increase due to recent drilling successes along with development work. Gulfsands is also involved in developing the nearby Yousefieh field, which is currently producing about 1,200 bbl/d and is expected to produce 6,000 bbl/d by . All of these activities have reportedly added more than 50,000 bbl/d of production over the past 2 years, and a further 15,000-20,000 bbl/d is set to come on stream in 2010 from fields discovered by India's ONGC and Russia's Tatneft.

Attempts to explore the offshore Mediterranean were unsuccessful in 2007, as no offers were confirmed for the four blocks tendered, reportedly because terms were deemed unfavorable and the blocks too small. However, in April 2010, it was announced that eight new blocks, located onshore mainly in the north and east of the country, are open for bidding before a September 15 deadline. And the SPC plans to reissue tenders for the offshore blocks in the near future.

Syria's Total Petroleum* Balance, 1990-2009

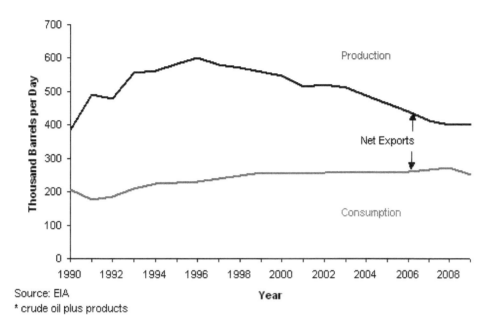

Source: EIA
* crude oil plus products

Exports

In 2009, Syria's net petroleum exports were estimated to be 148,000 bbl/d. All oil exports are marketed by Sytrol, Syria's state oil marketing firm, which sells most of its volumes under 12-month contracts. Syrian crude oil exports go mostly to OECD European countries, in particular Germany, Italy, and France, totaling an estimated 143,000 bbl/d in 2009, according to International Energy Agency (IEA) data.

Pipelines

Syria has a developed domestic pipeline system for transporting crude and petroleum products managed by the Syrian Company for Oil Transportation (SCOT). Pipelines include the 250,000-bbl/d, 347-mileTel Adas-Tartous crude line linking SPC and other fields to the port at Tartous with a connection to the refinery at Homs, and oil products pipelines linking the Homs refinery to Syria's major cities.

Syria has three Mediterranean oil export/import terminals, all managed by SCOT. Baniyas (7 berths) and Tartous (2 berths) are larger ports; Latakia handles smaller cargoes. The terminals are connected to refineries through the domestic pipeline network.

In 2009, it was reported that an initial agreement took place between Syria and Iraq to repair and reopen the Kirkuk-Banias oil pipeline, which extends 500 miles from oil fields in northern Iraq to the Syrian port of Banias on the Mediterranean. This pipeline, which could be used to export production from Iraq's northern fields, has been closed since 2003. However, to date no contract has been awarded.

Refining

According to The Oil and Gas Journal, Syria's total refining capacity was approximately 240,000 bbl/d as of January 2010. Syria's two state-owned refineries are located at Baniyas and Homs,

For additional analytical, business and investment opportunities information,
please contact Global Investment & Business Center, USA
at (703) 370-8082. Fax: (703) 370-8083. E-mail: ibpusa3@gmail.com
Global Business and Investment Info Databank - www.ibpus.com

which have 133,000 bbl/d and 107,000 bbl/d, respectively, of refining capacity. Syria faces shortages of gas oil and diesel, which are imported. A proposed new 100,000 bbl/d capacity refinery project by CNPC at Abu Khashab is currently under contract following the completion of an economic feasibility study in early 2010.

NATURAL GAS

Syria will almost double its natural gas production in 2010 , all of it slated for domestic use .

According to *The Oil and Gas Journal*, as of January 1, 2010, Syria's proven natural gas reserves were estimated at 8.5 trillion cubic feet (Tcf), about half of which is associated gas. Non-associated gas reserves are mainly located in the east and center of the country. Roughly 35 percent of Syrian natural gas production was reinjected into oilfields in 2008, about 2 percent was vented or flared, and the rest distributed to power generators and other domestic users.

Syria plans to substitute natural gas for oil in all of its domestic power generation and industrialuse by 2014. Over half of Syria's power generating facilities are still fueled by refined oil products, much of which must be imported due to inadequate refining capacity.

Production

In 2008, Syria produced an estimated 208 billion cubic feet per year (Bcf/y) of natural gas, imported 5 Bcf, and consumed 213 Bcf. Syria's natural gas production was declining from 2004 to 2008, but it is now poised to increase rapidly as a series of new projects come on stream. By the end of 2010, Syria reportedlyexpects to double its 2008 production level. According to Syrian Minister of Petroleum and Mineral Resources SufianAllao, reported by the Syrian Arab News Agency on April 14, 2010, Syrian natural gas production had reached 361 Bcf/y at that time and was expected to reach 412 Bcf/y by the end of 2010.

In November 2009, the South Central Area gas plant came online. Built by Russia's Stroytransgaz, the project produces about 88 Bcf per year of treated gas, thereby increasing Syria's total natural gas production by about 40 percent. Also in November 2009, an early production facility in Al Hayan gas field came onstream with the capacity to produce 7.8 Bcf per year. The main treatment plant at Al Hayan is being built by Petrofac, and is scheduled to start up in late 2010 with a capacity of about 50 Bcf per year. Suncor Energy (Petro-Canada) started up its Ebla gas plant in April 2010, producing about 29 Bcf per year from the Ebla gas fields. As natural gas production rises, gas demand for electric power generation grows and power plants switch from fuel oil to gas.

Natural Gas Imports and Pipelines

Syria is a natural gas importer since mid-2008, when it began importing an estimated 5 Bcf/y of natural gas from Egypt by way of the Arab Gas Pipeline (AGP). Syria's long-term aim is to become a transit state for Egyptian, Iraqi, Iranian, and even potentially Azerbaijani gas, which would gain it valuable transit revenues as well as help increase the availability of natural gas imports to Syria. According to a 2009 agreement with Turkey, Syria will import up to 35 Bcf of gas from Turkey starting in 2011 with the opening of the Syria-Turkey section of the Arab Gas Pipeline.

For additional analytical, business and investment opportunities information,
please contact Global Investment & Business Center, USA
at (703) 370-8082. Fax: (703) 370-8083. E-mail: ibpusa3@gmail.com
Global Business and Investment Info Databank - www.ibpus.com

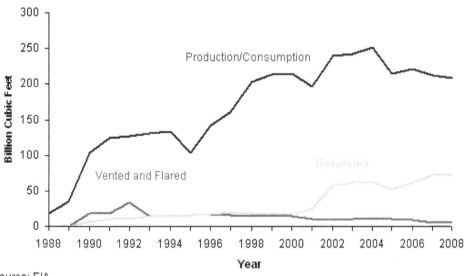

Syria's Natural Gas Balance, 1988-2008

Source: EIA

Arab Gas Pipeline

The AGP currently links Egypt with Jordan, Syria, and Lebanon. Limited gas supplies to Lebanon from Egypt began at the end of 2009. Completion of the pipeline to Turkey is projected for 2011. A memorandum of understanding with Turkey was signed in 2009, under which Turkey will build a 56-mile pipeline on its side of the border to link into the line Syria is currently building from Aleppo to Kilis on the border. The Aleppo-Kilis line is to be completed by March 2011. According to the agreement, Syria will receive between 17.5 and 35 Bcf of Turkish gas annually for 5 years starting in 2011.

Syria-Iraq Gas Pipeline

Discussions are reportedly under way between Syria and Iraq to construct a new natural gas pipeline from the Akkas gas field in Iraq's western province of Al-Anbar, about 30 miles from the Syrian border. The main sticking points are terms for exports and Iraq's own domestic need for gas. Akkas has the potential to contribute to the supply of gas to Europe through tying into the Arab gas pipeline that will run to the Turkish border via Syria.

Persian Pipeline

Syria and Iran reportedly signed a cooperation agreement in April 2009 which includes plans for a natural gas pipeline between Iran and Syria via Iraq. The main sticking point is the security of the line through Iraq.

SUPERVISION AND CONTROL COMPANIES APPROVED BY S.P.C

Name	SOEX (SOYUZEXPERTIZA of the Russian Federation Chamber of Commerce and Industry)
Type	SERVICES

Product	INSPECTION and Supervision Company
Address	Russian Federation,125009,Moscow,13/17,M.Dmitrovka street
Box	
Telex	
Phon	+7(495)660-58-68
Fax	+7(495)621-56-75
Email	inbox@soex.ru
WebSite	WWW.soex.ru

Name	Baxcounsel LTD
Type	SERVICES
Product	INSPECTION and Supervision Company
Address	301, Trade Avenue Bldg, Suren Road , Andheri (East), Mumbai 400069
Box	
Telex	Tel2-3951 4271/4347/4346
Phon	2683 4158/4231/4652
Fax	0091-22-2683 9250
Email	baxin@giasbm01.vsnl.net.in
WebSite	www.baxcounsel.com

Name	TUV NORD GmbH
Type	SERVICES
Product	INSPECTION and Supervision Company
Address	Amtuv1 30519 Hannover
Box	
Telex	
Phon	00494085572348
Fax	00494085571015
Email	imulisch@tuev-nord.de
WebSite	www.tuev-nord.de

Name	RBGLTD
Type	SERVICES
Product	INSPECTION and Supervision Company
Address	Norfolk house pitmeden road dyce Aberdeen AB21 ODP-UK
Box	TELEX
Telex	
Phon	0044(0)1224722888 (CONTACT PERSON:-ADRIAN PAYNE)
Fax	0044(0)1224723406

Email	Adrian.payne@rbgltd.com
WebSite	www.rpgltd.com

Name	2R Engineering Ravenna
Type	SERVICES
Product	INSPECTION and Supervision Company
Address	Via Trieste '227.48100 (RAVENNA) ITALY
Box	
Telex	
Phon	00390544420025
Fax	00390544421540
Email	Info@dueerreravenna.com
WebSite	www.dueerreravenna.com

Name	MOODY INTERNATIONAL
Type	SERVICES
Product	INSPECTION and Supervision Company
Address	69,Road 161,intersection with Road 104, Ground Floor ,Maadi ,Cairo-Egypt
Box	
Telex	
Phon	+2025253841 /+2025244745 /+2025276026 /+20106849648
Fax	+2025275985
Email	e.sherif@moodyint.com
WebSite	www.moodyint.com

Name	SGS
Type	SERVICES
Product	INSPECTION and Supervision Company
Address	1 ,Place Des Alipes CH-1211 Geneval
Box	2152
Telex	422140 SGS
Phon	(41-22)739.91.11
Fax	(41-22)739.98.86
Email	enquiries@sgs.com
WebSite	www.sgs.com

Name	QUALITY SERVICES GROUP
Type	SERVICES
Product	INSPECTION and Supervision Company
Address	Head Office: 9,Gamal Eldin AbulMahasen St.,Garden City,Cairo

Box	
Telex	
Phon	(202)7923043 [3lines]
Fax	002034248838
Email	inspect@qsgegypt.com
WebSite	www.qsgegypt.com

Name	INNOSPECTION LIMITED
Type	SERVICES
Product	INSPECTION and Supervision Company
Address	Unit 1,Howemoss Avenue Kirkhill Industrial Estate,Dyce Aberdeen,AB21 0GP UK
Box	
Telex	
Phon	+44-1224-724-744
Fax	+44-1224-774-087
Email	s.mo@innospection.com
WebSite	www.innospection.com

Name	VELOSI
Type	SERVICES
Product	INSPECTION and Supervision Company
Address	Velosi Limited Unit 1,Woodside Business Park,Whitley Wood Lane,Reading,Berkshine,RG2 8LW,UK
Box	
Telex	
Phon	44(0)1189207030
Fax	+44(0)1189869749
Email	
WebSite	www.velosi.com

Name	Apave International
Type	SERVICES
Product	INSPECTION and Supervision Company
Address	Siège social:8rue Jean Jacques Vemazza -ZAC Saumaty-Séon -BP 193-13322 MARSEILLE Société par Actions Simplifiée au capital de 6 502500 €-No SIREN:775581812
Box	
Telex	
Phon	0496152260
Fax	0496152261
Email	
WebSite	www.apave.com

For additional analytical, business and investment opportunities information,
please contact Global Investment & Business Center, USA
at (703) 370-8082. Fax: (703) 370-8083. E-mail: ibpusa3@gmail.com
Global Business and Investment Info Databank - www.ibpus.com

Name	Control Union
Type	SERVICES
Product	INSPECTION and Supervision Company
Address	GOLZHEIMER STR.120 Derendorf Deutschland
Box	40476 DUSSELDORF
Telex	
Phon	02115158590
Fax	0211483017
Email	info@controlunion.de
WebSite	www.controlunion.de

MINISTRY OF MINERAL RESOURCES CONTACTS

Name	mail-E	Website	Number Fax	Phone number	Site
of Ministry and Petroleum Mineral Resources Central) (Administration	mopmr-cor@mail.sy	www.petroleum.gov.sy	0114463942	0114451624	Damascus
Syrian Petroleum Company	spccom1@scs-net.org spccom2@scs-net.org	www.spc-sy.com	0113137979 0113137977	0113137913 0113137935	Damascus
Gas Syrian Company	syrgasco@mail.sy	www.sgc.gov.sy	0312451932 0312451933	0312451925 To 0312451931	Homs
AFPC	sy.net.afpc@afpc	www.afpc-sy.com	0116184444	0116183333	Damascus
oil Zour-Al Deir					Damascus
Hayan Petroleum Company		www.hpc.com.sy	0113349821	0113349820 0113349822	Damascus
oil the of Planet company	com.sskoc@sskochq		0116122770	0116122772 0116122773 0116122774	Damascus
Syrian Oil for Company Transport	org.net-scs@50scot	www.scot-syria.com	043710418		Banias
General for Company Refinery Homs	sy.mail@homsrefinery	www.homsrefinery.com	0312516410 0312516411	0312470101 0312516401	Homs
Refinery Banias Company	sy.tarassul@3brc	www.brc-sy.comwww.brc-sy.net	043712325	043	Banias
Company Fuel					
Syrian for Company	sy.gov.scdgaz@gaz_scd	www.scdgaz.gov.sy	0115812002	0115810939 0115811051	Damascus

For additional analytical, business and investment opportunities information,
please contact Global Investment & Business Center, USA
at (703) 370-8082. Fax: (703) 370-8083. E-mail: ibpusa3@gmail.com
Global Business and Investment Info Databank - www.ibpus.com

Distribution Gas					
General Establishment and Geology of Mineral Resources	org.sy-geology@geo	www.geology-sy.org	0114465947	0114447755 0114450507 0114455426	Damascus
General for Company and Phosphate Mines					
General for Company & Marble Asphalt	sy.mail@marble	www.marble.com.sy	041330102	041330106 To 041330109	Lattakia
Center National Earthquake for	sy.mail@snsn		0114429197	0114423578 0114420780	Damascus
Oil of Institute professional and in occupations Homs					

IMPORTANT DEVELOPMENTS

MINISTRY OF OIL AND MINERAL RESOURCES RESTRUCTURING

Decides as follows:

Article 1 - Amend label Directorate of planning and economic studies in the rules of procedure of the Ministry of Oil and Mineral Resources so that the "Directorate of Planning and International Cooperation."

Article 2 - Fold the International Cooperation Bureau of the organizational structure of the Ministry of Petroleum and Mineral Wealth. "

Article 3 - occur in the Directorate of Planning and International Cooperation Department called "Department of International Cooperation", assume the following tasks:

A - Preparation of correspondence with the countries and the Arab and foreign, institutions and international organizations.

B - Participation in the preparation of agreements and memorandums of understanding between the Ministry and the local, Arab and international, in the areas of the ministry's activities and its affiliates.

C - the follow-up implementation of agreements and memorandums of understanding signed between the Government of the Syrian Arab Republic and other countries, organizations and bodies, universities and institutes ..., in the work of the ministry and its affiliates.

D - participation in meetings of international cooperation, and preparation of correspondence relating thereto.

E - To undertake any other work assigned to them in the workplace.

And - the specific tasks book Presidency of the Council of Ministers No. 1997/15 date 08/02/2011.

Article 4 - A - Directorate of integrated services in the Directorate of Administrative Affairs.

Article 5 - In addition to the functions of the Directorate of Administration the following tasks:

A - Supervise the work of the reform of the electricity and plumbing, elevators and other services.

B - Supervision of the custodians and apportioned, cleaners and garden.

C - Directorate of Management consists of the following services:

1 - Service.

2 - Department of mechanisms: It consists of the Division and the Division of August Murr Register mechanisms.

3 - Department correspondence, consisting of Cabinet Division and the Division of Printing and Imaging Division archives.

D - circles and the people exercise their functions as specified in the rules of procedure.

Article 6 - A talk on behalf of the Directorate of the Directorate of Readiness Division of the tasks identified in the readiness and the presidency of the Council of Ministers Resolution No. 673 date 25.05.2009.

B - Readiness Directorate is composed of the following services:

1 - Department of Department of Readiness: The readiness of the Ministry and the headquarters and shelters, and related work queries.

2 - Department of Public Safety: and assume the functions of civil defense and fire services.

Article 7 - Works accompanying description card.

Article 8 - This resolution shall be and he is required to implement it.

OIL PRODUCTION

The total oil produced in Syria during the first quarter of 2011 amounted to 34.828 million barrels (of light and heavy oil and condensate) increased by the implementation of 100% or the rate of 387 thousand barrels per day, an increase of 4.7 thousand barrels per day for the first quarter of last year.

- The share of national companies (SPC - Syrian Gas) of the total production of oil 52% with the production of 18.341 million barrels, while the total production companies 16.487 million barrels, divided into companies (Euphrates, Deir Al-Zour, return, planet, Hayyan, the Tigris, Abu Kamal, Ebla)

- The total of the Muslim oil refineries 22.069 million barrels, of which 10.929 million barrels of light and 11.140 million barrels of heavy oil, while the total source of heavy oil and light 12.079 million barrels.

GAS PRODUCTION

- The total free gas and utilities product in the country during the first quarter of this year's 2.664 billion m 3 daily average of 29.6 million m 3, handed it to gas processing plants in Syria 2.497 billion m3 were produced 2.378 billion m 3 of clean gas were also imported 121 million m 3 of Egypt , The distribution of gas available to consumers of $ 2.008 billion m 3, as follows:

- Ministry of Electricity 1.789 billion m 3.

- Ministry of Industry 109 million m 3.

- Ministry of Oil and 116 million m 3.

Investment plan:

Report the total expenditure for the institution of public companies for oil for the same period 2.140 billion SP. O The distribution of expenditure in the following form:

- Syrian Petroleum Company: The total investment spending 1.168 billion SP. O.

- Syrian Company for Gas: 796 million for. O

- Syrian Company for Oil Transport: 176 million for. O.

Public Institution for refining

HRC:

Against the annual plan for HRC in 2011 to contribute to the realization of this plan economic and social development of Qatar by providing the local market's growing need of oil products and mineral oils.

Where the assumed production plan refining 1.296 million metric tons of crude oil during the first quarter of 2011 while the amounts of refined oil is actually 1.408 million metric tons by the implementation of 109% as the volume of oil produced is actually 11 799 metric tonnes compared to 15000 tons planned, an implementation rate of 79% .

With the volume of oil derivatives produced 1.351 million metric tons while the production quantities planned to 1.225 million metric tons by the implementation of 110% and total production of coke 42,000 tons while the total expenditure on the investment plan, the amount of $ 100 million for . o.

Banias Refinery:

Total crude oil refined in the Banias refinery for the first quarter of 2011, a total of 1.621 million metric tons compared to 1.620 million metric tons planned by the implementation of 100% while the total of derivatives processing 230,000 metric tons.

The total expenditure on the investment plan 55 million Syrian pounds by the implementation of 100% for the period included the replacement and renovation projects and the city center, unloading and project engineering solutions of the economics of refining

Fuel:

Total fuel sales for the first quarter of 2011, a total of 2.585 million tons of oil products, the following: (different kinds of gasoline, diesel, kerosene fuels), and total sales of (oil, grease, metal, asphalt fuel - gas, liquefied coke White Spirit and solvents) (1.771) million tons, bringing the total sales (3788) million tons (internally and externally), while the sales of bottled gas cylinders (20.070 million) and cylinder (25 416) a hollow cylinder.

Amounted to domestic purchases of the company (1178) million tons of (gasoline, diesel, kerosene fuels) and (1,400) million tons of (mineral oils, asphalt fuel - gas, liquefied coal and coke White Spirit solvent), bringing the total domestic purchases to (2578) million tons were imported in (1.168) million tons of "fuel oil - gasoline - fuel oil and liquid gas"

And has reached the value of total sales executed (84.411) billion Syrian pounds while the value of total purchases (133 479) billion Syrian pounds of them (45 837) billion Syrian pounds purchases of Foreign Affairs, ie that the value of purchases of the company's total increased value of sales for the first quarter of Alam current difference (49.068 billion) for. o to meet the needs of the local market of oil derivatives.

As for the investment plan amounted to actual expenditure (128 187) million Syrian pounds.

General Establishment of Geology and Mineral Resources

Raw materials and construction industry:

Produced the General Establishment of Geology and Mineral Resources, the amount of / 107 964 / tons of raw materials for marble / 140 230 / t the implementation of the scheme by 77%.

The company posted a rate of 161% for raw plaster with production of this article / 145 076 / tons, compared to / 90 000 / t while the total production of volcanic tuff / 254 171 / t, the planner / 232 000 / ton.

As has been the implementation of the insulation work for 75 282 m 2

As for the Quartz sand and rock salt has reached the amount of output generated from the rock salt / 16 386 / t, the planner / 17 500 / ton while the production quantity derived from the sand Quartz / 383 100 / t, the planner / 321 000 / ton.

The total sales of the corporation of building materials and raw materials industry (domestic + external) / 283 639 / l million. O.

Phosphate

Produced by the General Company for Phosphate and Mines during the first quarter of 2011 a total of 988,635 tons of phosphate compared to 809,800 tons by the implementation of planned and 122%, and the company's sales amounted to 882,724 tons of phosphate a value of 2.963 million for. O.

Investment plan:

Total actual expenditure of the Public Institution of Geology and Mineral Resources and the General Company for Phosphate for the same period to 121 million. O.

Said Sufian Al Alao Minister of Oil and Mineral Resources said that the technical committees completed the first phase of the international tender for oil exploration, development and production in eight blocks, covering about 40 percent of the area of Syria announced by the Oil Ministry and the General Organization of Petroleum last March.

The minister added in a statement to reporters on the sidelines of a workshop financing oil projects that Sunday, 13/3/2011 technical committees presented the results of studies on the

For additional analytical, business and investment opportunities information,
please contact Global Investment & Business Center, USA
at (703) 370-8082. Fax: (703) 370-8083. E-mail: ibpusa3@gmail.com
Global Business and Investment Info Databank - www.ibpus.com

High Commission was to identify companies that presented on appropriate terms, pointing out that the companies submitted their offers on four blocks, only block / 7 / and block / 3 / and block / 12 / and block / 5 / While not receive the remaining four blocks any view.

He pointed out that some of the presentations made by the companies were close to a large extent which made the request of these companies improve their offers are chosen to supply the most appropriate is supposed to be received replies companies and offers improved during the next few days as a prelude to announce the results of the tender before the end of this March .

On the subject of exploration in the sea, the minister explained that he was the processing and preparation of all necessary documentation for the Declaration and will write to companies qualified and receive the prequalification documents for companies wishing to participate in the announcement this month, pointing out that it has been divided into Syrian waters, which the ministry plans to ad to explore the three blocks .

He disclosed that the ministry plans to complete the procedures for Balsgel oil shale and blocks of advertising where to invest in the region has been divided into blocks in preparation for presentation to investors and qualified companies.

Referred to the results of prospecting and exploration for shale oil shale, which is an alternative source of energy in the long run showed the presence of more than 39 billion tons of raw shale oil shale in the area of Khanasser South honor of Aleppo on an area of 152 square kilometers and with a thickness ranging between 128-240 meters to the layers of raw The value of the thermal energy of the samples between 2466-5464 J / g has been divided to 14 blocks the site to be put on investment.

It is reported that 12 international companies from different nationalities made offers to tender blocks eight to explore for oil and gas and is the French company Total and Petro-Canada Canadian and Italy's Eni in partnership with Gulfsands British leading companies which submitted their offers for this tender as well as companies, CNPC of China and the color of Energy - Syria Branch Canadian and Dana UAE gas and HPC Tunisian and Egyptian and Pico Azvenska Swedish and American IPR and Sideragon French and Flournoy Energy Oil & Gas

/ Flournoy Oil & Gas /.

The General Organization of Petroleum indicated that the content of advertising aimed at the conclusion of a production-sharing for all the operations of prospecting and exploration for oil, develop and produce in the region, described the book of technical conditions and pursuant to the provisions, obligations and conditions contained in the draft contract attached to the book of the conditions prescribed for this purpose. The right of the viewer to bid separately for one block or more.

Eng Sufian Alao Minister of Oil and Mineral Resources, the workshop set up by the Arab Company for Petroleum Investments (APICORP) on the financing of oil projects and infrastructure projects for the oil industry in Syria and in the foundation building of the oil.

Participated in the workshop, specialists and technicians from the ministries of oil, finance and the economy and the State Planning Commission and the Central Bank of Syria and the Commercial Bank of Syria.

The Minister stressed that the company "APICORP" has considerable experience and wide in the area of project financing and how to obtain it and risks as well as ways and means of payment, insurance and all the related topics for pointing out that the exchange of experiences with "APICORP" in this area is very important particularly for large study for projects and securing funding.

He called on Minister of participants to take advantage of all the course topics and mainstream interest to the concerned departments in their organizations, pointing out that the Oil Ministry signed an agreement with APICORP to provide consultancy and expertise in the field of refineries or any other topics where you are sending experts and answer questions from the ministry in the areas agreed upon.

The aim of two-day workshop to give participants knowledge of application frameworks, structural study and analysis of major projects and to identify the key factors for the financing of mega projects and identify and assess key risks in project financing as well as the use and interpretation of the model of Mali is simple to evaluate the financing of projects.

The Chancellor spoke at the "APICORP" Richard Wilson on the basis of funding projects and frameworks, risk financing and study the structure of funding in addition to key aspects of the project agreements.

The «APICORP» Arab financial institution established in 1975 according to an international agreement between the Governments of Member States of the Organization of Arab Petroleum Exporting Countries, "OAPEC" including Syria, based in Saudi Arabia are classified Kmsrv multilateral development owned by the ten States members of the (OAPEC). The company contributed to the development and funding of Arab oil and energy sectors through funding, research and consultancy.

Oil Minister reviewed with the delegation of Polish economic aspects of cooperation in the field of oil, gas and mineral wealth

Engineer Sufian Alao Minister of Oil and Mineral Resources with the Polish economic delegation Monday, 21/02/2011 aspects of possible cooperation in oil and gas and refining industry and mineral wealth between the two countries.

And presentation of the Minister of events and activities the ministry and its institutions in the areas of prospecting and exploration for oil and gas and development of existing fields to increase the profitability of productivity and the transfer of crude oil in addition to oil refining and washing phosphate pointing to the importance of participation of companies of Poland in the tenders announced by the Ministry of Oil or one of its companies to supply equipment industry oil.

For his part, noted the potential of the Polish delegation, the Polish companies in the areas of extraction and production of oil and construction and development of refineries, as well as experience in the investment of Bologna, where shale gas reserves are estimated at this article in Bologna about 1500 billion cubic feet. Displaying a desire to enter the oil market, especially after the Syrian and the significant improvement witnessed by the investment climate in Syria in recent years.

The meeting was attended by Dr. Hassan Zeinab, Al-Din Hossam Abdo Associate Minister of Petroleum and Geological Ghzayel Jaber, head of marketing of oil and Ali Abbas, Director General of the Public Corporation for Oil and Omar Al Hamad, Director General of the Syrian Oil Company .

The end of the international tender for oil exploration in Syria .. And 12 international companies submitted their offers

Ended on last Wednesday on the eighth of this month, international tender for oil exploration and development and production in the eight new blocks, covering about 40 percent of the area of Syria announced by the Ministry of Petroleum and Mineral Resources and the General Organization of Petroleum last March.

It is located eight blocks in different parts in the north and south-east Syria, and an approximate area about 73 thousand km 2.

The announcement came in the framework of plans and programs of the Oil Ministry to increase production by expanding the exploration activities to include all the occupied Syrian and development of old fields, where it offered the ministry to new areas for exploration through a number of bids over the past years resulted in the signing of 12 contracts to explore new areas During the period from 2003 to 2007, with specialized international companies and qualified.

As they advanced 12 companies worldwide from different nationalities to their offers for this tender is the French company Total and Petro-Canada Canadian and Italy's Eni in partnership with Gulfsands British leading companies that made offers to this tender, as well as firms CNPC of China and the color of Energy - Syria Branch Canadian and Dana Gas, the UAE and HPC Tunisian and Picot Egyptian Azvenska Swedish and American IPR and Sideragon French and Flournoy Energy Oil & Gas / Flournoy Oil & Gas /.

The aim of the advertising content to the production-sharing contract to carry out all special operations for oil exploration, development and production in the region, described the book of technical conditions and pursuant to the provisions, obligations and conditions contained in the draft contract attached to the book of the conditions prescribed for this purpose. The right of the viewer to bid separately for one block or more.

The signing of a memorandum of understanding between Syria and Venezuela to complete the implementation of the joint refinery project Alfrekls

Signed and ministries of oil in Syria, Venezuela, Friday, 3/12/2010 Memorandum of Understanding for the development of operational steps to complete the refinery project Alfrekls joint studies through detailed design of the refinery project, which she could reach 140 thousand barrels per day and estimated cost of about $ 5 billion.

The Minister of Petroleum and Mineral Resources Sufian Al Alao, who signed the note on the Syrian side that the memorandum of understanding aims to document what has been agreed upon for the development of practical steps to follow up the refinery project Alfrekls where the program has been established time frame for completion of design studies and then move on to the stages of implementation and will be under this Memorandum of contract with global consulting firms through the evaluation of proposals by a joint committee to study the most appropriate selection and the best.

The minister added that the schedule notice subsequent steps to the subject of study for the conduct of this project forward as quickly as possible, pointing out that both the Syrian and Venezuelan will pay the cost of these studies in the event that the two sides of the Iranian and Malaysian did not approve it.

For his part, Minister of Energy and Petroleum of Venezuela Rafael Ramirez, the importance of implementing the directives of the leaderships of the two countries to accelerate the completion of the refinery joint pointing out that the Venezuelan side will select the best international companies specialized in the field of studies and consultations so that the end of the study before the end of the first half of next year to begin to take steps and measures following the preparation of financial studies of the project, from design to complete the two sides as soon as possible.

It is noteworthy that Syria, Iran and Venezuela, Bukhari Group of Malaysia and signed in the month of March 2008, the partnership agreement to establish a refinery for refining crude oil in the region Alfrekls east of the city of Homs and the project consists of financing and the establishment of a refinery integrated refining crude oil with a total capacity of 140 thousand barrels per day.

Attended the Engineer Hussam Abdo religion, Deputy Oil Minister, Eng Noureddine Makhlouf Director-General of the General Organization for refining and Jaber Ghzayel oil marketing head of the Office of the Council of Ministers and the Venezuelan ambassador in Damascus

Oil Minister: fact, the oil and gas in Syria is stable .. and the Declaration on the prospecting and exploration in the territorial waters beginning of the year

Said Sufian Al Alao Minister of Oil and Mineral Resources said that fact, the oil and gas in Syria is stable with high production slightly from previous years as a result there are plans to increase production and improve performance in addition to the apparent rise in the indicators of recoverable reserves in oil and gas.

The minister added in a press statement on the sidelines of a seminar the global financial crisis and its impact on oil and gas sector in the Arab States, which began its work in Damascus on Sunday, 22/11/2010 The stability of the current oil prices encouraged investors to establish projects and encouraging consumers not to search for alternative sources Energy explained that the ministry will receive special offers announce eight blocks for prospecting and exploration in wilderness areas until the end of next month and plans to announce that prospecting and exploration in the Syrian territorial waters at the beginning of next year.

He referred to the existence of projects for regional oil and gas through the presence of the Arab gas pipeline, which links between Syria, Lebanon, Jordan and Egypt, stressing that it will be delivered part complementary to link this line with the Turkish gas network during the month of March next year and the project will be linked with a network of European gas during the next year.

Indicating that the operational procedures for the implementation of vital projects and promising with Iraq began by announcing the request for a consultant to prepare studies and technical conditions for the implementation of projects on the principle of the / P or T / and include two lines for the transfer of Iraqi oil exports through Syrian ports, where the first line capacity 5.1 million barrels per day and the second 25.1 million barrels can be increased in addition to a pipeline to transport gas .

Minister of Oil in Libya, looking to develop cooperation in the field of oil and gas

Engineer Sufian Alao Minister of Oil and Mineral Resources during a meeting in Tripoli, Dr. Shukri Mohammed Ghanem, head of the Libyan National Oil bilateral relations between the two countries in the field of oil, gas and ways of developing them. The two sides expressed during the meeting, the desire to establish joint investment projects between the two countries and cooperation through the exchange of information and experiences and implementation of training programs for cadres in Syria, Libya.

The Minister said in remarks to reporters after the meeting that he discussed with the possible participation of Ghanem, the National Endowment for oil prospecting and exploration for oil and gas in Syria as well as exchange of expertise areas of marketing and development of gas fields and the training of cadres.

He added that it was the establishment of a national training center interview in Syria to cooperate with foreign companies with experience to train cadres in the areas of oil and gas industry, explaining that it had agreed to Ghanem, a delegation from the Libyan National Oil to visit Syria in the sending of the Ministry of Oil and Mineral Resources of Syria's documentation to identify place to send young Libyans to train in Syria.

He pointed out that it was discussed during the meeting to the methods of developing the performance of the Organization of Arab Petroleum Exporting Countries OAPEC also presented the "Draft Agreement", a draft bilateral agreement in the field of oil and gas between Syria and Libya, expressing his hope to study well and will be signed at the meeting of the Council of strategic cooperation joint to be held in December next in Damascus.

For his part, Ghanem said that there is cooperation between the two countries, especially in the international conferences that are to attend and participate in such meetings of the Organization of Petroleum Exporting Countries OPEC observers in OAPEC as permanent members, pointing out that it had been discussion of the topics to be presented at the meeting of OAPEC in December next year, when formatted views on some topics related to Arab cooperation in the field of petroleum projects .. With regard to oil market conditions were discussed international oil and gas market is international.

He said Mr. Ghanem, the Minister informed him that Syria will conduct a tour of the world's gas companies to participate in the processes of exploration of gas fields in addition to cooperation in the exchange of information and the oil activity in common and open the door for Arab companies and oil services company to work in Syria.

Ghanem said about the proposed memorandum of cooperation from the Syrian side that cooperation with Syria is under agreement and that the note presented by the Minister Alao is a project of cooperation between the two countries hope to sign during the meeting of Strategic Council Top Syrian Libyan to be held in Damascus later this year.

He pointed out that the essence of this agreement is to exchange information, exchange visits and training and joint projects in the field of oil and gas

Field trip to the Minister of Oil in the Fields: the return of company: good procedures to improve the environmental situation

Company Tigris: an increase in production and transportation of oil pipelines

Planet Company: unfair treatment of oil and re-soil to life

Said Sufian Al Alao Minister of Oil and Mineral Resources said that the Ministry pays great attention to the rehabilitation and training of human resources have a constant and growing to raise the professional competence and technical, linguistic and IT to keep pace with technological and technological development in the areas of oil and gas industry different, including a positive impact on production.

The Minister, during a tour to the oil and gas fields in the province on Thursday, 14/10/2010 Hasakah that the ministry recently established an institute Tghania average oil and gas field Taym in the province of Deir al-Zour began teaching with the beginning of the current academic year in addition to the opening of the national training center developed for those working in the field of gas and the refining industry in the region of Alfrekls in the province of Homs with the aim of qualifying the largest possible number of workers in this vital sector. along with many of the existing training centers in the Deir al-Zour, Hassake and Homs.

Mr.'s oil minister that his ministry is making great efforts to apply the rules of safety and security and to address all forms of pollution in the fields of production of the Syrian Oil Company and oblige all companies operating in Syria to abide by these rules in accordance with the specifications and global measures adopted.

And visited the stations return and October Committees of the company return to the oil joint-venture with Sinopec of China, which produces about 17,500 barrels per day and a look at the reality of work and listened to a briefing about the actions taken by the company to address the diversion of gas in the air through the installation of equipment surface new and the preparation of engineering designs and technical studies necessary for a number of projects aimed at improving the environmental situation in the production sites and the minister stressed the need to commit to a program schedule for the implementation of the company's projects as soon as possible.

He also briefed on the progress of work in the fields of company Tigris Petroleum shared between the Foundation of the oil company "Gulfsands" by Britain, the company produces from the station east of ruined and Yusufiyah about 21 thousand barrels per day The company has implemented recently a line for transporting oil produced from fields along the 22 km led to dispense with the process of transport tanks and take advantage of this solution is environmentally and economically.

He visited Mr. Minister station glomerulus, a subsidiary of Planet Petroleum, a joint venture between the General Organization of the Petroleum Corporation, CNPC of China where the company produces about 14 thousand barrels per day and see the sites address the inequities of oil in order to improve environmental conditions where it is the withdrawal of the remaining oil in the vicinity of the wells and then soil treatment and returned to the natural characteristics of investable agricultural.

Participated in the round Eng Abdo Hossam El Din, Deputy Oil Minister Ali Al-Abbas, Director General of the Public Corporation for Oil and Khalid Al-ahead with Deputy Director-General of the Syrian Oil Company and the heads of boards of directors and general managers of companies, the return of the Tigris and the planet and directors of the fields.

The Minister of Petroleum and Mineral Resources Sufian Al Alao on the a Ravae and Thursday toured a field to work sites and production in the fields Aljbsp and Rmelan and companies operating there and the field life of the AFPC will also convene a meeting with the staff working in operating companies and the Syrian Gas Company in the area of Deir Al-Zour for closely at the reality of work and ways to improve it.

Include the visit of Minister of Oil stations return and October Committees of the company return to the oil and stations ravaged eastern and Yusufiya subsidiaries of the company Tigris Petroleum and the station glomerulus, a subsidiary of Planet of the oil in addition to the opening of the project and the link between the systematic compilation of gas to gas plant age and Deir al-Zour.

OPERATION REGULATIONS OF FREE ZONE IN SYRIAN ARAB REPUBLIC

LEGISLATIVE DECREE NO. 18 ON THE FUNDAMENTAL REGULATIONS OF THE ESTABLISHMENT

The President of the Republic
Pursuant to the rules of the provisional constitution
Pursuant to decision no.18 issued by the council of ministers on 18.2.1971

ENACTS as follows:

Article 1
There shall be created a public establishment that enjoys the status of a juristic person and has a financial and administrative autonomy to be called the public establishment of free zones in the Syrian Arab Republic attached to the minister of economy and foreign trade.

The establishment shall be considered to be an establishment of an economic character and shall be governed in its dealing with third party by the provisions of the law of commerce.

The head office of the establishment shall be in the city of Damascus and the establishment may set up branches in other Syrian cities if and when necessary.

Article 2
The Establishment shall assume the following duties:

To run and operate the free zones, to set up such warehouses and stores as may be necessary for such free zones, and to develop them so as to contribute to the growth and prosperity of these zones.

To propose such projects so as to set up or to cancel free zone.

To organize the functions of the free zones and to coordinate their activities so as to serve economy and to develop international trade exchange.

To exercise all such powers that has been exercised by such bodies operating the free zones except such powers in relation to the affairs of customs control.

Generally to handle all matters concerning the management and operation of the free zones.

The Establishment shall observe such provisions and conditions concerning customs and currency control and shall provide such constructions as may be necessary for this purpose.

Article 3
The Establishment shall have a board of directors to be set up and its powers to be defined as provided for in the fundamental regulations.

The Establishment shall be run by a general manager to be appointed by a decree and his powers shall be defined in the fundamental regulations.

Article 4
The Fundamental regulations, the numerical strength and the operation regulations of the Establishment shall be issued by a decree with the approval of the Economic committee and these regulations may embody exclusions from the provisions of the laws and regulations in force.

For additional analytical, business and investment opportunities information,
please contact Global Investment & Business Center, USA
at (703) 370-8082. Fax: (703) 370-8083. E-mail: ibpusa3@gmail.com
Global Business and Investment Info Databank - www.ibpus.com

The other regulations of the Establishment shall be issued by an order from the minister of economy and foreign trade on a proposal by the board of directors provided that the approval by the minister of finance of the financial regulations shall be obtained.

Pending the issue of the regulations referred to in the two preceding clauses the internal, financial and appointment and employment regulations in force at present in the free zones shall continue to be in force in so far as they are not contrary to the provisions of this legislative decree.

Article 5
The Establishment shall follow the state financial year and shall keep its accounts in line with the principles of business accounting. The funds of the Establishment shall be considered as public funds for the purpose of the application of the provisions of the law of economic sanctions.
Article 6
For financing the Establishment depends in particular on:

Dues, rents and charges for temporary tenancy and services as defined in the operation regulations.

The appropriations annually set aside by the state for the Establishment.

Loans from third party.

Article 7
As regards court proceedings the Establishment shall be relieved from giving in a deposit in all such cases a deposit is required to be given in by law.

Article 8
There shall be transferred to the Establishment the free zones created prior to the issue of this legislative decree together with such constructions existing in such free zones. These constructions, the land attached thereto, their equipment and their value shall be determined by an agreement made for this purpose between the minister of finance and minister of economy and foreign trade.

Article 9
With due observance of the legal provisions in force persons in the employ of the free zones existing at the date of the coming into force of this legislative decree may be transferred or seconded to the Establishment by an order from the board of directors upon an agreement with the minister of finance and the government service in which such persons work.

Article 10
All provisions contrary to this legislative decree shall be deemed to be automatically amended.

Article 11
This legislative decree shall be published in the official Gazette and shall come into force immediately upon its issue.

Damascus, 23.12.1390 h.

18.02.1971 A.D.

President of the Republic

Decree No. 84

The President of the republic,

Pursuant to the rules of legislative decree no. 18 of 18.2.1971,

Enacts as follows:

Article 1
The operation regulations of free zones and duty free shops in the Syrian Arab Republic and its annex containing the operation tariffs shall be endorsed and shall be applied to all free zones and duty free shops in the country.

Article 2
The provisions contrary to these regulations shall be repealed.

Article 3
This Decree shall be published and shall be notified to whomsoever necessary for implementation.
Damascus, 24.11.1391 H.

10.01.1972 A.D.

President of the Republic

OPERATION REGULATIONS OF FREE ZONES IN SYRIAN ARAB REPUBLIC

General Provisions
Article 1
The following expressions shall have the meanings hereby assigned to them:

The Establishment: The public establishment of free zones

The board: The Board of directors of the establishment

The director: the General director of the establishment

Article 2
These regulations shall apply to all free zones and duty free shops that are set up or will be set up in the Syrian Arab Republic.

Article 3
The establishment shall have the exclusive power to operate all free zones and duty free shops and the board may upon a proposal by the director assign the duty to operate the markets to another administration upon such conditions as may be set by the board.

Article 4
The establishment shall have a right of priority over all movable and immovable property of the establishment's debtors lying within free zones and duty free shops.

Article 5
Free zones and duty free shops shall be governed by the laws and regulations concerning security, morals, public health and antismuggling.

ADMISSION OF GOODS

Article 6
Foreign goods of any description whatsoever, irrespective of their origin or source, shall be allowed to be admitted into and exited out of free zones and duty free shops, to the exclusion of the customs zone, and shall in this case be not subject to foreign trade regulations and shall not be chargeable to customs duties and taxes.

Domestic goods or goods that have become as such by placement for consumption shall be allowed to be admitted into free zones and duty free shops shall be governed by the regulations in force in this respect.

Goods lying in the free zone shall be allowed to be admitted into the customs zone to be placed for local consumption in accordance with the laws and regulations in force.

Article 7
As an exception to the provisions of article 6 the following goods shall be prohibited from being admitted into free zones and markets under pain of seizure without any indemnity, apart from such other legal measures as are provided for in the laws in force.

Goods of Israeli origin or source, goods prohibited to be imported under Israel boycott regulations and goods from such states with which economic dealing is prohibited.

Narcotics of any description and their derivatives to the exclusion of such narcotics and derivatives for medicines and pharmaceutical industry.

Arms, ammunitions and explosives of any description whatsoever to the exclusion of hunting arms and their ammunitions.

Rotten or inflammable materials as shown on such tables issued and upon such conditions specified by the establishment satisfy the requirement of public security, health and safety.

Article 8
The status of the free zone shall not preliminary require within the boundaries of this zone any measures to be taken by the customs other than such measures for the detection of goods prohibited from being admitted under the provisions of article 7 of these regulations in agreement and cooperation with the establishment whereupon the establishment shall report to the customs any and all things in violation of the provisions of the said article the establishment's officials or employees may perceive.

Article 9
Goods shall be admitted into the free zone on the strength of an application to be submitted by the person concerned or his legal representative showing the origin, source, nature, type, weight and value of the goods as well as the type, trademark, numbering and number of the parcels, and the application shall contain a declaration by the applicant to the effect that he is cognizant of the provisions of these regulations and all rules concerning the operation of free zones and undertakes to observe and comply with them.

Admission shall be as follows:

Admission by land:

From inside or outside the country: the customs formality accompanying the goods shall be attached to the application in question.

Admission by sea:

From outside the country direct into the free zone in the same seaport.

The original copy of the shipping manifest shall be attached to the documents and bills of lading.

If the destination of the goods is an inland free zone, apart from the manifest, the documents and bills of lading referred to in the preceding clause shall be attached to the customs formality.

For additional analytical, business and investment opportunities information,
please contact Global Investment & Business Center, USA
at (703) 370-8082. Fax: (703) 370-8083. E-mail: ibpusa3@gmail.com
Global Business and Investment Info Databank - www.ibpus.com

From a Syrian seaport into a free zone in another Syrian seaport or an inland free zone admission shall be subject to the same conditions referred to in the preceding clause.

Article 10
The Establishment shall submit to the customs lists of all materials admitted into or exited from the free zone within 36 hours.

Article 11
When goods are admitted into or exited from the free zone, they shall be entered into the admission and exit registers prepared by the establishment in such approved regular forms which shall contain all such data of the relevant goods as set out in article 9 and all such data that may facilitate the identification of the goods.

Article 12
The goods admitted into the free zone shall be deposited in general roofed warehouses, and where there are no places in such warehouses, they shall be put under sheds or, otherwise, in open yards, with due regard as far as possible to the nature of the goods. There shall be put in open yards in particular:

Such goods that are impossible to put in sheds or roofed warehouses by reason of shape, size or weight, and are not affected by atmospheric conditions.

However, if the goods are affected by such conditions, the owners of the goods or their legal representatives shall take the necessary precautions for their protection.

The Establishment may take, without being bound, at the expense of the owners of the goods, at its sole discretion, the precautionary measures in question, and shall, in exercising this right, advise the persons concerned of the measures that have been taken and the quantum of expenses due within 48 hours, and the owners of the goods shall have the right to apply to the Establishment in writing to lift such precautionary measures at their own responsibility.

Such goods whose owners apply for their deposit in such a manner especially when the warehouses and sheds are full provided that the owners of such goods shall submit a prior declaration in writing to the effect that such a deposit is at their own responsibility.

Article 13
There shall be deposited in free zones the goods whose particulars and types are set out in the applications for admission and the owners of such goods shall be held responsible for the correctness of the statements that have been submitted and for any fault or fraud that may be found therein.

HANDING & TAKING OVER

Article 14
The goods shall be handed over to the establishment if and when they are admitted into such places other than the private tenancy according to the following procedures there shall be registered in the presence of the owner of the goods or his legal representative the parcels that have been admitted according to their types, marks and numberings, the damaged and suspicious parcels shall be sorted out, weighed and plumbed, an outturn report shall be made under the signature of the representative of the establishment and the person concerned, and there shall be entered in the outturn report any contradiction between the statements and documents on the one hand and the goods that have been taken over on the other hand. Goods in bulk or goods impossible to count shall be admitted as a whole according to their relevant documents and a reference shall be made in this respect in the outturn report.

For additional analytical, business and investment opportunities information, please contact Global Investment & Business Center, USA at (703) 370-8082. Fax: (703) 370-8083. E-mail: ibpusa3@gmail.com Global Business and Investment Info Databank - www.ibpus.com

If the person concerned declines to sign the outturn report or enters a reservation as to the facts established therein and fails to approach the court of urgent affairs within a maximum period of 3 days as from the date of the outturn report, this outturn report shall have full effect and force as if it had been signed without any reservation.

Article 15
Handing and taking over shall be as follows:

Goods of identical units : by number or weight on the basis of the carton.

Goods in bulk or goods impossible to count: according to the relevant documents without counting or weighing (i.e. as a whole as they have been received).

Other goods: by number without weight.

The Establishment shall not be responsible upon handing and taking over the goods referred to in clause (2) for weight and number as well as the goods referred to in clauses (1) and (3) for number even if this is given in the documents of the goods unless the owner of the goods asks the Establishment for handing and taking over be made on the basis of actual weight. In this case the expenses for weighing upon admission and exit shall be borne by the owner of the goods and the properties and nature of the goods, the method of packing and other circumstances that may have an effect of the weight of the goods, increase or decrease, shall be taken into consideration, whereupon the Establishment shall not be held responsible for any shortage in weight as a result of such circumstances.

WAREHOUSE WARRANTS

Article 16
The owner of the goods that have been deposited shall be given at his own request a nominal warehouse warrant or a receipt to order. Both shall be extracted from a book with counterfoil in which there shall be entered:

The name, surname, calling and service address of the depositor.

The number and date of admission of the goods into the general warehouses.

The name and nationality of the carrier vessel, if and when necessary, or any other means of transport.

The type of insurance and the sum insured.

The number, marks and condition of the parcels and place of depositing.

The type of the goods declared, the contents of the parcels and their weight.

The depositor of the goods shall be solely held responsible for the correctness of these particulars.

Article 17
The goods for which a warehouse warrant or a receipt to order is given shall be deposited in one place. The holder of the warrant or receipt shall have the right to divide the quantity deposited into several independent parts and to apply for the warrant or receipt to be replaced by a number of warrants or receipts equal to the number of the parts of the goods provided that the necessary measures shall be taken to distinguish these parts and to prevent their being mixed if and when necessary.

Article 18
The nominal warehouse warrants shall not be endorseable. The goods for which nominal warrants have been given shall be assigned before the establishment according to such instructions as may be issued by the establishment provided that both the assignor and the assignee or their respective legal representatives shall appear and the warehouse warrants of the goods that have been assigned shall be returned for the issue of new warrants in the name of the new owner in substitution.

Article 19
In case of the loss of the nominal warehouse warrant another warehouse warrant in replacement may be given or the goods subject of the warrant may be handed over to the person in whose name they are entered against a receipt along a declaration in writing of the loss of the warrant.

Article 20
Prior to the registration of the assignment and the issue of a new warehouse warrant to the assignee the applicant shall pay all fees chargeable on the goods assigned up to the date of the registration of the assignment.

Article 21
The depositor shall have the right to endorse the receipt to third party with no need to obtain the approval of or to notify the establishment and the endorser's obligations in respect of the goods shall devolve on the endorsee.

All notifications and notices shall be served by the establishment on the depositor and the goods that are the property of the depositor or the ultimate endorsee shall remain as a security for all the establishment's entitlements.

Article 22
In case of the loss of the receipt to order neither a replacement may be issued nor the goods may be handed over save by decision from the competent court and the establishment shall be under no responsibility in consequence.

Article 23
Endorsement shall transfer the ownership of the goods and all rights and obligations of the endorser in respect of the goods shall devolve on the endorsee.

Article 24
The depositing of the goods in the free zone shall not primarily be limited to a specified period except in such cases that necessitate the exit of the goods by reason of their very nature or the failure by their owners to pay such amounts as may be due to the establishment from them or their violation of the provisions of these regulations.

Article 25
The establishment shall have the right, as the exigencies of operation may be require, move, with approval of the persons concerned, the goods from the place where they are lying to another place as the establishment may deem appropriate. Anyhow the establishment may remove, at the expense of the persons concerned, the goods that may be found deleterious to the neighborhood, public health or to the constructions of the establishment.

Article 26
The establishment shall arrange for the insurance of the goods deposited in the warehouses and yards against fire risks and civil liability. This insurance shall be obligatory.

For additional analytical, business and investment opportunities information,
please contact Global Investment & Business Center, USA
at (703) 370-8082. Fax: (703) 370-8083. E-mail: ibpusa3@gmail.com
Global Business and Investment Info Databank - www.ibpus.com

The establishment shall recover from the owners of the goods deposited the insurance premiums appropriate to the value of the goods deposited and duration of depositing.

Article 27

The establishment shall take such care as may be necessary to safeguard the goods deposited in the free zone and shall take such measures necessary for their maintenance. If it appears that the goods are susceptible to destruction or that the damage to the goods or to other goods by reason of the damage to the goods in question has become grave at the discretion of the establishment, then the establishment shall have the right to serve a notice in writing by registered mail to the person concerned to remove the goods out of the free zone within such a time limit as the establishment may set as the case may be, and in default the establishment shall have the right in agreement with the administration of customs to sell or to destroy such goods.

The establishment may take such measures as may be necessary to protect the goods, to re-pack the parcels that have suffered damage and change or repair the covers at the expense of the owner of the goods if and when the establishment may so deem necessary with the approval of the person concerned, and the establishment shall have the right to carry out such works spontaneously at the expense of the persons concerned if and when the establishment may so deem necessary.

The waste of the goods as a result of probing, packing and collection by reason of loose parcels shall be handed over to the owners provided that they shall pay for their collection and sweeping and for the bags and containers packed therein if and when necessary.

The establishment shall dispose as the establishment may wish in its own interest with the waste of the goods that have not been identified.

Article 28

The establishment shall not be responsible for blemish, damage or defect by reason of the nature of the goods, the form of their packing, their unpacking, and the ambient temperature or humidity throughout the period of depositing. Further the establishment shall not be responsible for damage by reason of strikes, commotion, riots, war operations and different sorts of force major as well as by reason of harmful animals the establishment have to fight.

The establishment shall be held responsible for damage to the goods if it is established that such damage is a result of any act or negligence on the part of its officials, employees or workers, or the bad condition of its warehouses or their being not suitable for storage, on the strength of a decision issued by the competent court of law. The board may reach an amicable settlement to indemnify for the damage without recourse of the court of law.

Article 29

There shall be allowed to be set up and to be carried out freely in the free zones with a prior license from the establishment different industries, plants and all converting processes. They are as an example not by way of limitation division, sorting, forming, processing, packing, packaging, mixing, purifying, cleaning, lubricating, distilling, acidifying, hammering, breaking, crushing, marking, placing and changing trademarks.

The above operations shall be primarily carried out in places of special operations and the establishment may allow some of such operations be carried out in its general warehouses, yards or in such places prepared for this purpose if and when the establishment finds it possible.

For additional analytical, business and investment opportunities information,
please contact Global Investment & Business Center, USA
at (703) 370-8082. Fax: (703) 370-8083. E-mail: ibpusa3@gmail.com
Global Business and Investment Info Databank - www.ibpus.com

DUTIES AND FEES

Article 30
The board shall have the right to endorse and set fees for such services that have not been envisaged in the tariff.

The board shall have the right to increase or to decrease the fees as set out in the tariff annexed to these regulations at a rate not over than 50%. The new fees shall apply to all beneficiaries.

The decisions adopted by the board under the provisions of (a) and (b) shall be published in the official Gazette.

Article 31
The establishment shall collect the following fees as set in the tariff of free zones annexed to these regulations:

Porterage and handling fees.

Storage fee.

Tenancy fee.

Entry fee.

Insurance fee.

Assignment fee.

Fee for other services and for use of equipment and plant.

Article 32
The establishment shall carry out porterage and handling operations and shall collect from the owner of the goods the fee on the basis of weight in package or on the basis of actual weight as the case may be.

As regards goods in bulk that are impossible to count, the fee shall be collected on the basis of the weight as given in the documents (manifest, customs declaration, or shipping document) whether porterage by hand labor by vehicles and equipment in the following cases:

Case 1: Transport of the goods from the quay or the entrance of the free zone to the allocated place inside the zone and their stowing and stacking according to their types and marks.

Case 2: Transport of the goods from the warehouses or yards of the free zone to the quay or the inspection room and their loading after survey for transport outside the free zone.

Case 3: Taking over the goods alongside the means of transport inside the free zone, their depositing at the allocated place in the warehouses or yards inside the free zone and their stowing and stacking according to their types and marks.

Case 4: Transport of the goods from the warehouses or yards in the free zone and their delivery alongside on board the means of transport inside the free zone.

Case 5: Unloading the goods from a means of land transport and onloading on board another means of land transport.

Article 33

The establishment shall collect from the owner of the goods fees for all porterage operations that are not within the definition in the previous article. They cover collecting, re-packing, changing and repair covers, weighing, sorting, handling, and such other services relating to porterage as defined in the tariff.

Article 34

If the owner of the goods applies for porterage or another service and then he withdraws his application in whole or in part, the establishment shall have the right, if the necessary measures have already been taken, (according to the circumstances), to collect a porterage fee at a maximum rate or 50% for the entire quantity handled by labour.

Article 35

The establishment shall collect storage fee for such goods deposited in such warehouses inside the free zone other than the warehouses occupied by tenants throughout the whole period of their stay in the warehouses without any period of exemption.

The storage fee shall be calculated on the basis of the gross weight, number or volume as set in the tariff.

Article 36

The establishment shall collect a tenancy fee for such private places as defined in the contracts made with the persons concerned. If and when tenancy fee is chargeable, the establishment shall not collect storage fee for such goods deposited in the private places of the tenants.

Article 37

The establishment shall collect a duty at a flat rate in respect of such goods admitted into the free zone.

Article 38

The establishment shall collect an assignment fee each time the goods, contracts of commercial or industrial tenancy, or vehicles and means of transport are assigned.

Article 39

The establishment shall collect from the persons concerned fees for the different materials, services, certificates or copies of documents the establishments provides at request and charges for the use of machines and equipment.

Article 40

The fees shall be chargeable for the whole period of the stay of the goods in the free zone up to the date of their actual exit.

The board shall fix, upon a proposal from the director, the dates for the payment of the fees and advances to be paid by the persons concerned on account of the fees.

The establishment shall have the right, if there is a delay on the part of the persons concerned for more than 6 months in paying such fees, to sell the goods by public auction following the service of a notice in writing and the lapse of a period of 15 days as from the date on which the persons concerned have been served the said notice.

As regards goods that have a small value, the establishment shall have the right, if and when the fees are not paid on the dates on which they become due and payable, to sell such goods by public auction after the persons concerned are served a notice and after the lapse of the time limit referred to above. Sale shall be effected on the basis of the customs status in the free zone.

For additional analytical, business and investment opportunities information,
please contact Global Investment & Business Center, USA
at (703) 370-8082. Fax: (703) 370-8083. E-mail: ibpusa3@gmail.com
Global Business and Investment Info Databank - www.ibpus.com

Article 41

If a dispute arises between the establishment and the persons concerned over the question of fees and charges, the persons concerned shall pay the amount claimed by the establishment and shall then have the right to appeal administratively to the competent authority in the establishment and to have recourse, if and when necessary, to the competent court of law.

Article 42

It is a condition precedent to the refunds of the difference in fees and charges erroneously collected that the difference shall be greater than five Syrian pounds and that an application in writing shall be filed within a maximum period of 6 months as from the date of collection.

Article 43

The establishment shall draft the forms of tenancy contracts and shall define the conditions of such tenancy. These contracts shall be considered temporary tenancy contracts and shall not be governed by the provisions of the law of rent.

The maximum period of the temporary tenancy contract shall be:

One year in respect of open places intended to be occupied for storage purposes without erecting buildings or installing industrial equipment.

Fifteen years in respect of open places intended to be occupied for the purpose of erecting buildings for storage.

Twenty years in respect of open places intended to be occupied for the purpose of erecting buildings for converting industries and processes.

The ownership of the buildings and appurtenances shall devolve on to the establishment after the expiry of the period as specified in the tenancy contracts.

These contracts shall be renewed, after the expiry of their period, from year to year for a rent to be paid in advance and to be fixed by mutual agreement unless the person concerned expresses his intention in writing not to renew the contract three months before the expiry of the term.

Article 44

If the establishment finds that the person concerned has suspended his activity for two consecutive years of five years at intermittent intervals without a lawful excuse, the establishment shall have the right, with the approval of the board, to determine the contract or to refuse the renewal of the contract, and this shall be attended by all consequences attending the expiry of the initial period of the contract.

Article 45

The industrial operation in free zones shall be mainly oriented for export. There may be allowed with the approval of the ministry of economy and foreign trade, upon a proposal by the establishment, the admission of a percentage of the exports of such industries into the Syrian markets by way of exclusion from the foreign trade laws and regulations and from the restrictions imposed on import except such restrictions relating to the limitation or restriction of import to a public sector body. For this portion of production there shall be granted automatic import licenses with no need to transfer the value abroad and this portion of production shall be exempt from duties pro rata the local materials incorporated in manufacture.

Article 46

It shall be observed that the industries set up in free zones shall not lead to the imitation or competition of such industries in the country except in such where they enter into a partnership with local industries .priority shall be given to the following industries with due regard to the industrial strategy and the requirements of the development plans in the Syrian Arab Republic:

Industries for which local raw materials or locally manufactured components are available.

Industries that integrate with locally existing industries.

New industries that are not locally existing and depend on modern technical production.

Industries that meet the need of local consumption and help to dispense with import from abroad.

Industries that help to employ a greater number of hand labour.

Article 47

The prospective tenant shall submit an application to the establishment in which he shall specify the purpose of tenancy, the types of goods intended to be stored or converted , the places intended to be occupied, and the buildings or the industrial enterprises and equipment he wishes to erect or set up thereon provided that the prospective tenant shall be residing in the city or town in which the free zone is situate, or shall have therein a service address or a representative.

Applications for tenancy submitted by foreign natural or juristic persons shall not be allowed unless such persons have established a head office or a branch in the Syrian Arab Republic or unless such persons have a representative who is a Syrian Arab Citizen.

In this latter case the application shall be accompanied by a copy of the contract made between the two parties provided that this contract shall, anyhow, be registered in accordance with the domestic laws.

The area of the land intended to be occupied by the prospective tenant shall not be more than 10% of the area allocated for private tenancy inside the free zone.

Article 48

The contracts made between the two parties shall specify the mode and dates of payment of the tenancy fee. There shall be collected from the prospective tenant a tenancy fee for at least one year in advance. As regards contracts for less than one year, the fee shall be collected in advance for the whole term of the contract.

Article 49

The director shall determine the applications submitted for tenancy of land for storage and the board shall determine, upon a proposal by the director, the applications submitted for tenancy of land to set up industrial enterprises.

Buildings and industrial enterprises shall be set up on the land tenanted as indicated on the drawing with all roads and means for protection from fire risks upon an approval by the establishment. There shall be observed the technical procedures as to storage, converting and manufacturing and any modification in these drawings shall be subject to an approval from the establishment.

Article 50

The tenants of private places shall observe and comply with the rules for protection from fire and explosion. Insurance shall cover civil liability to such an extent at the discretion of the establishment and shall be made with accredited insurance companies. This insurance shall be obligatory at the expense of the tenants.

Article 51

The goods shall be forwarded to the private places in the free zone at the request of the tenants provided that these goods shall be for the tenants or that these goods are regularly assigned to them. Further these goods shall be relevant to the purposes for which the place has been allocated in the tenancy contract and shall be entered in the registers of the places tenanted. Goods shall be chargeable in case of the violation of any of the conditions referred to herein to a double storage fee.

Article 52

If the tenants of the private places violate the provisions of these regulations or the terms of the tenancy contracts made with them , the establishment shall address a notice to them to remedy the violation within such a time limit as specified in the notice. In default to remedy the violation within the time limit as set in the notice, the establishment shall have the right , with the approval of the board , to rescind the contracts and to specify a reasonable period for eviction. In this case the buildings shall become the property of the establishment with no indemnity. If the persons concerned fail to remove their goods, machines and equipment within the stated time limit, the establishment shall have the right to do so at their own expense and the goods, machines and equipment shall be stored at their own expense in the general warehouses and yards.

Article 53

The tenants of private places shall be responsible for all damage caused by them, their representatives or their subordinates, or by reason of their enterprises or goods to other buildings or enterprises or the goods lying therein inside and outside the free zone, and their observance of the safety rules imposed on them shall not release them from liability.

Article 54

The tenants of private places shall keep and maintain registers to enter the incoming and outgoing goods. These registers shall be maintained in such forms as specified by the establishment.

Article 55

The tenants of private places shall keep and maintain records of the names and number of their employees and workers and the date of their employment in the free zone and lists thereof shall be sent direct to the establishment. All amendments to the particular of the records, increase or decrease, shall be notified to the establishment. The tenants shall hand each of their employees and workers a sign in such a uniform model to be specified by the establishment to carry the name of the employer and the number of the warehouse or the industrial enterprise and to be put on the arm when on duty inside the free zone. These signs shall be left with the establishment's watchmen at the gates of the free zone when they exit.

The tenants of private places shall be responsible for the behavior of their employees and workers. The establishment shall have the right to prevent any of such employees and workers from entering into the free zone if and when such person violates the regulations of work therein.

Article 56

The establishment may allow the tenants of private places to assign to third party the right of tenancy of the land they occupy and the enterprises erected on such land within the following conditions:

Assignment shall be made before the competent official of the establishment.

A new contract shall be made between the assignee and the establishment and shall be subject to all terms of the former contract with the assignor.

The assignment fee as set in the tariff of fees shall be paid.

For additional analytical, business and investment opportunities information, please contact Global Investment & Business Center, USA at (703) 370-8082. Fax: (703) 370-8083. E-mail: ibpusa3@gmail.com Global Business and Investment Info Databank - www.ibpus.com

Article 57

The tenants of private places who carry on an industrial activity in the free zone shall keep and maintain special records of the industrial machines used in such places to enter their admission and exit, with certain records assigned for machine from the domestic market, and there shall be entered therein such particulars as may be necessary such description, number, mark, origin, value, destination, type and such other useful data.

Article 58

The goods that have been admitted into the private places and have undergone converting processes shall be entered in special records to give all necessary clarifications of the converting, mixing and manufacturing processes and to show the type of the materials that have been used in the new production, their quantities, their origin and all such relevant data, and shall be cleared in such other records and registers referred to in these regulations. The products that have been converted or manufactured in the free zone shall carry the expression "free zone in ..." in a product the board resolves to be relieved from this expression.

FREE MARKETS

Article 59

The establishment may establish free markets inside the free zones, in the main cities in the country, in civil airports and in seaports.

The duty free shop shall consist of commercial stores for the wholesale or retailsale of foreign and national goods to passengers in transit and international passengers for re-export, diplomatic and consular corps, and the like, and the general rules of free zones shall apply to these duty free shops in with the nature of their composition and the purpose for which they have been established.

The establishment shall specify the types of goods, the sale conditions and the means of control in agreement with the administration of customs and the administration of the airport as the case may be provided that sale shall be in such acceptable foreign currency.

The operations allowed in the free markets shall be limited to the sorting, packing, division and grading operations and such operations as may be necessary for preservation.

Article 60

The body assigned the duty by the establishment to operate the duty free shop shall be responsible towards the establishment for all violations and faults committed direct by the said body, its agents or its subordinates.

EXIT OF GOODS

Article 61

Goods shall be exited from the free zone upon an application in writing by the person concerned to the establishment and the application shall show the type of the goods, their origin, and the number and types of parcels.

If the goods have undergone any of the converting or manufacturing operations referred to in these regulations, all clarifications of the operation in question shall be given, further, in case of mixing or new production, the types and sources of the parcels mixed shall be given, so that the customs service would be in a good position to exercise control and to compute the customs duties that may be chargeable on such materials.

Article 62

In exiting the goods the following shall be observed:

For additional analytical, business and investment opportunities information, please contact Global Investment & Business Center, USA at (703) 370-8082. Fax: (703) 370-8083. E-mail: ibpusa3@gmail.com Global Business and Investment Info Databank - www.ibpus.com

The fees due to the establishment for such goods shall be paid and the relevant customs formalities shall be channeled.

The nominal warehouse warrants or the receipts to order referred to in these regulations shall be returned.

The delivery orders and such other documents shall be produced, if and when necessary, according to such instructions issued by the establishment.

The goods shall be removed to the inspection room for survey and customs formalities. This room shall be set up at the expense of the establishment at such place to be agreed on with the administration of customs. This room shall be under the joint watchman service of both the establishment and the customs.

The owner of the goods or his representative shall sign a note in acknowledgement of receipt.

Article 63
If and when a parcel is opened for customs inspection or at the request of the person concerned, the soundness of the parcels shall be verified before opening, so that if it appears that a parcel is suspicious a customs report shall be made in cooperation with the establishment. If no customs report is made, this parcel that has been opened is considered to be intact. In this case the establishment shall not be responsible for any discrepancy that may transpire in the contents of the parcels when opened.

OPERATION OF BANKS

Article 64
Banking enterprises may be licensed to be established within free zones to exercise functions in financing different commercial and industrial activities and operations and in rendering different bank services as may be required for the activities of the operators in these zones.

Article 65
There shall be specified by an order from the board the tenancy fee and duration.

Article 66
The board shall formulate the provisions concerning the operation of banks, especially the provisions:

To regulate the granting of loan

To specify the capital and reserve of the bank

To specify the bank operations allowed

To specify such date and information to be submitted to the establishment to verify the sound standing and activity of the bank

To specify the role of the establishment in exercising control and supervision of the bank operations

To regulate the liquidation of the bank

To specify the securities to safeguard the rights of the customers of the bank and the provisions for the regulation of the operation of bank

To specify the violations, fines and administrative penalties.

In formulating such provisions there shall be observed that they are consistent with the purpose of creating free zones and the nature of operation without due observance of the provisions of laws governing bank operations in the country.

GENERAL & MISCELLANEOUS PROVISIONS

Article 67
Foreign goods shall not be allowed to be consumed in the free zones for personal use before payment of such customs duties and other taxes and duties chargeable.

Further residence in free zones shall not be allowed save by a special permission from the establishment as may be required for running the work.

Article 68
All national and foreign vessels may arrange for the supply of all marine equipment as they may require from the free zone.

National and foreign vessels, load over 150 net marine tons, may arrange for the supply of foodstuffs, cigarettes, drinks, oil, and all materials as necessary for their machines from the free zone. The establishment shall have the right suspend the supply operation if and when fraud and abuse are established.

Article 69
Any person who enters into the free zone, or deals with it, or uses its constructions and facilities shall observe and comply with these regulations.
Article 70
No person shall be allowed to enter into the free zone unless he holds a special permit from the director of the free zone for this purpose to the exclusion of the customs guards and the competent customs officials if and when necessary for the exigencies of work.
Article 71
Working hours and procedures to enter into and exit from the free zone shall be specified by the director of the establishment.

TRAVEL TO SYRIA

SYRIA – US STATE DEPARTMENT SUGGESTIONS

COUNTRY DESCRIPTION: The Syrian Arab Republic has a developing, mixed-sector economy. The ruling Ba'th party espouses a largely secular ideology, but Islamic traditions and beliefs provide a conservative foundation for the country's customs and practices. The constitution refers to Islamic jurisprudence as a
principal source of legislation, but the legal system remains influenced by French practice. Tourist facilities are widely available, but vary in quality depending on price and location. The workweek in Syria is Saturday through Thursday. The U.S. Embassy is open Sunday through Thursday.

ENTRY REQUIREMENTS: A passport and a visa are required. Visas must be obtained prior to arrival in Syria. Entry to Syria is not granted to persons with passports bearing an Israeli visa or entry/exit stamps, or to persons born in the Gaza region or of Gazan descent. Entry into Syria via the land border with Israel is not possible. Foreigners who wish to stay 15 days or more in Syria must register with Syrian Immigration by their 15th day in Syria. Americans between the ages of 18 and 45 who are of Syrian birth or recent descent are subject to the Syrian compulsory military service requirement, unless they receive an exemption from the Syrian Embassy in the United States prior to their entry into Syria. An AIDS test is not required for foreigners prior to arrival in Syria. However, tests are mandatory for foreigners (age 15 to 60) wishing to reside in Syria. The AIDS test must be conducted in Syria at a facility approved by the Syrian Ministry of Health. A residence permit will not be issued until the absence of the HIV virus has been determined. Foreigners wishing to marry Syrian nationals must also be tested for HIV. For further entry information, travelers may contact the Embassy of the Syrian Arab Republic, 2215 Wyoming Ave. N.W., Washington, D.C. 20008, tel. (202) 232-6313.

American citizens are cautioned that the Syrian government rigidly enforces restrictions on prior travel to Israel. Travelers with Israeli stamps in their passports, Jordanian entry cachets or cachets from other countries which
suggest prior travel to Israel, or the absence of any entry stamps from a country adjacent to Israel which the traveler has just visited, will cause Syrian immigration authorities to refuse the traveler admission to Syria. In one case in 1998, a group of American citizen travelers suspected of traveling to Israel were detained overnight for questioning.

Although Syria is a signatory to the Vienna Convention, consular notification and access to arrested Americans is problematic. Syrian officials generally do not notify the American Embassy when American citizens are arrested. When the American Embassy learns of arrests of Americans and requests consular access, individual police officials have, on their own initiative, responded promptly and allowed consular officers to visit the prisoners. However, security officials have also in the past denied Embassy requests for consular access.

MILITARY SERVICE: Syrian-American males of draft age who are planning to visit Syria are strongly urged to check with the Syrian Embassy in Washington concerning their requirement for compulsory military service. Even Americans who have never resided in or visited Syria before may be considered Syrian and required to complete military service if their fathers were Syrian. Possession of a U.S. passport does not absolve the bearer of this obligation.

IRAQ: Syrian security officials are sensitive about travel to Iraq. There have been past instances of Iraqi-Americans or Americans believed to have traveled to Iraq being detained for questioning at ports of entry/exit.

For additional analytical, business and investment opportunities information,
please contact Global Investment & Business Center, USA
at (703) 370-8082. Fax: (703) 370-8083. E-mail: ibpusa3@gmail.com
Global Business and Investment Info Databank - www.ibpus.com

MEDICAL FACILITIES: Basic medical care and medicines are available in the principal cities of Syria, but not necessarily in outlying areas. Doctors and hospitals often expect immediate cash payment for health care services. The Medicare/Medicaid program does not always provide for payment of medical services outside the United States. U.S. medical insurance is not always valid outside the United States. Supplemental medical insurance with specific overseas coverage, including a provision for emergency evacuation, has proven useful. Information on health problems can be obtained from the Centers for Disease Control and Prevention at 1-877-FYI-TRIP (1-877-394-8747), fax: 1-888-CDC-FAXX (1-888-232-3299), or on the Internet at http://www.cdc.gov.

INFORMATION ON CRIME Crime is generally not a serious problem for travelers in Syria. The loss or theft of a U.S. passport abroad should be reported immediately to local police and the nearest U.S. Embassy or Consulate. Useful information on safeguarding valuables, protecting personal security, and other matters while traveling abroad is provided in the Department of State pamphlets, A Safe Trip Abroad and Tips for Travelers to the Middle East and North Africa. They are available from the Superintendent of Documents, U.S. Government Printing Office, Washington, D.C. 20402, via the Internet at http://www.access.gpo.gov/su_docs, or via the Bureau of Consular Affairs home page at http://travel.state.gov.

Syria is included on the Department of State's list of state sponsors of terrorism. There is no record of terrorist attacks against Americans in Syria and Syrian government officials have repeatedly stated their commitment to protect Americans. However, a number of terrorist groups which oppose U.S. policies in the Middle East have a presence in this country.

CUSTODY/FAMILY ISSUES: Children under the age of eighteen whose fathers are Syrian must have the father's permission in order to depart Syria, even if the mother has been granted full custody by a Syrian court. Women in Syria are often subject to strict family controls; on occasion families of Syrian/American women visiting Syria have attempted to prevent them from leaving the country. This can be a particular problem for young single women of marriageable age. Finally, although this occurs only rarely, a Syrian husband is permitted to take legal action to prevent his wife from leaving the country, regardless of her nationality.

DRUG PENALTIES: U.S. citizens are subject to the laws and legal practices of the country in which they travel. Penalties for possession of even small amounts of illegal drugs for personal use are severe in Syria. The penalty in Syria for growing, processing or smuggling drugs is the death penalty, which may be reduced to a minimum of 20 years imprisonment.

TRAFFIC SAFETY AND ROAD CONDITIONS: Driving in Syria requires great caution. Although drivers generally follow traffic signs and signals, they often maneuver aggressively and show little regard to vehicles traveling behind them. Lane markings are usually ignored. Unlike the U.S., vehicles within Syrian traffic circles must give way to oncoming traffic. Pedestrians must also exercise caution. Parked cars, deteriorating pavement, and guard posts present obstacles on sidewalks, often forcing pedestrians to walk in the street.

CURRENCY REGULATIONS: Syrian currency cannot be exchanged for any other currency except at government-approved exchange centers within Syria. Travelers must declare all foreign currency when they enter Syria. Amounts in excess of $5,000 (US) [or $2,000 (US) for those holding dual Syrian-American
nationality] are subject to confiscation upon leaving Syria.

AVIATION SAFETY OVERSIGHT: As there is no direct commercial air service by local carriers at present, or economic authority to operate such service, between the U.S. and Syria, the U.S. Federal Aviation Administration (FAA) has not assessed Syria's Civil Aviation Authority for compliance with international aviation safety standards for oversight of Syria's air carrier operations. For further information, travelers may contact the Department of Transportation within the U.S. at 1-800-322-7873, or visit the FAA Internet home page at http://www.faa.gov/avr/iasa/index.htm. The U.S. Department of Defense (DOD) separately assesses some foreign air carriers for suitability as official providers of air services. For information regarding the DOD policy on specific carriers, travelers may contact DOD at 618-256-4801.

Y2K INFORMATION: As a consequence of the so-called Y2K "bug," on or about January 1, 2000, some automated systems throughout the world may experience problems, including unpredictable system malfunctions. In countries that are not prepared, the Y2K problem could affect financial services, utilities, health
services, telecommunications, energy, transportation and other vital services. American citizens who are traveling to any country during this time period should be aware of the potential for the disruption of normal medical services. Travelers with special medical needs should consult with their personal physician and take appropriate precautions. While travelers do not necessarily need to alter their travel plans, being informed and prepared for possible disruptions is prudent.

Syria is not heavily reliant on computerized systems and is working with the international community to minimize any impact as a result of Y2K. While Syria appears to be generally prepared to deal with the Y2K problem, remediation and contingency planning continue. Critical systems in sectors such as aviation, water distribution and chlorination, electricity generation and distribution, maritime transport and telecommunications are either expected to be Y2K-compliant, or are based on manual or non-date-dependent systems. Syrian officials acknowledge the potential for unexpected problems and said they are preparing contingency plans in all critical sectors. Without further remediation, interest payments on current accounts at the Commercial Bank of Syria may also be affected. U.S. citizens traveling to or residing in Syria in late 2004 or early 2000 should be aware of these potential difficulties.

It is difficult to predict the severity or duration of Y2K-related disruptions. U.S. citizens in Syria should take practical precautions, anticipate the potential for disruptions to their daily activities, and be prepared to cope with the impact of such disruptions. Information about personal preparedness and Y2K is available in the Department of State Worldwide Public Announcement of July 26, 2004, which is accessible on the Department of State, Bureau of Consular Affairs home page at http://travel.state.gov/y2kca.html.

Aviation and Y2K: The Department of Transportation is heading an international Year 2000 civil aviation evaluation process to review information on Y2K readiness in aviation based on reports to the International Civil Aviation Organization and other available sources. The Federal Aviation Administration is working with the industry and its international partners to encourage sharing of Y2K readiness and contingency planning information so that air carriers will be able to make appropriate decisions. Consult your airline about contingency plans in the event of unforeseen Y2K-related delays, cancellations, or disruptions. See the Department of Transportation Y2K home page at http://www.dot.gov/fly2k for updated information on Y2K and aviation issues.

As January 1, 2000, draws nearer, we will provide updated information available to us about important Y2K issues in Syria on the Consular Affairs home page at http://travel.state.gov/y2kca.html.

REGISTRATION/U.S. EMBASSY LOCATION: U.S. citizens are encouraged to register at the U.S. Embassy and obtain updated information on travel and security within Syria. The U.S. Embassy in Damascus, Syria, is located in Abu Roumaneh, Al-Mansur St. No. 2; P.O. Box 29.

Telephone numbers are (963) (11) 333-2814, 332-0783, 333-0788, and 333-3232. Fax number is (963) (11) 331-9678.

BUSINESS CUSTOMS

TRAVEL ADVISORY AND VISAS

1. Personal entry requirements

Passport: Required
Visa: Required
Health & Immunization: Certificates are required of all travelers arriving from infected areas. There are not currently any AIDS test requirements for short-term visitors to Syria. The Syrian government will not grant entry to persons with passports bearing an Israeli visa or entry/exit stamp, or to persons born in the Gaza region or of Gazan descent.

2. Embassy information

Syrian Embassy in the United States:
Address: Embassy of the Syrian Arab Republic,
2215 Wyoming Ave., Washington, D.C. 20008
Telephone: (202) 232-6313, Fax: (202)234-9548

U.S. Embassy in Syria:
Address: Abou Roumaneh, 2 Al-Mansour Street, P.O. Box 29,
Damascus, Syria
Telephone: 963-11-3332814/3330416/3330788, Fax: 963-11-2247938

HOLIDAYS

Syrians will observe the following holidays

July 15	(Prophet's Birthday)1/
October 6	(Tishrin War)
December 25	(Christmas Day)
January 1	(New Year's Day)
January 29-31	(Al-Fitr Holiday)1/
March 8	(Revolution Day)
March 21	(Mothers' Day)
April 7-10	(Al-Adha Holiday)1/
April 12	(Easter)
April 17	(Independence Day)
April 19	(Orthodox Easter)
April 29	(Muslim New Year)1/

May 1	(Labor Day)
May 6	(Martyr Day)
July 5	(Prophet's Birthday)1/
October 6	(Tishrin War)
December 25	(Christmas Day)

1/ Based on lunar calendar. Exact date to be confirmed.

SYRIA, THE CIVILIZATION AND HISTORY

Syria is an ancient Tourist country. It is the land of continuous and uninterrupted history. It has known most of the prophets and conquerors. It is the land on which greatest empires accumulated.

This has not affected its inhabitants who were sometimes known as Amorites and sometimes the Arameans, but were all the time known as Arab who remained trade mediators all over the world and emissaries combining human education and cooperation.

This land does not only embody human efforts and hopes, including the civilization above and beneath it, but it was a landmark of antiquity throughout all ages. It was also eternal paradise in all times, and dreamful desert covered by sand dunes around abandoned cities that have once ruled the near east region as a whole. It is a land of dense forests that almost prevented sunshine to beam over their feet. It is also a beautiful coastline that curves along soft-sanded shores, and it is a superior climate that is affected by mountains, forests, sea and desert making tourism and enjoyment. It is first and for all the country of human being who has turned cooper into artistic tools and mud into embroidered containers, whereby changing the shepherd life into a stable agricultural life which witnessed the construction of cities and civilizations.

It is the land of the Arabs who introduced the alphabet in the form of language and simplified writing that has turned to be political and trade apparatus through the world conveying thought from era to era.

It is the land of the Arabs who accomplished all these achievements and who are currently leading a civilized process and dignity under a wise and inspiring leadership.

The Syrian Arab republic is located in the western part of Asia overlooking the Mediterranean Basin. Its area is 184,000 square Kilometers with 12 million inhabitants.

It is surrounded by Turkey from the north, Iraq from the east, Jordan from and Palestine from the south and the Mediterranean sea and Lebanon from the west.

Syrian is known for being a land containing many historical ruins. The national Museum in Damascus is famous for the valuable historical belonging. It is similar to an active exhibition showing evidences of human development on the Syrian territories.

There, one can find astonishing ruins with stands for Syrian oriental ruins and other ruins belonging to the Greek, Roman, and Byzatine eras as well as Arab and Islamic ruins.

It also contahall, whichis a symbol of beauty. In Damascus also, there is the Ommayad Mosque, which is viewed as one of the marvelous Arab architecture. Beside it lies the tomb of Salah din al-

For additional analytical, business and investment opportunities information, please contact Global Investment & Business Center, USA at (703) 370-8082. Fax: (703) 370-8083. E-mail: ibpusa3@gmail.com Global Business and Investment Info Databank - www.ibpus.com

Ayyouby in another area in the city, lies the Takiyeh Suleimanieh with its wonderful engraving and architecture.

Al-Azim palace is also a touritic gift of Damascus where the straight street extends with nearby churches of Saint Hanania and Saint Paul in the palace vicinity, lie the old markets of Damascus, which reflect the flavor of an oriental history, in addition to a large number of Monastries, churches, mosques, schools, gates, inns and old beautiful Damascus houses.

In the outskirts of Damascus, there is the site of Sayeda Zeinab, grand daughter of prophet Mohammad and Koukab the place where Saint Paul viewed, there is also Maalola historical city with its Monastry which is considered one of the oldest Christian Monastries in the world. Then comes Sydnaya town, which still maintains its famous monastry. In Aleppo to the north, which is a city full of touristic places, there stands Aleppo citadel with all its great landmarks and the wonderful museum, which contains most valuable historical richness.

In this city, one can also find old oriental markets, which enjoy a special charming attraction derived from its famous industries. There are also numerous oriental houses, mosques, inns, and Bathrooms. In the outskirts of Aleppo, stands Saint Simon citadel with its historical church and monastry and to the southwest also stands the famous historical city of Ebla which goes back to the third thousand B.C. This old city is considered one of the oldest civilization centers where a prosperous kingdom was established.

Homs city, which is located to the north of Damascus, is famous with Zennar church which contains the belt of virgin Mary and Khaled Bin Al-Walid mosque where the tomb of this great leader lies. In Hums province (Muhafazet) lies crac de chevaliers, one of the greatest military castles of the middle ages.

The historical city of Palmyra, the capital of the great Arab queen of Zennobia, is located in the central Syrian desert. This city became famous worldwide because of its historical temples, pillars and engravings which are kept in Palmyra museum and under the city's cemetries, status and the arches of victory.

In Hama city there is Al-Azem palace which is an immitation of Al-Azem palace of Damascus. It was turned into a museum containing ruins and precious belonging.

Hama waterwheels still stand as giants defying the burdens of the time and carrying water from the orontes river to the surrounding plantations and nursaries.

In Bosra, located in Derra muhafazet south of Damascus, lies the Roman stadium with its unique theater and Bosra Islamic citadel. In this town there is a number of Roman ruins that have been recently discovered.

In Sweidaa, east of Bosra, a collection of Roman, Arab, and Islamic ruins scatter in nearly Shahba, Al-Hiet, Al-Hiyat, Zukeir, and Ariqa. There, you can also find Salkhad citadel, which lies on a big hill overlooking the plateaues of Salkhad in addition to landmarks of antiquity scattered here and there.

The Syrian coastal area comprises Lattakia and Tartous Muhafazets with their fascinating landscape and Furullouq Forests and Kassab area, which contains wonderful Arab and crusade citadels and castles. It also contains Ugarit city in Ras Shamra near Lattakia, where the oldest alphabet known in the world was found. On the Syrian coast, soft sand shores stretch. It is one of the places where tourists can enjoy their time fautastically throughout the year.

In Al-Raqqa and Deir Ezzor muhafazet east of Syria, lies the Rusafa of Hicham Bin Abdul Malik, which turns the sun beams to the Rainbw colors on its walls. This place is very away from Jaaber

For additional analytical, business and investment opportunities information,
please contact Global Investment & Business Center, USA
at (703) 370-8082. Fax: (703) 370-8083. E-mail: ibpusa3@gmail.com
Global Business and Investment Info Databank - www.ibpus.com

citadel which floats inside Al-Assad lake formed by the great Euphrates Dam. Other historical sites which lie along the banks of the Euphrates river are Mary, Doura, Orobos, Halabieyeh, Zilbiyeh, and Al-Rahba citadel in Al-Mayadin town.

In general, Syria with its beautiful summer resorts, fruit trees and fresh air has been bestowed with all natural beauty and weather variance which make the country a fascinating place.

The people of Syria, who have been famous for hospitality and generosity throughout history, now invite you to get acquainted with the consecutive civilization erected over this beautiful land. They also open their arms and hearts to embrace all Arab and foreign tourists to see on spot the Syria of civilization and glory and to view the Syria of president Hafez Al-Assad, the country of loving, fraternity and peace.

FORMALITIES TO ENTER AND LEAVE SYRIA

- All individuals who wish to travel to Syria must posses a valid passport .

- Passports must contain a valid entry visa for Syria , delivered by the Syrian embassy or consulate accredited to the country of the holder of passport .

- If there is not a Syrian mission in the country of the passport holder, a visa can be obtained at any Syrian foreign mission or upon arrival at the Syria border .

- A collective visa, free of charge , is given to tour groups consisting of ten persons or more . This visa is attached to a list of the members of the tour group ; however , each individual in the tour group must also carry a valid passport .

- If the duration of an individual's stay in Syria exceeds fifteen days, he or she must contact the Syrian authorities to obtain an extension of stay on his or her passport .

- Passports must not contain an Israeli visa .

- The cost of a visa is a calculated on the basis of the current reciprocal relationship between Syria and the country of the passport holder .

- Travellers do not need an exit visa if the duration of their stay in Syria does not exceed fifteen days .

CUSTOMS REGULATIONS FOR TRAVEL

- Clothing and personal effects which are accompanying travellers are exempt from customs and do not need to be declared .

- The following consumable materials accompanying travellers are exempt from customs but must be declared :

  - One litre of eau de Cologne

  - One litre of an alcoholic beverage .

  - Two hundred cigarettes or fifty cigars or two hundred grams of tobacco .

- The following products accompanying travellers must be declared , but are exempt from customs on the condition that they are used and that the travellers agrees that the goods will leave Syria with him or her :

- photographic camera

- video camera , for non-professional use .

- pair of binoculars

- portable musical instrument

- portable tape recorder

- baby carriage or stroller

- portable typewriter

- camping equipment

- individual sports equipment

- bicycle

- small iron for pressing clothing

- medical instruments that are commonly carried by a doctor

- toilet accessories

- travelling blankets and sleeping bags .

Customs agent at the Syrian border are permitted , according to their personal judgement , to authorise the entry of other objects for personal use mentioned above.

To bring a car to Syria , the owner must carry an international driver's licence , an international grey card , and a triptych . A car can stay in Syria for three to four months , on one or more trips .

Cars that are fuelled by diesel can stay in Syria for four months , but the driver must pay an entry tax . For more information , please contact the Syrian customs authorities . Cars that run on gasoline do not require an entry tax .

It is possible , in all cases , to acquire detailed information concerning customs , transit formalities and recent change to customs regulations from Syrian embassies and consulates , and from the customs offices located on the Syrian boeder .

IMPORTANT TO REMEMBER WHEN IN SYRIA

Don't accept food in a social setting the first time it's offered. It's polite to   decline at least once before accepting.

Do offer a guest food or drink several times (as he or she may decline the first offer)

Do feel free to talk politics with your guests, but don't hammer home a point or be insensitive to local and national traditions. Feel free to debate issues such as   democracy, the price of coffee, etc., but don't say negative things about the ruler of the country, even if asked. Syrians feel very upset about their country's negative reputation. They will spend a lot of time defending their country's good name.

Don't admire a specific item in a host's home or office - or the host may feel obliged to give it to you, something neither of you really wants. Keep your compliments general.

Do expect to see Syrian women riding on the back of motorbikes, wearing jeans and fashionable clothes. Not all will be veiled or covered in black. Don't assume that there is anything unusual about men walking arm in arm or hand in hand. Men are much more physically affectionate with their male friends and relatives than men are in the West

Do be careful at security checkpoints when traveling inside Syria. Move slowly and obey the authorities. Don't expect your phone conversations to be private (the phones may be bugged).

Don't point at people or use your hands to give direction, as to do so is considered rude. Also, be careful that the soles of your shoes don't show when you're sitting.

Do make appointments and be on time, but don't be offended by a lack of punctuality by others. Also, don't be offended if the person you're meeting for business conducts other business during "your" appointment. Don't show irritation when everything stops five times a day for prayers. Do shake hands and say marha-bah, keif halak, when greeting people. Don't expect stores, offices or markets to be open on Friday, the Muslim Sabbath (the work week is Saturday through Thursday).

Do take along a small gift when invited to a home (don't bring liquor, or artwork that contains images of people).

Don't inquire about a host's wife. If you meet her, shake hands only if she offers   hers first.

Do be sure to dress appropriately (no bare arms or legs) when visiting a mosque and remove your shoes before entering. However, you should carry your shoes with you during your visit, as thieves have been known to steal shoes left at the mosques' entrances.

Don't let two days go by without visiting a hammam. The spa treatment is basic, but the atmosphere and prices are unbeatable.

Do choose Damascus's Omayyad Mosque over Aleppo's and Aleppo's suq and citadel over Damascus's if time is limited.

Don't photograph veiled women (unless permission is granted first), airports, military establishments or bridges.

Don't talk business during social visits with a business host.

Do attend one of the numerous cultural festivals if you get the chance.
Don't exchange money in the black market. Its illegal, unsafe and the exchange   rate is not that much higher than in banks. And don't exchange more money than you have to if you are crossing over from the Turkish land border. The rate is lousy.

Don't pass anything (especially food) with your left hand.

For additional analytical, business and investment opportunities information,
please contact Global Investment & Business Center, USA
at (703) 370-8082. Fax: (703) 370-8083. E-mail: ibpusa3@gmail.com
Global Business and Investment Info Databank - www.ibpus.com

Do take along toilet paper. But don't flush it: Place it in the basket provided next to the toilet.

Don't be surprised if, when you shake your head side to side to mean "no," it's interpreted as meaning "I don't understand." If you want to say "no," shake your head upward, while making a "tut" sound.

Don't go beyond the iconostasis when visiting an Orthodox church.
Don't drink or smoke in public during Ramadan, the Islamic holy month.
Do expect to see pictures of President Assad and his late son Basil on every storefront, office, street lamp and car in the country.

Do expect to see old Buicks and Dodges from the 1940s and '50s still working as shared taxis on the routes to Beirut and Amman.

Don't be surprised if it seems like every time you turn around you're tipping someone. Pay is low, and tipping is expected nearly everywhere.

MONEY & COSTS

Currency: Syrian pound (£S)
Relative costs:

Budget meal: US$1-4
Moderate restaurant meal: US$5-10
Top-end restaurant meal: $10-15

Budget room: US$4-10
Moderate hotel: US$10-20
Top-end hotel: US$200 and upwards

Syria is still a pretty cheap place to visit, but it's definitely getting more expensive. It is possible (but you'd have to be pretty desperate) to get by on US$15-20 a day, if you're prepared to sleep in fleabags and live on felafel and juice. If you'd prefer to stay in a room with its own bathroom and eat in restaurants once a day, you'll need to budget about US$30-40 a day.

Cash is king in Syria, but travelers' checks, of course, are safer. There's no commission for changing cash, but you'll pay per transaction for checks. You're unlikely to get a cash advance on your credit card, but plastic is   increasingly accepted by bigger hotels and stores, and for buying air tickets or renting cars.

Tipping is the oil that keeps the Middle East running smoothly. Waiters in better restaurants expect a tip, and if you don't give one they'll probably short change you anyway. People who open doors for you and people who carry your luggage will also expect a tip, but it's up to you to decide if it's worth it. Bargaining is integral when buying souvenirs - you won't have to try very hard to get the asking price halved.

HOW TO GET THERE

Syria has two international airports, one 35km (22mi) south-east of Damascus, the other just north-east of Aleppo. Both have regular connections to Europe, the Middle East, Africa and Asia. Flights tend to be quite expensive. There's a departure tax of about US$5.

Buses run between Aleppo or Damascus and Istanbul (Turkey), between Damascus and Amman (Jordan), Damascus and Beirut or Tripoli (Lebanon) and Damascus and Riyadh (Saudi Arabia).

For additional analytical, business and investment opportunities information,
please contact Global Investment & Business Center, USA
at (703) 370-8082. Fax: (703) 370-8083. E-mail: ibpusa3@gmail.com
Global Business and Investment Info Databank - www.ibpus.com

Trains go from Aleppo to Istanbul and from Damascus to Amman. Service taxis also run from Damascus to most of the neighboring countries. You can bring your own vehicle into Syria, but you will need a carnet de passage and local third-party insurance. If you prefer the ferry, there's a weekly service from Lattakia for Alexandria (Egypt) via Beirut. In summer, the ferry also stops in Cyprus.

GETTING AROUND

There are internal flights between Damascus and Aleppo, Qamishle, Lattakia and Deir ez-Zur. Syria's road network is excellent, and buses are frequent and cheap - most Syrians use the bus, as very few have their own car. Distances are short and most trips take under four hours. Bus types include the traditional coach, minibuses and Japanese vans known as microbuses. Service taxis operate on the major bus routes but are considerably more expensive than microbuses.

Syria's trains are a modern lot, made in Russia. They're cheap and punctual, but the stations are usually a fair way out of town. The main line connects Damascus, Aleppo, Deir ez-Zur, Hassake and Qamishle, with a secondary line along the coast. There are a few car rental companies in Syria, but rates are around 50% higher than in the West and petrol is expensive and hard to find. Syrians drive on the right.

For additional analytical, business and investment opportunities information, please contact Global Investment & Business Center, USA at (703) 370-8082. Fax: (703) 370-8083. E-mail: ibpusa3@gmail.com Global Business and Investment Info Databank - www.ibpus.com

SUPPLEMENTS

SELECTED CONTACTS

FOREIGN EMBASSIES

EUROPEAN UNION

DELEGATION OF THE EUROPEAN COMMISSION

P. O. Box 11269, Abou Roumaneh, Rue Chekib Arslan, Immeuble du Patriarcat Grèc Catholique, Damascus
Tel. 3327640; Tel. 3327641; Fax 3320683

REPUBLIC OF AUSTRIA

P. O. Box 5634, Rue Chafic Al-Mouàyd, Immeuble Sabri, Malki Damascus
Tel. 3327691; Tel. 337528; Fax 3329232

COMMERCIAL SECTION

Tel. 2124616; Tel. 2124771

KINGDOM OF BELGIUM

P.O. Box 31, Rue Ata Ayoubi, Immeuble Hachem, Damascus
Tel. 3332821; Tel. 3338098; Fax 3330426

KINGDOM OF DENMARK

P.O. Box 2244, Rue Chekib Arslan, Abou Roumaneh Immeuble du Patriarcat Grèc Catholique, Damascus
Tel. 3331008; Tel. 3337853; Fax 3337928

REPUBLIC OF FINLAND

P.O. Box 3893, Malki West, Hawakir, Immeuble Yacoubian, Damascus
Tel. 3338809; Tel. 3338670

REPUBLIC OF FRANCE

P.O. Box 769, Rue Ata Ayoubi, Damascus
Tel. 3327992/3/4/5

COMMERCIAL SECTION

1st, Cham Palace Hotel, Rue Maysaloun, Damascus
Tel. 2213414; Tel. 2213987

FEDERAL REPUBLIC OF GERMANY

P.O. Box 2237, 53 Rue Ibrahim Hanano, Immeuble Kotob, Damascus
Tel. 3323800/1/2; Fax 3323812

For additional analytical, business and investment opportunities information, please contact Global Investment & Business Center, USA at (703) 370-8082. Fax: (703) 370-8083. E-mail: ibpusa3@gmail.com
Global Business and Investment Info Databank - www.ibpus.com

REPUBLIC OF GREECE

P.O. Box 30319, Mezzeh, east Villas, Opp. Al-Farabi Gardens, Damascus
Tel. 2233009; Tel. 2233035

COMMERCIAL SECTION

P.O. Box 3792, Rue Ata Ayoubi, Damascus
Tel. 3338258

RUSSIAN FEDERATION

Rue Omar Ben Al Khattab, Damascus
Tel. 4423155; Tel. 4423156

COMMERCIAL SECTION

Tel. 3712238; Tel. 3718884; Fax 3710243

SWITZERLAND

P.O. Box 234, Rue Mehdi Ben Baraka, Damascus
Tel. 3715474; Tel. 3321137

REPUBLIC OF ITALY

P.O. Box 2216, 82 Avenue Al-Mansour, Damascus
Tel. 3332621; Tel. 3338338; Tel. 3332537; Fax 3320325

KINGDOM OF NETHERLANDS

P.O. Box 702, Rue Abou Roumaneh, Damascus
Tel. 3336871; Tel.. 3337661; Tel. 3338069;
Fax. 3339369

KINGDOM OF SPAIN

Rawda Al-Jallah, Immeuble Al-Kabbani, Damascus
Tel. 3332126; Tel. 3335178

COMMERCIAL SECTION

61 Hidjaz Al-Jadid, Rawda, Damascus
Tel. 3330015; Tel. 3333619S

KINGDOM OF SWEDEN

P.O. Box 4266, Rue Chekib Arslan, Abou Roumaneh,
Immeuble du Patriarcat Catholique, Damascus
Tel. 3327261/1/2/3

UNITED KINGDOM OF GREAT BRITAIN AND NORTHERN IRELAND

P.O. Box 37, Malki, Rue Kurd Ali, Immeuble Kotob, Damascus
Tel. 3712561/2/3; Fax 3713592

For additional analytical, business and investment opportunities information,
please contact Global Investment & Business Center, USA
at (703) 370-8082. Fax: (703) 370-8083. E-mail: ibpusa3@gmail.com
Global Business and Investment Info Databank - www.ibpus.com

IRELAND, PORTUGAL AND LUXEMBOURG

Not currently represented through their own embassies in Syria. Queries should be addressed to embassies in neighbouring countries or the appropriate ministry of foreign affairs.

COMMONWEALTH OF AUSTRALIA

P.O. Box 3882, Mezzeh, East Villas, 128/A Rue Al Farabi Damascus
Tel. 6664317; Tel. 6660238; Fax. 6621195

CANADA

P.O. Box 3394, Mezzeh Autostrad, near Razi Hospital, Damascus
Tel. 2236892; Tel. 3330535; Tel. 3332409

PEOPLE'S REPUBLIC OF CHINA

83 Rue Ata Ayoubi, Damascus
Tel. 3339594; Tel. 2247968

JAPAN

P.O. Box 3366, Rue Mehdi Ben Baraka, Damascus
Tel. 3338273; Tel. 3332553; Tel. 3339781; Fax. 3335314

HASHEMITE KINGDOM OF JORDAN

Abou Roumaneh, Rue Al Aljalaà, Damascus
Tel. 3334642; Tel. 3339313

RUSSIAN FEDERATION

Rue Omar Ben Al Khattab, Damascus
Tel. 4423155; Tel. 4423156

COMMERCIAL SECTION

Tel. 3712238; Tel. 3718884; Fax 3710243

SWITZERLAND

P.O. Box 234, Rue Mehdi Ben Baraka, Damascus
Tel. 3715474; Tel. 3321137

TURKEY

58 Avenue Ziad Bin Abou Soufian, Damascus
Tel. 3331411; Tel. 3334253; Tel. 3331370

COMMERCIAL SECTION

Tel. 3333142

UNITED STATES OF AMERICA

P.O. Box 29, Rue Al Mansour, Damascus
Tel. 3332315; Tel. 3332814; Fax. 2247938

Tel. 3714108

MINISTRIES

SYRIAN CABINET

Cabinet of Ministers
(Includes Ministries of state and of State for Cabinet and Services Affairs)
Shahbandar Street

Tel 2226001, 2221000, 2110212
Tlx. 411020

Ministry of the Interior
Al Bahsah Street

Tel. 2238682
2238683
Fax 2246921
Tlx. 412752

Ministry of Housing and Utilities
Al-Salheyeh, Yousef
Azmeh Square

Tel 3722552
2217571
2217572
3722552
Fax 2217570

Ministry of Information
Mezzeh Autostrad,
Dar al Ba'th Building

Tel 6664600
6664601
Fax 6620052
Tlx. 412620

Ministry of Economy and Foreign Trade
Maysaloun Street

Tel 2213514
2213515
Fax. 2225695
Tlx. 411982

Ministry of Construction
and Building
Sa'dallah al-Jaberi
Street in Front of
the Mail Center

Tel. 2223595
2227966

2223196
2223597

Ministry of Al Awkaf
Rukeneddin

Tel. 4419079
4419080
Fax. 419969

Ministry of Education
Al Mazraa,
Al Shahbandar
Square

Tel. 4444703/4/2
4444800
Fax. 4420435
Tlx. 421959

Ministry of Higher Education
Al Rawda, Kasem
Amin Avenue

Tel. 3330700/1/2/3
Fax. 3337719

Ministry of Supply and Internal Trade
Al Salheyeh

Tel. 2219044
2219241
Fax. 2219803
Tlx. 411908

Ministry of Culture
Al Rawda, George
Haddad Street

Tel 3331556
3338633
338600
Fax 3320804
Tlx. 411944

For additional analytical, business and investment opportunities information,
please contact Global Investment & Business Center, USA
at (703) 370-8082. Fax: (703) 370-8083. E-mail: ibpusa3@gmail.com
Global Business and Investment Info Databank - www.ibpus.com

Ministry of Foreign Affairs
Muhajereen,
Shora Avenue

Tel. 3331200/4
      3337200
Fax. 3320686
Tlx. 411975
      419123

Ministry of the Interior
Al Shuhadaa Square

Tel. 2211001
      2219401
Fax.2223428

Ministry of Defense

Omayad Square

Tel. 7770700
      880980
      3710980
      3720936

Ministry of Environment
Al Salheyeh

Tel. 2222600/1/2/3/4
Fax. 3335645
Tlx. 412686

Ministry of Irrigation
Fardoss Street

Tel. 2212741
      2221400
Fax. 3320691
Tlx. 411059

Ministry of Agriculture and Agrarian Reform
Sa'dallah Al Jaberi
Street

Tel. 2213613
      2222513
Fax. 2244078
      2244023
Tlx. 411643

Ministry of Tourism
Kwatli Street,
Barada bank

Tel. 2210122
      2237940
Fax. 2242636
Tlx. 411672

Ministry of Social Affairs and Labor

Al Salheyeh, Yousef
Azmeh Square

Tel. 2210355
      2225948
Fax.2247499

Ministry of Health
Parliement Street

Tel. 3339600/1/2
Fax. 2223085
Tlx. 412655

Ministry of Industry
Maysaloun Street

Tel. 2231834
Fax. 2231096
Tlx. 411115

Ministry of Justice
al-Nasre Street

Tel. 2214105
      2220302
Fax. 2246250

Ministry of Electricity
Kwatli Street

Tel. 2223086
      2229654
Fax.2223686
Tlx. 411938

Ministry of Finance
Al Sabee Bahrat Square, Baghdad Street.

Tel. 2219600/1/2/3
Fax. 2224701
Tlx. 411932

Ministry of Communications
Al Salheyeh

Tel. 2227033/34
Fax. 2246403
Tlx. 411933

Ministry of Oil and Mineral Resources
Adawi, Insha'at

Tel. 4445610
      4451624
Fax 4457786
Tlx. 411006

Ministry of Transport
Al Jalaa Street

For additional analytical, business and investment opportunities information,
please contact Global Investment & Business Center, USA
at (703) 370-8082. Fax: (703) 370-8083. E-mail: ibpusa3@gmail.com
Global Business and Investment Info Databank - www.ibpus.com

Tel. 3336801/2/3
Fax. 3323317
Tlx. 411994

SELECTED GOVERNMENT AND BUSINESS CONTACTS

Syrian Petroleum Company (SPC)
Contact Name: Dr. Muhammad Khaddour
Contact Title: Director General
Address: Fardos, Mutanabi St., P.O. Box
2849, Damascus, Syria
Telephone: 2227095, 2227007, 2226984,
2226245
Fax: 2225648
Telex: 411031 sypco SY

Al-Furat Petroleum Company (AFPC)
John Darley
General Manager
Mazzeh, Writers' Union Building, P.O. Box
7660, Damascus,
Telephone: 6183333
Fax: 2238104, 2244010
Tlx: 412088 SY or 412089 SY

Syrian Petroleum Transport Company
Mohammad Douba
Director General
P.O. Box 13, Banias, Syria/ P.O. Box 51,
Homs, Syria/ P.O. Box 310, Damascus,
Syria
Telephone: (43) 711300
Fax: (43) 710418
Tlx: 441012 scot SY

**Public Establishment for Power
Generation and Distribution**
Zeki Odeh
Director General
P.O. Box 3386, Damascus, Syria
Telephone: 2227981, 2229654, 2223086,
2228334, 2246472
Fax: 2229062
Tlx: 411056 syrlec SY

**General Organization for Engineering
Industries**
Issa Dawood
Director General
P.O. Box 3120, Damascus, Syria
Telephone: 2123438, 2121889, 2121824,
2121825

Fax: 2123375
Tlx: 411035 SY

**Syrian Telecommunications Corporation
(STE)**
Makram Obeid
Director General
Mezzeh, Damascus, Syria
Telephone: 2240300, 6122210
Fax: 2242000
Tlx: 411015 gentel SY

**General Organization for Cement and
Building Material**
Ahmad Al-Hamo
General Director
Mazzeh, Western Villas, P.O. Box 5265,
Damascus, Syria
Telephone: 6117666, 6117444, 611333,
6118444, 6117503
Fax: 6117111
Tlx: 411369 SY

**General Organization for Textile
Industries**
Hussein Al-Zu'bi
Director General
P.O. Box 620, Damascus, Syria
Telephone: 2216200, 2227158
Fax: 2216201
Tlx: 412036 nasige SY

**General Organization for Chemical
Industries**
Zaid Al-Hariri
Director General
Baramkeh, P.O. Box 5447, Damascus, Syria
Telephone: 2127654, 2123363, 2122743,
2122917, 2122362
Fax: 2128289
Tlx: 419145 SY

General Organization for Food Industries
Ali Kamel Salman
Director General
P.O. Box 105, Damascus, Syria
Telephone: 2225290, 2225291

For additional analytical, business and investment opportunities information,
please contact Global Investment & Business Center, USA
at (703) 370-8082. Fax: (703) 370-8083. E-mail: ibpusa3@gmail.com
Global Business and Investment Info Databank - www.ibpus.com

Fax: 2245374
Tlx: 419154 SY

Ministry of Health
Dr. Iyad Chatti
Minister of Health
Najmeh Square, Parliament Street,
Damascus, Syria
Telephone: 3339602, 3333801,
3311020/1/2/3
Fax: 3311114

**Foreign Trade Organization for
Machinery and Equipment** (SAYARAT)
Muhammad Salim Dalloul
General Director
P.O. Box 3130, Damascus, Syria
Telephone: 2218223, 2218156, 2232190,
2232199
Fax: 2211118
Tlx: 411036 SY

**Country Trade Associations/ Chambers
of Commerce**

**The Federation of Syrian Chambers of
Commerce and Industry:**
President: Dr. Rateb Shallah
P.O. Box 5909
Damascus, Syria
Telephone: 3337344, 3311504
Fax: 963-11-3331127

Damascus Chamber of Commerce
President: Dr. Rateb Shallah
P.O. Box 1040
Damascus, Syria
Telephone: 223-2348, 223-2360, 2211339,
2218339
Fax: 963-11-222-5874

Damascus Chamber of Industry
President: Dr. Yahya Hindi
P.O. Box 1305
Damascus, Syria
Telephone: 222-2205, 221-3475, 221-5042,
221-3475
Fax: 963-11-224-5981

Aleppo Chamber of Commerce
President: Mr. Mohammad Saleh Al-Mallah
P.O. Box 1261
Aleppo, Syria

Telephone: 963-21-238-236, 238-237
Fax: 963-21-213-493

Aleppo Chamber of Industry
President: Mr. Muhammad Oubari
P.O. Box 1859,
Aleppo, Syria
Telephone: 963-21-620-600/1/2, 639-700
Fax: 963-21-620-040

Homs Chamber of Commerce and Industry
President: Mr. M. Walid Tuleimat
P.O. Box 440
Homs, Syria
Telephone: 963-31-228-605, 231-000
Fax: 963-31-224-247

**Hama Chamber of Commerce and
Industry**
President: Mr. Abd Al-Salam Al-Sabe'
P.O. Box 147
Hama, Syria
Telephone: 963-33-233-304, 517-700
Fax: 963-33-517701

**Latakia Chamber of Commerce and
Industry**
President: Mr. Kamal Ismail Al-Assad
P.O. Box 124
Latakia, Syria
Telephone: 963-41-239-530
Fax: 963-41-238-526

Country Market Research Firms

The Syrian Consulting Bureau
Dr. Nabil Succar
P.O. Box 12574, Damascus, Syria
Tel: 2225946
Fax: 2231603

Commerce and Engineering Consultants
Mr. Ramez Raslan
Malki, P.O. Box 6136, Damascus, Syria
Tel: 3733956, 3730771
Fax: 3733955

**Consulting, Management, and
Contracting Company**
Mr. Hani Sawaf
P.O. Box 3858, Damascus, Syria
Tel: 3331226
Fax: 3333031

For additional analytical, business and investment opportunities information,
please contact Global Investment & Business Center, USA
at (703) 370-8082. Fax: (703) 370-8083. E-mail: ibpusa3@gmail.com
Global Business and Investment Info Databank - www.ibpus.com

Financial, Economic, & Consulting Services
Dr. M. Ayman Midani

P.O. Box 7825, Damascus, Syria
Tel: 3316075
Tlx: 411044 Midani SY

FOREIGN EMBASSIES IN SYRIA

Name of Embassy	Address	Telephone
Argentina	Al-Rawda	3334167
Armenia	Abu-Roumaneh	3711357
Spain	Abu-Roumaneh	3332126
Australia	Mezzeh - Farabi Str.	6664317
Germany	Malki - Hanano Str.	3323800
U.S.A	Abu-Roumaneh	3332315
Iran	Mezzeh - Autostrad	2227675
Italy	Malki - al-Mansour Str.	3332537
Pakistan	Mezzeh - Farabi Str.	6662391
Brazil	Al-Rawda	3337770
U.K.	Malki - Kurd ali Str.	3712561
Belgium	Abu-Roumaneh	3332821
Czech	Mezzeh - Farabi Str.	3331383
Greece	Mezzeh - Farabi Str.	2123009
Turkey	Al-Rawda	3331383
Russia	Omar ben Al-khattab Str.	4423156
Romania	Abu-Roumaneh	3327570
Sweden	Abu-Roumaneh	3327261
Switzerland	Omar ben Al-khattab Str.	3311871
China	Malki - al-Mansour Str.	3339594
France	Affif Atta-Ayoubi Str.	3327993
Cyprus	Abu-Roumaneh	3332919
Canada	Mezzeh - Autostrad	6116870
Cuba	Mezzeh Al-Rashid Str.	3339624
Austria	Mezzeh - Farabi Str.	6624732
India	Malki Square	3719580

Netherlands	Abu-Roumaneh	3337661
Japan	Abu-Roumaneh	3332533
United Arab Emirates	Al-Mehdi ben Barakeh Str.	3330308
Jordan	Abu-Roumaneh	3334642
Tunisia	Mezzeh East Villas	6617509
Algeria	Al-Rawda	3334548
Saudi Arabia	Abu-Roumaneh	3334914
Sudan	White Bridge	2247046
Qattar	Abu-Roumaneh	3327451
Kuwait	Malki - Hanano Str.	3714760
Libya	Abu-Roumaneh	3333914
Egypt	Abu-Roumaneh	3332932
Morocco	Mezzeh - Farabi Str.	6620839
Yemen	Mezzeh East Villas	6622706
Mauritania	Malki Karameh Str.	3339317

SELECTED U.S. AND COUNTRY CONTACTS FOR SYRIA

SYRIAN CONTACTS

Organization: Syrian Petroleum Company (SPC)
Contact Name: Dr. Muhammad Khaddour
Contact Title: Director General
Address: Fardos, Mutanabi St., P.O. Box 2849, Damascus, Syria
Telephone: 2227095, 2227007, 2226984, 2226245
Fax: 2225648
Telex: 411031 sypco SY

Al-Furat Petroleum Company (AFPC)
John Darley
General Manager
Mazzeh, Writers' Union Building, P.O. Box 7660, Damascus,
Telephone: 6183333
Fax: 2238104, 2244010
Tlx: 412088 SY or 412089 SY

Syrian Petroleum Transport Company
Mohammad Douba
Director General
P.O. Box 13, Banias, Syria/ P.O. Box 51, Homs, Syria/ P.O. Box310, Damascus, Syria
Telephone: (43) 711300

Fax: (43) 710418
Tlx: 441012 scot SY

Public Establishment for Power Generation and Distribution
Zeki Odeh
Director General
P.O. Box 3386, Damascus, Syria
Telephone: 2227981, 2229654, 2223086, 2228334, 2246472
Fax: 2229062
Tlx: 411056 syrlec SY

General Organization for Engineering Industries
Issa Dawood
Director General
P.O. Box 3120, Damascus, Syria
Telephone: 2123438, 2121889, 2121824, 2121825
Fax: 2123375
Tlx: 411035 SY

Syrian Telecommunications Establishment (STE)
Makram Obeid
Director General
Mezzeh, Damascus, Syria
Telephone: 2240300, 6122210
Fax: 2242000
Tlx: 411015 gentel SY

General Organization for Cement and Building Material
Ahmad Al-Hamo
General Director
Mazzeh, Western Villas, P.O. Box 5265, Damascus, Syria
Telephone: 6117666, 6117444, 611333, 6118444, 6117503
Fax: 6117111
Tlx: 411369 SY

General Organization for Textile Industries
Hussein Al-Zu'bi
Director General
P.O. Box 620, Damascus, Syria
Telephone: 2216200, 2227158
Fax: 2216201
Tlx: 412036 nasige SY

General Organization for Chemical Industries
Zaid Al-Hariri
Director General
Baramkeh, P.O. Box 5447, Damascus, Syria
Telephone: 2127654, 2123363, 2122743, 2122917, 2122362
Fax: 2128289
Tlx: 419145 SY

General Organization for Food Industries
Ali Kamel Salman
Director General
P.O. Box 105, Damascus, Syria
Telephone: 2225290, 2225291

For additional analytical, business and investment opportunities information,
please contact Global Investment & Business Center, USA
at (202) 546-2103. Fax: (202) 546-3275. E-mail: rusric@erols.com

Fax: 2245374
Tlx: 419154 SY

Ministry of Health
Dr. Iyad Chatti
Minister of Health
Najmeh Square, Parliament Street, Damascus, Syria
Telephone: 3339602, 3333801, 3311020/1/2/3
Fax: 3311114

Foreign Trade Organization for Machinery and Equipment (SAYARAT)
Muhammad Salim Dalloul
General Director
P.O. Box 3130, Damascus, Syria
Telephone: 2218223, 2218156, 2232190, 2232199
Fax: 2211118
Tlx: 411036 SY

COUNTRY TRADE ASSOCIATIONS/ CHAMBERS OF COMMERCE

The Federation of Syrian Chambers of Commerce and Industry:
President: Dr. Rateb Shallah
P.O. Box 5909
Damascus, Syria
Telephone: 3337344, 3311504
Fax: 963-11-3331127

Damascus Chamber of Commerce
President: Dr. Rateb Shallah
P.O. Box 1040
Damascus, Syria
Telephone: 223-2348, 223-2360, 2211339, 2218339
Fax: 963-11-222-5874

Damascus Chamber of Industry
President: Dr. Yahya Hindi
P.O. Box 1305
Damascus, Syria
Telephone: 222-2205, 221-3475, 221-5042, 221-3475
Fax: 963-11-224-5981

Aleppo Chamber of Commerce
President: Mr. Mohammad Saleh Al-Mallah
P.O. Box 1261
Aleppo, Syria
Telephone: 963-21-238-236, 238-237
Fax: 963-21-213-493

Aleppo Chamber of Industry
President: Mr. Muhammad Oubari
P.O. Box 1859,
Aleppo, Syria
Telephone: 963-21-620-600/1/2, 639-700
Fax: 963-21-620-040

For additional analytical, business and investment opportunities information,
please contact Global Investment & Business Center, USA
at (202) 546-2103. Fax: (202) 546-3275. E-mail: rusric@erols.com

Homs Chamber of Commerce and Industry
President: Mr. M. Walid Tuleimat
P.O. Box 440
Homs, Syria
Telephone: 963-31-228-605, 231-000
Fax: 963-31-224-247

Hama Chamber of Commerce and Industry
President: Mr. Abd Al-Salam Al-Sabe'
P.O. Box 147
Hama, Syria
Telephone: 963-33-233-304, 517-700
Fax: 963-33-517701

Latakia Chamber of Commerce and Industry
President: Mr. Kamal Ismail Al-Assad
P.O. Box 124
Latakia, Syria
Telephone: 963-41-239-530
Fax: 963-41-238-526

COUNTRY MARKET RESEARCH FIRMS

The Syrian Consulting Bureau
Dr. Nabil Succar
P.O. Box 12574, Damascus, Syria
Tel: 2225946
Fax: 2231603

Commerce and Engineering Consultants
Mr. Ramez Raslan
Malki, P.O. Box 6136, Damascus, Syria
Tel: 3733956, 3730771
Fax: 3733955

Consulting, Management, and Contracting Company
Mr. Hani Sawaf
P.O. Box 3858, Damascus, Syria
Tel: 3331226
Fax: 3333031

Financial, Economic, & Consulting Services
Dr. M. Ayman Midani
P.O. Box 7825, Damascus, Syria
Tel: 3316075
Tlx: 411044 Midani SY

COMMERCIAL BANKS

Commercial Bank of Syria: Director General: Mr. Riad Hakim, YousefAl-Azmah Square, P.O. Box 933, Damascus, Syria; Telephone: 221-4508;Fax: 221-6975, 222-8524

U.S. Embassy Trade Personnel: Telephone: (963)(11) 333-3232

Anne Bodine: Economic/Commercial Attache
Donna Vandenbroucke: Economic/Commercial Officer
Jamal Aliah: Economic/Commercial Officer
Jonathan Rice: Economic/Commercial Officer

WASHINGTON-BASED USG CONTACTS

Office of Syrian Affairs
E. Candace Putnam
U.S. Department of State
Washington, D.C. 20520
Telephone: (202)647-7216
Fax: (202)647-0989

Office of Syrian Affairs
Thomas A. Sams
U.S. Department of Commerce
Washington, D.C.
Telephone: (202)482-1860
Fax: (202)482-0878

ATTORNEYS IN SYRIA

Damascus

Mazhar Anbari: Sanjakdar Street, tel: 2217017. Citizenof the SAR. Born in Damascus 1923. Graduate of Damascus Law School1948; practicing since 1948. Specializes in criminal and civilcases, insurance, and international arbitration. Former Ministerof Justice. Former Vice-Speaker of the Parliament. Former Presidentof the Syrian Bar Association. Languages: Arabic, English, and French.

Farid Arslanian: Balkis Street, telephone: 2218321 and3331676. Citizen of the SAR. Born in Turkey in 1915. Graduateof Damascus Law School. Specializes in criminal, civil, and insurancecases. Secretary General of the Committee of Damascus Bar Association.Controller, 1960-1971. Elected Deputy in the Syrian Parliament.Legal consultant since 1964 for the United Nations Relief andWorks Agency in the SAR. Languages: Arabic, French, English, Armenian,and Turkish.

Ghazi Al-Ghazzi: 69 Salhieh street, Tibi & Sulo Building,P.O. Box 4238, tel: 2224036 (office), fax: 2229798, 3327648 (home).Citizen of the SAR. Born in 1937. Graduate of Damascus Law School.Represents a number of foreign firms in Syria. Languages: Arabic,English, and French.

Jacques Hakim: Victoria Bridge, Mardam Building, P.O. Box5788. Telex 412033 Sy (drobco); tel: 2223577 (office), 3710554(home). Citizen of the SAR. Born in Damascus in 1931. Doctor ofLaw (France), graduate in economics (Economics Institute, Univ.of Colorado). Professor, Head of the Commercial Law Department, Damascus University. Practicing since 1952. Specializes in commercial,and finance cases along with international arbitration. Languages:Arabic, English, and French.

Hazem Jazzar: Salhieh Street, Cinema Amir's Building, Tel:4421069 (home), 2225286 (office). Citizen of the SAR. Born inDamascus in 1948. Graduate of Damascus Law School 1971. Has practicedlaw since 1971. Specializes in commercial and criminal cases.Languages: Arabic and English.

For additional analytical, business and investment opportunities information,
please contact Global Investment & Business Center, USA
at (202) 546-2103. Fax: (202) 546-3275. E-mail: rusric@erols.com

Zouheir Al-Midany: Abou-Roumaneh Street, tel: 2213100 (office),3332075, 3330650 (home). Citizen of the SAR. Born in Damascusin 1923. Graduate of Damascus Law School 1947. Has practiced lawsince 1947. Specializes in civil, commercial, and criminal cases.Former head of the Syrian Bar Association and former Vice-Presidentof the International Bar Union. Languages: Arabic and French.

Mamdouh Rahaby: Salhieh, Dentists' Syndicate Building,3rd floor, tel: 2221428 (office), 3332905 (home). Citizen of theSAR. Born in Damascus in 1932. Graduate of Damascus Law School1966. Specializes in civil, real estate, and commercial cases. Languages: Arabic and English.

Souheil Sarkis: 7 Fountain Square, Adel Sharaf Building,2nd floor, tel: 4428240, 4420049, telex 412464. Citizen of theSAR. Born in Damascus in 1934. Graduate of Damascus Law School1960. Has practiced law since 1961. Specializes in civil and commercialcases. Languages: Arabic, English, and French.

Sami Wardeh: Marjeh Square, Kabbani building, P.O. Box10355, tel: 2211767 (office), 3714892 (home). Citizen of the SAR.Born in Damascus in 1942. Graduate of Damascus Law School 1965.Has practiced law since 1965. Specializes in commercial and realestate cases. Languages: Arabic, French and English.

Aleppo

Miss Ghada Bismarji: Kostaki Homsi Street, Azizieh, telephone219428. Citizen of the SAR, graduate of Damascus Law School 1962. Has practiced law since 1962. Sworn translator English-Arabic,and vice-versa. Handles all types of cases. Languages: English, Arabic, French, and some Armenian.

Ihsan Kayali: Baron Street, tel: office 215811, home 219403.Citizen of the SAR. Born in Aleppo in 1925. Graduate of DamascusLaw School in 1949. Handles all cases with specialization in commercialand insurance cases. Languages: Arabic, English, and French.

Simon Bashkhamji: P.O. Box 67, Azizieh, tel: office 247074,home 217624. Citizen of the SAR. Graduate of the University ofAleppo 1969. General practice. Languages: Arabic, French, andsome English.

Homs

Mouhammad Mounir Amoudi: P.O. Box 362, tel: 223115 (office),222683 (home). Citizen of the SAR. Born in 1928. Graduate of DamascusLaw School 1949. Has practiced law since 1949. Specializes incriminal, civil, banking, and insurance cases. Languages: Arabic,French, and English.

Antoun Trabulsi: tel: 224406 (office), 225286, 224655 (home).Citizen of the SAR. Born in 1919. Graduate of Damascus Law School1940. Has practiced law since 1940. Lawyer of the Municipality of Homs. Head of Homs Bar Association. General practice. Languages: Arabic and French.

Hama

Fathallah Alloush: Al-Alamien Street, tel: 223206 (office).Citizen of the SAR. Born in Hama in 1932. Graduate of DamascusLaw School in 1955, practicing law since 1955. Specializes incivil, banking, and criminal cases. Languages: Arabic and French.

Khaled Al-Keylani: Kowatly Street, tel: 222536, 221299.Citizen of the SAR. Born in Hama in 1929. Graduate of DamascusLaw School in 1954. No specialization, handles all cases. Languages:Arabic, French, and some English.

For additional analytical, business and investment opportunities information, please contact Global Investment & Business Center, USA at (202) 546-2103. Fax: (202) 546-3275. E-mail: rusric@erols.com

Latakia

Hassan Makhlouf: P.O. Box 1025, tel: 338055 (office), 226089(home). Citizen of the SAR. Born in 1930. Graduate of DamascusLaw School 1960. Has practiced law since 1960. No specialization, handles all cases. Languages: Arabic, French, and English.

INTERNATIONAL AGREEMENTS

AGREEMENTS SIGNED WITH FOREIGN STATES ON PROTECTION AND GUARANTEE OF INVESTMENT

State	Type of Agreement	Date of Signing	Instrument of Ratification and Date	Remarks
United States of America	Exchanged Notes on Manner of Guaranteeing American Investments in Syria	09.08.1976	Legislative Decree No.33 dated 01.08.1977	
Swiss Federation	Accord on Encouraging and protecting Investments	22.06.1977	Legislative Decree No.24 dated 12.07.1978	Most Favoured Nation
France	Agreement on Reciprocal Encouragement and Protection of Investments	28.11.1977	Legislative Decree No.30 dated 31.07.1978	Most Favoured Nation
Federal Germany	Agreement on Reciprocal Encouragement and Protection of Investments	02.08.1977	Legislative Decree No.34 dated 11.09.1978	Most Favoured Nation
Pakistan	Accord on Reciprocal Encouragement and Protection of Investments	25.04.1996	Law No. 5 dated 02.07.1997	
People's Republic of China	Accord on Reciprocal Encouragement and Protection of Investments and Appended Protocol	09.12.1996	Law No. 11 dated 04.08.1998	Protocol treats investment formalities and the transfers resulting from investment
Indonesia	Accord on Reciprocal Encouragement and Protecting Investments and Appended protocol	27.06.1997	Law No. 19 dated 31.12.1996	Most Favoured Nation. Protocol regulates transfers resulting from investment
Iran	Accord on Reciprocal Encouragement and Protection of Investments	05.02.1998	Legislative Decree No.3 dated 11.02.1998	Most Favoured Nation
Belorussia	Accord on Reciprocal Encouragement and	11.03.1998	Legislative Decree No.8 dated	

	Protection of Investments		04.08.1998	

Trade Agreements Signed with Foreign States :

State	Type of Agreement	Date of Signing	Instrument of Ratification and Date	Remarks
Russian Federation	Technical, Economic and Commercial Cooperation	15.04.1993	Law No. 11 dated 22.06.1993	
Bulgaria	Trade	02.05.1974	Legislative Decree No.54 dated 24.07.1974	New trade agreement was initialed by the two states on 13.03.1996
Hungary	Syrian side notified Hungarian side of its decision to nullify the trade agreement of 1974			New trade agreement has been initialed by the two sides
Albania	Trade	17.06.1979	Decree No.1252 dated 08.02.1980	
Cuba	Trade	27.03.1974	Decree No.167 dated 24.07.1974	It provides for exemption from Consular legalization. New trade agreement was initialed on .03.1998
Poland	Trade	20.08.1974	Decree No.303 dated 04.12.1974	
Czech	Syrian side nullified the trade agreement of 1975 signed with Czechoslovakia when the latter broke up as of 01.01.1993			The two sides have not agreed to signing new trade agreement
Slovak	Long term trade agreement	29.08.1995	Law No. 7 dated 03.07.1996	
Romania	Trade	13.04.1993		
Korea	Trade	28.06.1982	Law No.5 dated 08.02.1983	It provides for exemption from Consular Legalization
Vietnam	Trade	12.05.1994	Legislative Decree No.12 dated 27.06.1994	
People's Republic of China	Trade	16.03.1982	Law No. 23 of 1982	
Byelorussia	Technical, Economic and Commercial	11.03.1998	Legislative Decree No.9 dated 04.08.1998	
Armenia	Trade	30.03.1992	Legislative Decree	

			No.7 dated 11.07.1992	
Turkmenistan	Trade	26.03.1992	Legislative Decree No.8 dated 11.07.1992	
Kazakhstan	Trade	27.03.1992	Legislative Decree No.9 dated 11.07.1992	
Azerbaijan	Trade	28.03.1992	Legislative Decree No.10 dated 11.07.1992	
Tajikistan	Trade	19.03.1992	Legislative Decree No.11 dated 11.07.1992	
Republic of Tanzania	Trade	15.02.1974	Decree No.166 dated 15.03.1974	
Republic of Niger	Trade	26.06.1980	Decree No.2661 dated 22.12.1980	
Republic of Nigeria	Trade	17.09.1969	Decree No.242 dated 23.12.1969	
Republic of Guinea	Trade	22.01.1979	Decree No.1209 dated 23.01.1979	
Republic of Senegal	Economic, Commercial, Cultural, and Technological	04.11.1975	Decree No.589 dated 03.03.1976	
Cyprus	Long term trade agreement	23.02.1982		
Pakistan	Trade Annex to trade agreement	11.08.1969 25.04.1996	Legislative Decree No.342 dated 23.11.1969	
Sri Lanka	Trade and Payments	09.10.1966	Legislative Decree No.29 dated 09.04.1966	
Turkey	Trade	17.09.1974	Decree No.31 dated 02.12.1974	
India	Trade	09.10.1969	Decree No.345 dated 23.12.1969	
Indonesia	Trade	18.03.1976	Decree No.1220 dated 09.07.1977	
Argentina	Trade	06.09.1989		
Grenada	Trade	22.01.1980	Decree No.1144 dated 27.05.1980	
Chile	Trade	27.02.1990	Legislative Decree No.12 dated 24.05.1990	
Iran	Trade	21.08.1996	Decree No.241 dated 10.11.1997	

European Union	Cooperation	18.01.1977	Legislative Decree No.14 dated 05.07.1977	

[

LIST OF BILATERAL AGREEMENTS SIGNED WITH ARAB STATES AND THE ADVANTAGES GRANTED THEREBY

State	Name & date of Agreement	Exemptions for Syrian Commodities	Exemptions for Arab Commodities
Saudi Arabia	Economic and Trade Agreement of 1972 Still valid	- Agricultural products and livestock and the produce of natural resources are exempted from customs duties according to list No.1 appended to the agreement - Syrian industrial products are exempted from customs duties according to list No.2 appended to the agreement - Syrian industrial products as per list No.3 appended to the agreement are exempted from two thirds of customs duties.	- Agricultural and animal products and livestock and the produce of natural resources are exempted from duties as per list No.1 appended to the agreement - All Saudi industrial products are exempted from duties
Kuwait	Economic and Commercial Cooperation Agreement of 1991 Still valid	- Agricultural and livestock products and the produce of natural resources are exempted from customs duties and other fees of similar effect - Syrian industrial products are exempted from duties and fees of similar effect except for the following: 1- Cast iron covering 2- Welded black steel pipes 3- oxygen gas for medical or industrial purposes	- Agricultural and livestock products and the produce of Kuwaiti natural resources are exempted from duties and fees of similar effect. - Kuwaiti industrial products are exempted from duties and fees of similar effect except for : 1- Cars. 2- Raw tobacco and byproducts. 3- cotton yarns locally produced.
Qatar	Economic and Commercial Cooperation Agreement of 1990 Still valid.	Agricultural, livestock and industrial products and raw materials that will be agreed upon in lists by the joint committee are exempted from	Agricultural, livestock and industrial products and raw materials that will be agreed upon in lists by the joint committee are

		customs duties.	exempted from customs duties.
Bahrain	Economic and Commercial Cooperation Agreement of 1994 Still valid.	-Syrian agricultural and livestock products are exempted from customs duties and fees of similar effect. - Syrian industrial products according to lists prepared by the joint committee as stated in the agreement are exempted from customs duties and fees of similar effect.	-Bahraini agricultural and livestock products are exempted from customs duties and fees of similar effect. - Industrial products according to lists prepared by the joint committee as stated in the agreement are exempted from customs duties and fees of similar effect.
United Arab Emirates	Economic and Commercial Cooperation Agreement of 1990 endorsed by Syria but not endorsed by U.A.E.Consultations are underway with the U.A.E for the purpose.	No advantages of preferences or exemptions for the products of each country. Yet, the agreement provides for offering facilities that support the movement of export and import between the two countries.	No advantages of preferences or exemptions for the products of each country. Yet, the agreement provides for offering facilities that support the movement of export and import between the two countries.
Oman	Economic and Commercial Cooperation Agreement of 1991 Still valid.	Agreement does not give any performances or exemptions from customs duties.	Agreement does not give any performances or exemptions from customs duties.
Jordan	Agreement on Economic Cooperation and Regulating Trade Exchange of 1975. Minutes of meeting of the joint committee of 1986.	The 1975 agreement provides for exemption from customs duties for agricultural, livestock products and the produce of natural resources and exchanged industrial products. The two sides agreed on two lists, one for prompt implementation and the other is a guideline. The "prompt" list benefits From exemption from customs duties in each country according to certain banking arrangements , the guidelines list does not benefit from customs exemptions.	The agreement provides for total exemption from customs duties for Jordanian products.
Yemen	Trade agreement signed in 1996, ratified by Yemen, procedures of ratification in Syria are under way.	Agreement does not provide for any advantage of preference. The joint committee will discuss preferences which each party can offer for the purpose of promoting and developing trade Exchange between the two	Agreement

For additional analytical, business and investment opportunities information,
please contact Global Investment & Business Center, USA
at (202) 546-2103. Fax: (202) 546-3275. E-mail: rusric@erols.com

		countries.	
Iraq	An agreement on economic cooperation and regulation of trade exchange, signed in 1979 (frozen at present)	All Syrian Products are exempted from customs duties. Free zone products are exempted from duties within the limits of local costs used in the manufacture of those products.	All Iraqi products are exempted from customs duties. Free zone products are exempted from duties within the limits of local costs used in the manufacture of those products.
Egypt	Trade agreement signed in 1991 (Valid)	Exemption from customs duties and relevant taxes (except local taxes and fees and taxes on sales) for the Syrian commodities and products as listed in Table A appended to the agreement. (This list contains 19 commodities)	Exemption from customs duties and relevant taxes (except local taxes and fees and taxes on sales) for the Egyptian commodities listed in Table B appended to the agreement. (This list contains 20 commodities)
Morocco	Agreement on regulating trade exchange and economic cooperation signed in1972 (Valid)	Each side treats the other side as a most favoured nation. Excluded from this condition are the relations binding either side to other countries that form with it customs union or economic unity or common market and the advantages granted by either side to facilitate cross-border trade.	Each side treats the other side as a most favoured nation. Excluded from this condition are the relations binding either side to other countries that form with it customs union or economic unity or common market and the advantages granted by either side to facilitate cross-border trade.
Libya	Agreement on regulating trade exchange and economic cooperation signed in1978 (Valid)	All Syrian agricultural, livestock products, produce of natural resources and industrial products are exempted from customs duties and other taxes and fees.	All Libyan agricultural, livestock products, produce of natural resources and industrial products are exempted from customs duties and other taxes and fees.
Sudan	An agreement on trade and economic cooperation signed in 1974 (Valid)	Exemption from customs duties and additional fees for Syrian agricultural and animal products and livestock except for a fee of 5%. - Syrian industrial products as listed in Table 1 are subject to reduced duties as explained in the said table (ranging between 10% and 100%) .	Exemption from customs duties and additional fees for Sudanese agricultural and animal products and livestock except for a fee of 2%. - Sudanese industrial products as listed in Table 2 are subject to reduced duties as explained in the said table (ranging

For additional analytical, business and investment opportunities information, please contact Global Investment & Business Center, USA at (202) 546-2103. Fax: (202) 546-3275. E-mail: rusric@erols.com

		- Most favoured nation.	between30% and 100%) . - Most favoured nation.
Tunisia	Trade agreement signed in 1977 (Valid)	All Syrian products are exempted from customs duties (agricultural, animal products, livestock, produce of natural resources and industrial products).	All Tunisian products are exempted from customs duties (agricultural, animal products, livestock, produce of natural resources and industrial products).
Algeria	Trade agreement signed in 1979, valid until the concluding of a new agreement in 1997 and notes of ratification are exchanged. Ratification is being followed up.	Old Agreement: Syrian agricultural products and livestock are exempted from customs duties. - Syrian industrial products as listed in Table 1 appended to the agreement are exempted from customs duties. New Agreement: No provision for most favoured nation for either country.	Old Agreement: Algerian agricultural products and livestock are exempted from customs duties. - Algerian industrial products as listed Table 2 appended to the agreement are exempted from customs duties. New Agreement: No provision for most favoured nation for either country.

Somalia	Trade agreement signed in 1973 (valid)	Most favoured nation with regard to customs duties and other taxes and fees on imports, exports, storage, transit, unloading and shipment of goods. Excluded are: 1- Advantages and benefits granted to facilitate cross-border trade. 2- Goods of non-Syrian or non-Somali origin. 3- Advantages and benefits resulting from customs union, free trade area, common market or any special agreements.	Same advantages

| Lebanon | Economic agreement signed in 1953, still valid by virtue of the provisions of agreement on social and economic cooperation and coordination of 1992 duly ratified by the two countries and being implemented by both of them | - Syrian agricultural and livestock products as listed in Table 1 appended to the agreement are exempted from customs duties.

- Syrian industrial products as listed in Table 2 appended to the agreement are exempted from customs duties.

-Exempted from half the duties are Syrian industrial products as listed in Table 3 appended to the agreement. | - Lebanese agricultural and livestock products as listed in Table 1 appended to the agreement are exempted from customs duties.

- Lebanese industrial products as listed in Table 2 appended to the agreement are exempted from customs duties.

-Exempted from half the duties are Lebanese industrial products as listed in Table 3 appended to the agreement. |

MAJOR EXPORT-IMPORT PRODUCTS

EXPORT & IMPORT BY CLASSIFICATION OF COMMODITY OF S.I.T.C.(Rev.3)
EXPORT & IMPORT BY CLASSIFCATION OF COMMODITY OF S.I.T.C.(REV.3) (Quantity in tons and value in "000" S.P.)

S.I.T.C. Rev.(3)	Sections	Divisions	Description of Goods	IMPORT Quant.	IMPORT Value	EXPORT Quant.	EXPORT Value
	0		Food & live Animals	1296533	7374798	1382088	6957868
		"00"	Live animals other than animals of div.03	15278	709256	208	1079268
			Sheeplive, live "000 heads"	NO.5969	5396	524	989970
"001.21"		"01"	Meat & meat preparations	2309	38642	87	662
		"02"	Dairy products and birds, eggs	13061	409501	4716	75157
		"03"	Fish	2931	262230	0	0
		"04"	Cereals and cereal preparations	406988	1224086	836730	1676225
"041.0"			Wheat & meslin, unmilled	–	–	278191	652686
"043.0"			Barley unmilled	–	–	556495	998871
		"05"	Vegetables and fruit	65003	583301	454034	3632990
"054.24"			Lentils	–	–	160665	602076
"054.40"			Tomatoes fresh or chilled	"000"	1	83104	512701
"057.93"			Stone fruit n.e.s. fresh	–	–	26843	397265
		"06"	Sugar preparations & hlney	528284	2144764	34327	145266

"061.10			Sugars beet or cane	124898	479175	_	_
		"07"	Coffee, tea, cocoa, spices,and manuf.thereof	48508	1230409	20977	303235
		"08"	Feeding stuff for animals	209033	668350	30837	42500
		"09"	Miscellaneous edible products and preparations	5138	104259	172	2565
	1		beeverages and tobacco	2918	342155	6160	30065
		11	Beverages	869	33626	4178	17429
		12	Tobacco and tobacco manufactures	2049	308529	1982	12636
	2		Crude Materials, linedible except fuels	264073	1899151	1537302	2484344
		21	Hides, Skins and furskins, raw	4289	51068	598	19050
		22	Oil seeds and oleaginous fruits	26500	237286	377	440
		23	Crude rubber	6062	86100	27	701
		24	Crok and wood	148750	888039	1473	860
		25	Pulp and waste paper	13688	73637	1	35
		26	Textile fibers	4946	120872	121605	2026421
"263.10			cotton (other than linters), not carded or combed	60	8058	99708	1914002
		27	Crude fertilizers, other than those of divison 56&crude				
			mineral (excluding coal, petroleum,&precious stones)	37660	92033	1408823	305500
		28	Metalliferous & metal scrap				
				19280	209992	94	1415
		29	Crude animal and vegetable materials	2898	140124	4304	126222
	3		Mineral fuels, lubricants and related materilas	487098	1081488	1.9E+07	3.1E+07
		32	Coal,coke and briquettes	5873	14013	1070	1121
		33	Petroleum, petroleum products and related materials	373727	807741	1.9E+07	3.1E+07
"333.00			petroleom oils and oils obtained from bituminous minerals cude	"000	25	1.7E+07	2.9E+07

For additional analytical, business and investment opportunities information,
please contact Global Investment & Business Center, USA
at (202) 546-2103. Fax: (202) 546-3275. E-mail: rusric@erols.com

334.11			Motor spririt(gasolene)including aviation spirit	44	1167	467245	923933
		34	Gas natural and manufactured	107498	259734	0	0
	4		ANIMAL AND VEGETABLE OILS, FATS & WAXES	151700	1191062	6183	184024
		41	Animal oils and fats	59702	579951	18	152
		42	Fixed vegetable fats and oils crude	74765	518199	6163	183846
421.1			soya hean oil and its fractions	38005	329582		
421.49			oil and their fractions obtained solely from olives	5572	35653	28	1712
		43	animal of vegetable fats and oils, processed, waxes of				
			animal of vegetable origin, inedible mixtures of preparati				
			of animal of vegetable fats of oils. N.E.S	17233	92912	2	26
	5		chemicals and related prodcucts N.E.S	927765	7248508	12843	113382
		51	organic chemicals	140839	915114	108	1517
		52	inorganic chemicals	99835	468754	666	4346
		53	dyeing, tanning & colouring mater	19010	423452	202	1695
		54	medicianl & farmaceutical products	3262	740650	819	18786
		55	essential oils and resionoids and perfume materials,				
			toilet, polishing & cleaning preparations	10295	153877	7742	78719
		56	fertilizers (other than those of group 272)	434539	706026	4	43
		57	plastices in primary forms	181532	2693543	2868	5660
571.1			polyethylene	58672	570068	7	65
573.1			polyvinyl chloride	27062	793648	21	223
		59	chemical materials and predicts N.E.S	38453	1147092	434	2616
	6		manufactured goods	2289116	1.9E+07	89306	1222880

For additional analytical, business and investment opportunities information, please contact Global Investment & Business Center, USA at (202) 546-2103. Fax: (202) 546-3275. E-mail: rusric@erols.com

			classified chefly by materei				
		61	leather, leather manufactured, N.E.S. and dressed				
			furskins	1032	10479	4285	134284
		62	ruber manufactures,n.e.s.	27799	809427	491	4120
625.1			tyres, pneumatic, new, of akind used on motor cars	1137	33847		
625.2			tyres, pneumatic, new, of akind used on buses, lor.	11790	384507	2	29
		63	cork and wood manufactures (excluding furniture	12670	89080	430	6532
		64	paper, paperboard and articles of paper pulp, of pape or				
			of paperboard	151839	957111	3435	52257
		65	textile yarn, fabrics, made-up articles, n.e.s. and				
			related products	199639	4844425	17771	885271
651.5			synthetic filament yarn not put up for retail sale	68055	1343858	35	1636
651.59			other synthetic filament yarn (other than sweing thread)	40913	1112549	1	1961
655.23			other fabrics, warp knit	70	7256	7205	399570
		66	non-metallic mineral manufactures, n.e.s.	811161	1856593	36309	38971
661.22			portland cement	627246	974419		
		67	iron and steel	984079	7832861	330	3037
676.00"			iron and steel bars, rods, angles, shapes and sections				
			(includings sheet piling)	564061	3691951	3	43
679.3			other tubes and pipes	76445	1855630	100	819
		68	non ferrous metals	15897	544185	22280	35164
		69	menufactures of metals n.e.s	85000	2248305	3975	43244
	7		machinery and transport equipment	245308	1.9E+07	9772	80734
		71	power geerating machinery and	24669	2137947	28	866

For additional analytical, business and investment opportunities information,
please contact Global Investment & Business Center, USA
at (202) 546-2103. Fax: (202) 546-3275. E-mail: rusric@erols.com

			equipment				
		72	machinery specialized particular industries	40813	1736762	1483	25666
728.49			machinery having individual functions n.e.s.	3176	396461	192	3323
		73	metalworing machinery	2386	162472	108	1849
		74	general industrial machinery and equipment				
			n.e.s. and machine parts, n.e.s.	46960	4756336	6594	36443
741.89			other machinery, plant or equipment	639	522763	5	151
748.2			bearing housings and plain shaft bearings	4147	798097	41	524
		75	office machines and automatic data processing				
			machines	836	469026	5	109
		76	telecommunications & sound recording & reproducing	3106	854459	3	46
			apparatus & equipment				
		77	electrical machinery, apparyatus and appliances, n.e.s	43897	3308748	365	6607
			and electrical parts hereof (including non-electrical				
			counterpants, n.e.s.				
773.1			insulated wire, cable and other insulated electric	18262	1191459	45	511
			conductors, whether or not fitted with connectors,				
			optical fiber cables made up of individually sheathed,				
			whether or noyt assemble with electric conductors or				
			fitted with conductors				
		78	road vehicles (including air-cushion vehicles)	55686	5134045	1141	8626
782.1			motor vehicles for the transport of goods	28430	3268280		

		79	other transport equipment	26955	571452	45	522
	8		miscellaneous manufactured articles	30511	1398473	44689	3101932
		81	prefabricated buildings sanitary, blumbing, heating and	596	44466	150	4174
			lighting fixtures and fittings, n.e.s.				
		82	furniture and parts thereof, bedding mattresses,	628	80280	1274	26843
			supports, cushions and similar stuffed furnishings				
		83	travel goods, handbags and similar containers	1	155	1699	43495
		84	articles of apparel clothing accessories	713	26288	28650	2578520
842.00"			womens and girls coats, capes, jackets, shirts	3	209	5730	619696
846.93			shawls, scarves, mufflers mautillas, veils and the like	5	1310	8857	702152
		85	footwear	28	5873	6849	357112
		87	professional, scientific & controlling instruments &	1755	572407	26	1298
			apparatus, n.e.s				
		88	photographic apparatus, equipment and supplies and	11517	235425	58	5198
			optical goods, n.e.s. watches and clocks				
		89	miscellaneous manufactured articles n.e.s.	15273	433579	5983	85292
	9		commodities and transactions not classified	22	2527	0	2
			elsewhere in the sitc				
		91	postal packages not classified according to kind				
		93	special transactions & commodities not classified				
			according to kind				

		96	coin (other than gold coin) not being legal tender	19	2252		
		97	gold, non-monetary (excluding gold ores and	3	275	0	2
			concentrates)				
			by passengers		1523505		
			GRAND TOTAL	5695045	60385380	22196902	44886991

LARGEST EXPORTERS

- **General company for fruits and vegetables**

Damascus P.O.Box: 5603
Tel 5422926-5422824-5422928
Fax 5423001
Tlx: 411914,412734
Cable :KHODAR
Products: Vegetables, Fruits, Fresh, Fruits, and Dehydrated

- **General Establishment For Food Industries**

Damascus P.O.Box :105
Tel :2225290-2234426-2234428
Fax :224537
Products: Soda , Conservatives, Jams, Arak, Oil, and Biscuits

- **General Establishment For Tobacco**

Damascus P.O.Box :616
Tel :2323125-2323126
Fax : 2233805
Tlx :411301   Cable :MONTAB
Products :Tobacco Tobacco Wholly , (Tombac)

- **General Company Leather Industries**

Damascus   P.O.Box :2994
Tel 5121808-5121809-5121810
Tlx :411628
Cable :AHZEAH
Products :Leather Footwear for men & women

- **General organization for fish**

Jableh
Tel :821677-833112-831367
Fax :831367
Tlx :451025
Products :FISH , CARP, FISH ,TILAPIA

- **General Establishment For Cows**

Hama, P.O.Box :48
Tel :410985
Fax :422984
Products: Meat frish, (Frezian,Holoshtin)

- **General Company For Matches ,Chipbord**

Damascus   P.O.Box :2672
Tel :5435734
Fax : 5437337
Tlx :41526 KEBRET SY
Cable :KEBRET-Damascus
Products :Matches ,Playwood, Chipboard ,Pencils (Graphite & Color)

- **General Establishment For Foreign Trade Of Food & Chemical Materials**

Damascus ,Jumhuryah St.
P.O.Box :893
Tel: 2218919-2225421
Fax:2226927
Productes: Cotton Linters,Onion (dried)

- **General Organization For Sugar**

Homs   P.O.Box :4290
Tel :227600-227602- Damascus 2212329
Fax :237899
Tlx :441123-441006 GOFS Cable :GOFS
PRODUCTS :MOLASSES,YEST DRY ,AL-COHOL, MEDICAL

- **"Orient" Company For Underwear**

Damascus   P.O.Box :1100
Tel :5436001-5436003
Fax :5436000
Tlx :412436 O.U.M.C.SY
Products :Ccoton Underwear

- **General Establishment For Cereal Processing And Trade**

Damascus   P.O.Box :4106
Tel :2238364-2238397-2237818
Fax :2232368
Tlx :412511-411027-411391
Cable :HOBOB-Damascus
Products: :Seed Of Lentils ,Lentils, Chick-Peas ,Barley

- **CARPET MANUFACTURING GENERAL CORPORATION**

Damascus   P.O.Box :1400
Tel :8880100 –8816973
Fax :8887002
Tlx :412514 CARP

For additional analytical, business and investment opportunities information,
please contact Global Investment & Business Center, USA
at (202) 546-2103. Fax: (202) 546-3275. E-mail: rusric@erols.com

Cable :CARPETCO
Products :Carpets , Woolen

- **HAMA COTTON YARN COMPANY**

Hama   P.O.Box :11
Tel :511092-551093-511091
Fax :511096
Tlx :431037 HAYC
Cable :GHAZEL Hama
Products :Cotton Carded Or Combed

- **Dry Battery Fabric**

Damascus   P.O.Box :3120
Tel: 6311643-8880789
Fax:2123375
Products: Dried battery

- **GENERAL ESTABLISHMENT FOR TIRES PRODUCTIONS**

Damascus   P.O.Box :12175
Tel :2210355 -2778808
Fax :2247499
 Poducts :Carpets, hand-made rug , carpets, hand made woolen , knit Faber. wool/fine hair

- **GENERAL ESTABLISHMENT FOR TIRES PRODUCTIONS**

Hama, Salamyah rood
Tel:424533-424532
Fax:424531
Tlx:431039
Products:Tires (different kinds)

- **General Company For Asphalt**

Lataquia   P.O.Box :6
Tle: 473121-475826
Fax : 475674
Tlx :451150
Cable :ASPEL
Products :,Nat. Asphalt Bituminous Mixtures Raw Stones

- **General Establishment For Porcelain**

Syria,Hama
P.O.Box : 161
Tel :510896-510996
Fax :511707
PRODUCTS : Porcelain , SANITARY WARE

- **General Organization For Poultry**

Damascus   P.O.Box :5597
Tel :2211968 -2212876

For additional analytical, business and investment opportunities information,
please contact Global Investment & Business Center, USA
at (202) 546-2103. Fax: (202) 546-3275. E-mail: rusric@erols.com

Fax :2217473
Tlx :412423 G.O.P. SYR
Cable :G.O.P. Damascus
Products :POULTRY LIVE, POULTRY FRESH
,EGGS BIRDS IN SHELL (HATCHING) ,EGGS BIRDS IN SHELL (TABLE)

- **Productive Projects Administration**

Damascus   P.O.Box :4703
Tel :2131499-212990-3314790
Fax :2205210
Tlx :412914 SY PRODUC
Products :, ,HONEY (flowred),HONEY (zalloo) ,MEDICAL PLANETS

- **General Establishment For Panting & Chemical Industries**

P.O.Box:1276
Tle : 5435511-5435512
Fax:5431088
Tlx:411299
Products Paints (deferent)

- **General Establishment For Chemical Industries**

Damascus
Tle:2127654-2123363
Fax :2128289
Products :Sport & leather shoes,Plastic houses, Chinaware

- **General Establishment For Engineering Industries**

Damascus
P.O.Box: 3120
Tle :212825-2122650
Fax :2123375
Products: Refrigerators, Household, Appliances, color TV Telephone sets, Cables

- **General Establishment For Textile Industries**

Fardous St.,Damascus
P.O.Box : 620
Tel :2216200-2215624-2215262
Fax :2216021
Tlx:411011
Products :Cotton yarns, Cotton Fabric, Socks , wool Carpets

- **General Establishment For Cleaners chemical Industry**

Damascus, Adra
P.O.Box: 682
Tel : 5810163- 5810164
Fax : 581062
Tlx : 412694 jecoda
PRODUCTS: Cleaners (Powders & Liquid), selphonic aside

- **General Electric Motors Manufacturing Company**

Lataquia   P.O.Box :190
Tel :421850 -421533
Fax :410761
Tlx :451090
Cable :MOTORS
Products :ELICTRICAL CABLE,TRANSFORMER (FLORESANT)

- **GENERAL COMPANY FOR Tanning**

Damascus ,Zablatani road
P.O.Box : 2019
Tel: 457840-454863
Fax : 4424935
Products :Raw & processed leather,leather jacets.

- **General Company For Transformation Industry**

Damascus P.O.Box :2803
Tel :6714574
Fax :6714572
Products :Sanitary Paper (For Baby & Women)

MAJOR NEWSPAPERS

Tishrin
Midan Street, P.O. Box 5452
Damascus, Syria
fax: 963-11-223-1374
phone: 224-7359, 224-7049, 889-6902/3/4.

Al-Thawra
Kaffar-Souseh Square, P.O. Box 2448
Damascus, Syria
fax: 963-11-221-6851
phone: 222-2399, 221-0850, 222-2911.

Al-Baath
Mazzeh Street, P.O. Box 9389
Damascus, Syria
fax: 963-11-662-2099
phone: 662-2142, 661-7616, 661-7683.

Golan
(the daily bulletin of official tenders)
P.O. Box 2842
Damascus, Syria
fax: 963-11-222-0754
phone: 222-5219.

Syria Times
(an English language daily newspaper targeted at the Western audience)
Midan Street, P.O. Box 5452
Damascus, Syria
fax: 963-11-223-1374

phone: 224-7359, 224-7049, 889-6902/3/4.

Commercial Bank of Syria:

Director General: Mr. Riad Hakim,

Yousef Al-Azmah Square, P.O. Box 933, Damascus, Syria; Telephone: 221-4508; Fax: 221-6975, 222-8524

U.S. Embassy Trade Personnel: Telephone: (963)(11) 333-3232

Anne Bodine: Economic/Commercial Attache
Donna Vandenbroucke: Economic/Commercial Officer
Jamal Aliah: Economic/Commercial Officer
Jonathan Rice: Economic/Commercial Officer

WASHINGTON DC - BASED CONTACTS FOR SYRIA

Office of Syrian Affairs
E. Candace Putnam
U.S. Department of State
Washington, D.C. 20520
Telephone: (202)647-7216
Fax: (202)647-0989

Office of Syrian Affairs
Thomas A. Sams
U.S. Department of Commerce
Washington, D.C.
Telephone: (202)482-1860
Fax: (202)482-0878

The Syrian for Exhibitions & International Conferences (SEIC)
P.O. Box 16046
Damascus, Syria
Tel. 963-11-613-3295
Fax: 963-11-613-3296.

United for Exhibitions and Media Services:
P.O. Box 6454, Damascus, Syria.
Tel. 963-11-331-2123
Fax: 963-11-331-2423.

The Arabian Group:
P.O. Box 2683, Damascus, Syria
Tel. 963-11-3737444/8/9
Fax: 963-11-3737446.

The International Group:
P.O. Box 35222, Damascus, Syria
Tel: 963-11-4428217
Fax: 963-11-4454510

BILATERAL AGREEMENTS SIGNED WITH ARAB STATES AND THE ADVANTAGES GRANTED THEREBY

State	Name & date of Agreement	Exemptions for Syrian Commodities	Exemptions for Arab Commodities
Saudi Arabia	Economic and Trade Agreement of 1972 Still valid	- Agricultural products and livestock and the produce of natural resources are exempted from customs duties according to list No.1 appended to the agreement - Syrian industrial products are exempted from customs duties according to list No.2 appended to the agreement - Syrian industrial products as per list No.3 appended to the agreement are exempted from two thirds of customs duties.	- Agricultural and animal products and livestock and the produce of natural resources are exempted from duties as per list No.1 appended to the agreement - All Saudi industrial products are exempted from duties
Kuwait	Economic and Commercial Cooperation Agreement of 1991 Still valid	- Agricultural and livestock products and the produce of natural resources are exempted from customs duties and other fees of similar effect - Syrian industrial products are exempted from duties and fees of similar effect except for the following: 1- Cast iron covering 2- Welded black steel pipes 3- oxygen gas for medical or industrial purposes	- Agricultural and livestock products and the produce of Kuwaiti natural resources are exempted from duties and fees of similar effect. - Kuwaiti industrial products are exempted from duties and fees of similar effect except for : 1- Cars. 2- Raw tobacco and byproducts. 3- cotton yarns locally produced.
Qatar	Economic and Commercial Cooperation Agreement of 1990 Still valid.	Agricultural, livestock and industrial products and raw materials that will be agreed upon in lists by the joint committee are exempted from customs duties.	Agricultural, livestock and industrial products and raw materials that will be agreed upon in lists by the joint committee are exempted from customs duties.
Bahrain	Economic and Commercial Cooperation Agreement of 1994 Still valid.	-Syrian agricultural and livestock products are exempted from customs duties and fees of similar effect. - Syrian industrial products according to lists prepared by the joint committee as stated in the agreement are exempted from customs duties and fees of similar effect.	-Bahraini agricultural and livestock products are exempted from customs duties and fees of similar effect. - Industrial products according to lists prepared by the joint committee as stated in the agreement are exempted from customs duties and fees of similar effect.

Country	Agreement	Syrian products	Partner products
United Arab Emirates	Economic and Commercial Cooperation Agreement of 1990 endorsed by Syria but not endorsed by U.A.E. Consultations are underway with the U.A.E for the purpose.	No advantages of preferences or exemptions for the products of each country. Yet, the agreement provides for offering facilities that support the movement of export and import between the two countries.	No advantages of preferences or exemptions for the products of each country. Yet, the agreement provides for offering facilities that support the movement of export and import between the two countries.
Oman	Economic and Commercial Cooperation Agreement of 1991 Still valid.	Agreement does not give any performances or exemptions from customs duties.	Agreement does not give any performances or exemptions from customs duties.
Jordan	Agreement on Economic Cooperation and Regulating Trade Exchange of 1975. Minutes of meeting of the joint committee of 1986.	The 1975 agreement provides for exemption from customs duties for agricultural, livestock products and the produce of natural resources and exchanged industrial products. The two sides agreed on two lists, one for prompt implementation and the other is a guideline. The "prompt" list benefits From exemption from customs duties in each country according to certain banking arrangements , the guidelines list does not benefit from customs exemptions.	The agreement provides for total exemption from customs duties for Jordanian products.
Yemen	Trade agreement signed in 1996, ratified by Yemen, procedures of ratification in Syria are under way.	Agreement does not provide for any advantage of preference. The joint committee will discuss preferences which each party can offer for the purpose of promoting and developing trade Exchange between the two countries.	Agreement
Iraq	An agreement on economic cooperation and regulation of trade exchange, signed in 1979 (frozen at present)	All Syrian Products are exempted from customs duties. Free zone products are exempted from duties within the limits of local costs used in the manufacture of those products.	All Iraqi products are exempted from customs duties. Free zone products are exempted from duties within the limits of local costs used in the manufacture of those products.
Egypt	Trade agreement signed in 1991 (Valid)	Exemption from customs duties and relevant taxes (except local taxes and fees and taxes on sales) for the Syrian commodities and products as listed in Table A appended to the agreement. (This list contains 19 commodities)	Exemption from customs duties and relevant taxes (except local taxes and fees and taxes on sales) for the Egyptian commodities listed in Table B appended to the agreement. (This list contains 20

			commodities)
Morocco	Agreement on regulating trade exchange and economic cooperation signed in1972 (Valid)	Each side treats the other side as a most favoured nation. Excluded from this condition are the relations binding either side to other countries that form with it customs union or economic unity or common market and the advantages granted by either side to facilitate cross-border trade.	Each side treats the other side as a most favoured nation. Excluded from this condition are the relations binding either side to other countries that form with it customs union or economic unity or common market and the advantages granted by either side to facilitate cross-border trade.
Libya	Agreement on regulating trade exchange and economic cooperation signed in1978 (Valid)	All Syrian agricultural, livestock products, produce of natural resources and industrial products are exempted from customs duties and other taxes and fees.	All Libyan agricultural, livestock products, produce of natural resources and industrial products are exempted from customs duties and other taxes and fees.

Sudan	An agreement on trade and economic cooperation signed in 1974 (Valid)	Exemption from customs duties and additional fees for Syrian agricultural and animal products and livestock except for a fee of 5%. - Syrian industrial products as listed in Table 1 are subject to reduced duties as explained in the said table (ranging between 10% and 100%) . - Most favoured nation.	Exemption from customs duties and additional fees for Sudanese agricultural and animal products and livestock except for a fee of 2%. - Sudanese industrial products as listed in Table 2 are subject to reduced duties as explained in the said table (ranging between30% and 100%) . - Most favoured nation.
Tunisia	Trade agreement signed in 1977 (Valid)	All Syrian products are exempted from customs duties (agricultural, animal products, livestock, produce of natural resources and industrial products).	All Tunisian products are exempted from customs duties (agricultural, animal products, livestock, produce of natural resources and industrial products).

For additional analytical, business and investment opportunities information, please contact Global Investment & Business Center, USA at (202) 546-2103. Fax: (202) 546-3275. E-mail: rusric@erols.com

Algeria	Trade agreement signed in 1979, valid until the concluding of a new agreement in 1997 and notes of ratification are exchanged. Ratification is being followed up.	Old Agreement: Syrian agricultural products and livestock are exempted from customs duties. - Syrian industrial products as listed in Table 1 appended to the agreement are exempted from customs duties. New Agreement: No provision for most favoured nation for either country.	Old Agreement: Algerian agricultural products and livestock are exempted from customs duties. - Algerian industrial products as listed Table 2 appended to the agreement are exempted from customs duties. New Agreement: No provision for most favoured nation for either country.
Somalia	Trade agreement signed in 1973 (valid)	Most favored nation with regard to customs duties and other taxes and fees on imports, exports, storage, transit, unloading and shipment of goods. Excluded are: 1- Advantages and benefits granted to facilitate cross-border trade. 2- Goods of non-Syrian or non-Somali origin. 3- Advantages and benefits resulting from customs union, free trade area, common market or any special agreements.	Same advantages
Lebanon	Economic agreement signed in 1953, still valid by virtue of the provisions of agreement on social and economic cooperation and coordination of 1992 duly ratified by the two countries and being implemented by both of them	- Syrian agricultural and livestock products as listed in Table 1 appended to the agreement are exempted from customs duties. - Syrian industrial products as listed in Table 2 appended to the agreement are exempted from customs duties. -Exempted from half the duties are Syrian industrial products as listed in Table 3 appended to the agreement.	- Lebanese agricultural and livestock products as listed in Table 1 appended to the agreement are exempted from customs duties. - Lebanese industrial products as listed in Table 2 appended to the agreement are exempted from customs duties. -Exempted from half the duties are Lebanese industrial products as listed in Table 3 appended to the agreement.

BASIC TITLES FOR SYRIA

IMPORTANT!
All publications are updated annually!
Please contact IBP, Inc. at ibpusa3@gmail.com for the latest ISBNs and additional information
Global Business and Investment Info Databank: www.ibpus.com

title
Syria A "Spy" Guide
Syria A Spy" Guide"
Syria Air Force Handbook
Syria Air Force Handbook
Syria Business and Investment Opportunities Yearbook
Syria Business and Investment Opportunities Yearbook
Syria Business and Investment Opportunities Yearbook Volume 1 Strategic Information and Opportunities
Syria Business and Investment Opportunities Yearbook Volume 1 Strategic Information and Opportunities
Syria Business Intelligence Report
Syria Business Intelligence Report
Syria Business Law Handbook
Syria Business Law Handbook
Syria Constitution and Citizenship Laws Handbook - Strategic Information and Basic Laws
Syria Constitution and Citizenship Laws Handbook - Strategic Information and Basic Laws
Syria Country Study Guide
Syria Country Study Guide Volume 1 Strategic Information and Developments
Syria Country Study Guide Volume 1 Strategic Information and Developments
Syria Customs, Trade Regulations and Procedures Handbook
Syria Customs, Trade Regulations and Procedures Handbook
Syria Diplomatic Handbook
Syria Diplomatic Handbook
Syria Ecology & Nature Protection Handbook
Syria Ecology & Nature Protection Laws and Regulation Handbook
Syria Economic & Development Strategy Handbook
Syria Economic & Development Strategy Handbook
Syria Energy Policy, Laws and Regulation Handbook
Syria Energy Policy, Laws and Regulations Handbook
Syria Energy Policy, Laws and Regulations Handbook
Syria Export Import & Business Directory
Syria Export Import & Business Directory
Syria Export Import & Business Directory
Syria Export Import & Business Directory
Syria Export Import & Business Directory
Syria Foreign Policy and Government Guide
Syria Foreign Policy and Government Guide
Syria Immigration Laws and Regulations Handbook - Strategic Information and Basic Laws
Syria Investment and Business Guide

For additional analytical, business and investment opportunities information,
please contact Global Investment & Business Center, USA
at (202) 546-2103. Fax: (202) 546-3275. E-mail: rusric@erols.com

title
Syria Investment and Business Guide
Syria Investment and Business Guide
Syria Investment and Business Guide
Syria Labor Laws and Regulations Handbook - Strategic Information and Basic Laws
Syria Labor Laws and Regulations Handbook - Strategic Information and Basic Laws
Syria Land Ownership and Agriculture Laws Handbook
Syria Land Ownership and Agriculture Laws Handbook
Syria Land Ownership and Agriculture Laws Handbook
Syria Mineral & Mining Sector Investment and Business Guide
Syria Mineral & Mining Sector Investment and Business Guide
Syria Mining Laws and Regulations Handbook
Syria National Development Strategy Handbook: Important Programs and Developments
Syria Oil & Gas Sector Business & Investment Opportunities Yearbook
Syria Oil & Gas Sector Business & Investment Opportunities Yearbook
Syria Oil and Gas Exploration Laws and Regulation Handbook
Syria President, Political System and Reforms Handbook
Syria Recent Economic and Political Developments Yearbook
Syria Recent Economic and Political Developments Yearbook
Syria Taxation Laws and Regulations Handbook
Syria Transportation Policy and Regulations Handbook

For additional analytical, business and investment opportunities information,
please contact Global Investment & Business Center, USA
at (202) 546-2103. Fax: (202) 546-3275. E-mail: rusric@erols.com

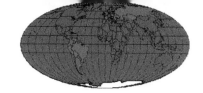

WORLD INVESTMENT AND BUSINESS PROFILES LIBRARY

World Business Information Catalog, USA: http://www.ibpus.com
Email: ibpusa@comcast.net.
Price: $49.95 Each

TITLE
Abkhazia (Republic of Abkhazia) Investment and Business Profile - Strategic, Practical Information and Contacts for Starting Business
Afghanistan Investment and Business Profile - Strategic, Practical Information and Contacts for Starting Business
Aland Investment and Business Profile - Strategic, Practical Information and Contacts for Starting Business
Albania Investment and Business Profile - Strategic, Practical Information and Contacts for Starting Business
Algeria Investment and Business Profile - Strategic, Practical Information and Contacts for Starting Business
Andorra Investment and Business Profile - Strategic, Practical Information and Contacts for Starting Business
Angola Investment and Business Profile - Strategic, Practical Information and Contacts for Starting Business
Anguilla Investment and Business Profile - Strategic, Practical Information and Contacts for Starting Business
Antigua and Barbuda Investment and Business Profile - Strategic, Practical Information and Contacts for Starting Business
Antilles (Netherlands) Investment and Business Profile - Strategic, Practical Information and Contacts for Starting Business
Argentina Investment and Business Profile - Strategic, Practical Information and Contacts for Starting Business
Armenia Investment and Business Profile - Strategic, Practical Information and Contacts for Starting Business
Aruba Investment and Business Profile - Strategic, Practical Information and Contacts for Starting Business
Australia Investment and Business Profile - Strategic, Practical Information and Contacts for Starting Business
Austria Investment and Business Profile - Strategic, Practical Information and Contacts for Starting Business
Azerbaijan Investment and Business Profile - Strategic, Practical Information and Contacts for Starting Business

For additional analytical, business and investment opportunities information,
Please contact Global Investment & Business Center, USA

TITLE
Bahamas Investment and Business Profile - Strategic, Practical Information and Contacts for Starting Business
Bahrain Investment and Business Profile - Strategic, Practical Information and Contacts for Starting Business
Bangladesh Investment and Business Profile - Strategic, Practical Information and Contacts for Starting Business
Barbados Investment and Business Profile - Strategic, Practical Information and Contacts for Starting Business
Belarus Investment and Business Profile - Strategic, Practical Information and Contacts for Starting Business
Belgium Investment and Business Profile - Strategic, Practical Information and Contacts for Starting Business
Belize Investment and Business Profile - Strategic, Practical Information and Contacts for Starting Business
Benin Investment and Business Profile - Strategic, Practical Information and Contacts for Starting Business
Bermuda Investment and Business Profile - Strategic, Practical Information and Contacts for Starting Business
Bhutan Investment and Business Profile - Strategic, Practical Information and Contacts for Starting Business
Bolivia Investment and Business Profile - Strategic, Practical Information and Contacts for Starting Business
Bosnia and Herzegovina Investment and Business Profile - Strategic, Practical Information and Contacts for Starting Business
Botswana Investment and Business Profile - Strategic, Practical Information and Contacts for Starting Business
Brazil Investment and Business Profile - Strategic, Practical Information and Contacts for Starting Business
Brunei Investment and Business Profile - Strategic, Practical Information and Contacts for Starting Business
Bulgaria Investment and Business Profile - Strategic, Practical Information and Contacts for Starting Business
Burkina Faso Investment and Business Profile - Strategic, Practical Information and Contacts for Starting Business
Burundi Investment and Business Profile - Strategic, Practical Information and Contacts for Starting Business
Cambodia Investment and Business Profile - Strategic, Practical Information and Contacts for Starting Business
Cameroon Investment and Business Profile - Strategic, Practical Information and Contacts for Starting Business
Canada Investment and Business Profile - Strategic, Practical Information and Contacts for Starting Business

TITLE
Cape Verde Investment and Business Profile - Strategic, Practical Information and Contacts for Starting Business
Cayman Islands Investment and Business Profile - Strategic, Practical Information and Contacts for Starting Business
Central African Republic Investment and Business Profile - Strategic, Practical Information and Contacts for Starting Business
Chad Investment and Business Profile - Strategic, Practical Information and Contacts for Starting Business
Chile Investment and Business Profile - Strategic, Practical Information and Contacts for Starting Business
China Investment and Business Profile - Strategic, Practical Information and Contacts for Starting Business
Colombia Investment and Business Profile - Strategic, Practical Information and Contacts for Starting Business
Comoros Investment and Business Profile - Strategic, Practical Information and Contacts for Starting Business
Congo Investment and Business Profile - Strategic, Practical Information and Contacts for Starting Business
Congo, Democratic Republic Investment and Business Profile - Strategic, Practical Information and Contacts for Starting Business
Cook Islands Investment and Business Profile - Strategic, Practical Information and Contacts for Starting Business
Costa Rica Investment and Business Profile - Strategic, Practical Information and Contacts for Starting Business
Cote d'Ivoire Investment and Business Profile - Strategic, Practical Information and Contacts for Starting Business
Croatia Investment and Business Profile - Strategic, Practical Information and Contacts for Starting Business
Cuba Investment and Business Profile - Strategic, Practical Information and Contacts for Starting Business
Cyprus Investment and Business Profile - Strategic, Practical Information and Contacts for Starting Business
Czech Republic Investment and Business Profile - Strategic, Practical Information and Contacts for Starting Business
Denmark Investment and Business Profile - Strategic, Practical Information and Contacts for Starting Business
Djibouti Investment and Business Profile - Strategic, Practical Information and Contacts for Starting Business
Dominica Investment and Business Profile - Strategic, Practical Information and Contacts for Starting Business
Dominican Republic Investment and Business Profile - Strategic, Practical Information and Contacts for Starting Business

TITLE
Ecuador Investment and Business Profile - Strategic, Practical Information and Contacts for Starting Business
Egypt Investment and Business Profile - Strategic, Practical Information and Contacts for Starting Business
El Salvador Investment and Business Profile - Strategic, Practical Information and Contacts for Starting Business
Equatorial Guinea Investment and Business Profile - Strategic, Practical Information and Contacts for Starting Business
Eritrea Investment and Business Profile - Strategic, Practical Information and Contacts for Starting Business
Estonia Investment and Business Profile - Strategic, Practical Information and Contacts for Starting Business
Ethiopia Investment and Business Profile - Strategic, Practical Information and Contacts for Starting Business
Falkland Islands Investment and Business Profile - Strategic, Practical Information and Contacts for Starting Business
Faroes Islands Investment and Business Profile - Strategic, Practical Information and Contacts for Starting Business
Fiji Investment and Business Profile - Strategic, Practical Information and Contacts for Starting Business
Finland Investment and Business Profile - Strategic, Practical Information and Contacts for Starting Business
France Investment and Business Profile - Strategic, Practical Information and Contacts for Starting Business
Gabon Investment and Business Profile - Strategic, Practical Information and Contacts for Starting Business
Gambia Investment and Business Profile - Strategic, Practical Information and Contacts for Starting Business
Georgia Investment and Business Profile - Strategic, Practical Information and Contacts for Starting Business
Germany Investment and Business Profile - Strategic, Practical Information and Contacts for Starting Business
Ghana Investment and Business Profile - Strategic, Practical Information and Contacts for Starting Business
Gibraltar Investment and Business Profile - Strategic, Practical Information and Contacts for Starting Business
Greece Investment and Business Profile - Strategic, Practical Information and Contacts for Starting Business
Greenland Investment and Business Profile - Strategic, Practical Information and Contacts for Starting Business
Grenada Investment and Business Profile - Strategic, Practical Information and Contacts for Starting Business

For additional analytical, business and investment opportunities information, Please contact Global Investment & Business Center, USA

TITLE
Guam Investment and Business Profile - Strategic, Practical Information and Contacts for Starting Business
Guatemala Investment and Business Profile - Strategic, Practical Information and Contacts for Starting Business
Guernsey Investment and Business Profile - Strategic, Practical Information and Contacts for Starting Business
Guinea Investment and Business Profile - Strategic, Practical Information and Contacts for Starting Business
Guinea-Bissau Investment and Business Profile - Strategic, Practical Information and Contacts for Starting Business
Guyana Investment and Business Profile - Strategic, Practical Information and Contacts for Starting Business
Haiti Investment and Business Profile - Strategic, Practical Information and Contacts for Starting Business
Honduras Investment and Business Profile - Strategic, Practical Information and Contacts for Starting Business
Hungary Investment and Business Profile - Strategic, Practical Information and Contacts for Starting Business
Iceland Investment and Business Profile - Strategic, Practical Information and Contacts for Starting Business
India Investment and Business Profile - Strategic, Practical Information and Contacts for Starting Business
Indonesia Investment and Business Profile - Strategic, Practical Information and Contacts for Starting Business
Iran Investment and Business Profile - Strategic, Practical Information and Contacts for Starting Business
Iraq Investment and Business Profile - Strategic, Practical Information and Contacts for Starting Business
Ireland Investment and Business Profile - Strategic, Practical Information and Contacts for Starting Business
Israel Investment and Business Profile - Strategic, Practical Information and Contacts for Starting Business
Italy Investment and Business Profile - Strategic, Practical Information and Contacts for Starting Business
Jamaica Investment and Business Profile - Strategic, Practical Information and Contacts for Starting Business
Japan Investment and Business Profile - Strategic, Practical Information and Contacts for Starting Business
Jersey Investment and Business Profile - Strategic, Practical Information and Contacts for Starting Business
Jordan Investment and Business Profile - Strategic, Practical Information and Contacts for Starting Business

For additional analytical, business and investment opportunities information, Please contact Global Investment & Business Center, USA

TITLE
Kazakhstan Investment and Business Profile - Strategic, Practical Information and Contacts for Starting Business
Kenya Investment and Business Profile - Strategic, Practical Information and Contacts for Starting Business
Kiribati Investment and Business Profile - Strategic, Practical Information and Contacts for Starting Business
Korea, North Investment and Business Profile - Strategic, Practical Information and Contacts for Starting Business
Korea, South Investment and Business Profile - Strategic, Practical Information and Contacts for Starting Business
Kosovo Investment and Business Profile - Strategic, Practical Information and Contacts for Starting Business
Kurdistan Investment and Business Profile - Strategic, Practical Information and Contacts for Starting Business
Kuwait Investment and Business Profile - Strategic, Practical Information and Contacts for Starting Business
Kyrgyzstan Investment and Business Profile - Strategic, Practical Information and Contacts for Starting Business
Laos Investment and Business Profile - Strategic, Practical Information and Contacts for Starting Business
Latvia Investment and Business Profile - Strategic, Practical Information and Contacts for Starting Business
Lebanon Investment and Business Profile - Strategic, Practical Information and Contacts for Starting Business
Lesotho Investment and Business Profile - Strategic, Practical Information and Contacts for Starting Business
Liberia Investment and Business Profile - Strategic, Practical Information and Contacts for Starting Business
Libya Investment and Business Profile - Strategic, Practical Information and Contacts for Starting Business
Liechtenstein Investment and Business Profile - Strategic, Practical Information and Contacts for Starting Business
Lithuania Investment and Business Profile - Strategic, Practical Information and Contacts for Starting Business
Luxembourg Investment and Business Profile - Strategic, Practical Information and Contacts for Starting Business
Macao Investment and Business Profile - Strategic, Practical Information and Contacts for Starting Business
Macedonia Investment and Business Profile - Strategic, Practical Information and Contacts for Starting Business
Madagascar Investment and Business Profile - Strategic, Practical Information and Contacts for Starting Business

TITLE
Madeira Investment and Business Profile - Strategic, Practical Information and Contacts for Starting Business
Malawi Investment and Business Profile - Strategic, Practical Information and Contacts for Starting Business
Malaysia Investment and Business Profile - Strategic, Practical Information and Contacts for Starting Business
Maldives Investment and Business Profile - Strategic, Practical Information and Contacts for Starting Business
Mali Investment and Business Profile - Strategic, Practical Information and Contacts for Starting Business
Malta Investment and Business Profile - Strategic, Practical Information and Contacts for Starting Business
Man Investment and Business Profile - Strategic, Practical Information and Contacts for Starting Business
Marshall Islands Investment and Business Profile - Strategic, Practical Information and Contacts for Starting Business
Mauritania Investment and Business Profile - Strategic, Practical Information and Contacts for Starting Business
Mauritius Investment and Business Profile - Strategic, Practical Information and Contacts for Starting Business
Mayotte Investment and Business Profile - Strategic, Practical Information and Contacts for Starting Business
Mexico Investment and Business Profile - Strategic, Practical Information and Contacts for Starting Business
Micronesia Investment and Business Profile - Strategic, Practical Information and Contacts for Starting Business
Moldova Investment and Business Profile - Strategic, Practical Information and Contacts for Starting Business
Monaco Investment and Business Profile - Strategic, Practical Information and Contacts for Starting Business
Mongolia Investment and Business Profile - Strategic, Practical Information and Contacts for Starting Business
Montserrat Investment and Business Profile - Strategic, Practical Information and Contacts for Starting Business
Montenegro Investment and Business Profile - Strategic, Practical Information and Contacts for Starting Business
Morocco Investment and Business Profile - Strategic, Practical Information and Contacts for Starting Business
Mozambique Investment and Business Profile - Strategic, Practical Information and Contacts for Starting Business
Myanmar Investment and Business Profile - Strategic, Practical Information and Contacts for Starting Business

For additional analytical, business and investment opportunities information,
Please contact Global Investment & Business Center, USA

6

TITLE
Nagorno-Karabakh Republic Investment and Business Profile - Strategic, Practical Information and Contacts for Starting Business
Namibia Investment and Business Profile - Strategic, Practical Information and Contacts for Starting Business
Nauru Investment and Business Profile - Strategic, Practical Information and Contacts for Starting Business
Nepal Investment and Business Profile - Strategic, Practical Information and Contacts for Starting Business
Netherlands Investment and Business Profile - Strategic, Practical Information and Contacts for Starting Business
New Caledonia Investment and Business Profile - Strategic, Practical Information and Contacts for Starting Business
New Zealand Investment and Business Profile - Strategic, Practical Information and Contacts for Starting Business
Nicaragua Investment and Business Profile - Strategic, Practical Information and Contacts for Starting Business
Niger Investment and Business Profile - Strategic, Practical Information and Contacts for Starting Business
Nigeria Investment and Business Profile - Strategic, Practical Information and Contacts for Starting Business
Niue Investment and Business Profile - Strategic, Practical Information and Contacts for Starting Business
Northern Cyprus (Turkish Republic of Northern Cyprus) Volume 1 Strategic Information and Developments
Northern Mariana Islands Investment and Business Profile - Strategic, Practical Information and Contacts for Starting Business
Norway Investment and Business Profile - Strategic, Practical Information and Contacts for Starting Business
Oman Investment and Business Profile - Strategic, Practical Information and Contacts for Starting Business
Pakistan Investment and Business Profile - Strategic, Practical Information and Contacts for Starting Business
Palau Investment and Business Profile - Strategic, Practical Information and Contacts for Starting Business
Palestine (West Bank & Gaza) Investment and Business Profile - Strategic, Practical Information and Contacts for Starting Business
Panama Investment and Business Profile - Strategic, Practical Information and Contacts for Starting Business
Papua New Guinea Investment and Business Profile - Strategic, Practical Information and Contacts for Starting Business
Paraguay Investment and Business Profile - Strategic, Practical Information and Contacts for Starting Business

8

For additional analytical, business and investment opportunities information,
Please contact Global Investment & Business Center, USA

TITLE
Peru Investment and Business Profile - Strategic, Practical Information and Contacts for Starting Business
Philippines Investment and Business Profile - Strategic, Practical Information and Contacts for Starting Business
Pitcairn Islands Investment and Business Profile - Strategic, Practical Information and Contacts for Starting Business
Poland Investment and Business Profile - Strategic, Practical Information and Contacts for Starting Business
Polynesia French Investment and Business Profile - Strategic, Practical Information and Contacts for Starting Business
Portugal Investment and Business Profile - Strategic, Practical Information and Contacts for Starting Business
Qatar Investment and Business Profile - Strategic, Practical Information and Contacts for Starting Business
Romania Investment and Business Profile - Strategic, Practical Information and Contacts for Starting Business
Russia Investment and Business Profile - Strategic, Practical Information and Contacts for Starting Business
Rwanda Investment and Business Profile - Strategic, Practical Information and Contacts for Starting Business
Sahrawi Arab Democratic Republic Volume 1 Strategic Information and Developments
Saint Kitts and Nevis Investment and Business Profile - Strategic, Practical Information and Contacts for Starting Business
Saint Lucia Investment and Business Profile - Strategic, Practical Information and Contacts for Starting Business
Saint Vincent and The Grenadines Investment and Business Profile - Strategic, Practical Information and Contacts for Starting Business
Samoa (American) A Investment and Business Profile - Strategic, Practical Information and Contacts for Starting Business
Samoa (Western) Investment and Business Profile - Strategic, Practical Information and Contacts for Starting Business
San Marino Investment and Business Profile - Strategic, Practical Information and Contacts for Starting Business
Sao Tome and Principe Investment and Business Profile - Strategic, Practical Information and Contacts for Starting Business
Saudi Arabia Investment and Business Profile - Strategic, Practical Information and Contacts for Starting Business
Scotland Investment and Business Profile - Strategic, Practical Information and Contacts for Starting Business
Senegal Investment and Business Profile - Strategic, Practical Information and Contacts for Starting Business

For additional analytical, business and investment opportunities information,
Please contact Global Investment & Business Center, USA

TITLE
Serbia Investment and Business Profile - Strategic, Practical Information and Contacts for Starting Business
Seychelles Investment and Business Profile - Strategic, Practical Information and Contacts for Starting Business
Sierra Leone Investment and Business Profile - Strategic, Practical Information and Contacts for Starting Business
Singapore Investment and Business Profile - Strategic, Practical Information and Contacts for Starting Business
Slovakia Investment and Business Profile - Strategic, Practical Information and Contacts for Starting Business
Slovenia Investment and Business Profile - Strategic, Practical Information and Contacts for Starting Business
Solomon Islands Investment and Business Profile - Strategic, Practical Information and Contacts for Starting Business
Somalia Investment and Business Profile - Strategic, Practical Information and Contacts for Starting Business
South Africa Investment and Business Profile - Strategic, Practical Information and Contacts for Starting Business
Spain Investment and Business Profile - Strategic, Practical Information and Contacts for Starting Business
Sri Lanka Investment and Business Profile - Strategic, Practical Information and Contacts for Starting Business
St. Helena Investment and Business Profile - Strategic, Practical Information and Contacts for Starting Business
St. Pierre & Miquelon Investment and Business Profile - Strategic, Practical Information and Contacts for Starting Business
Sudan (Republic of the Sudan) Investment and Business Profile - Strategic, Practical Information and Contacts for Starting Business
Sudan South Investment and Business Profile - Strategic, Practical Information and Contacts for Starting Business
Suriname Investment and Business Profile - Strategic, Practical Information and Contacts for Starting Business
Swaziland Investment and Business Profile - Strategic, Practical Information and Contacts for Starting Business
Sweden Investment and Business Profile - Strategic, Practical Information and Contacts for Starting Business
Switzerland Investment and Business Profile - Strategic, Practical Information and Contacts for Starting Business
Syria Investment and Business Profile - Strategic, Practical Information and Contacts for Starting Business
Taiwan Investment and Business Profile - Strategic, Practical Information and Contacts for Starting Business

For additional analytical, business and investment opportunities information,
Please contact Global Investment & Business Center, USA

TITLE
Tajikistan Investment and Business Profile - Strategic, Practical Information and Contacts for Starting Business
Tanzania Investment and Business Profile - Strategic, Practical Information and Contacts for Starting Business
Thailand Investment and Business Profile - Strategic, Practical Information and Contacts for Starting Business
Timor Leste (Democratic Republic of Timor-Leste) Investment and Business Profile - Strategic, Practical Information and Contacts for Starting Business
Togo Investment and Business Profile - Strategic, Practical Information and Contacts for Starting Business
Tonga Investment and Business Profile - Strategic, Practical Information and Contacts for Starting Business
Trinidad and Tobago Investment and Business Profile - Strategic, Practical Information and Contacts for Starting Business
Tunisia Investment and Business Profile - Strategic, Practical Information and Contacts for Starting Business
Turkey Investment and Business Profile - Strategic, Practical Information and Contacts for Starting Business
Turkmenistan Investment and Business Profile - Strategic, Practical Information and Contacts for Starting Business
Turks & Caicos Investment and Business Profile - Strategic, Practical Information and Contacts for Starting Business
Tuvalu Investment and Business Profile - Strategic, Practical Information and Contacts for Starting Business
Uganda Investment and Business Profile - Strategic, Practical Information and Contacts for Starting Business
Ukraine Investment and Business Profile - Strategic, Practical Information and Contacts for Starting Business
United Arab Emirates Investment and Business Profile - Strategic, Practical Information and Contacts for Starting Business
United Kingdom Investment and Business Profile - Strategic, Practical Information and Contacts for Starting Business
United States Investment and Business Profile - Strategic, Practical Information and Contacts for Starting Business
Uruguay Investment and Business Profile - Strategic, Practical Information and Contacts for Starting Business
Uzbekistan Investment and Business Profile - Strategic, Practical Information and Contacts for Starting Business
Vanuatu Investment and Business Profile - Strategic, Practical Information and Contacts for Starting Business
Vatican City (Holy See) Investment and Business Profile - Strategic, Practical Information and Contacts for Starting Business

TITLE
Venezuela Investment and Business Profile - Strategic, Practical Information and Contacts for Starting Business
Vietnam Investment and Business Profile - Strategic, Practical Information and Contacts for Starting Business
Virgin Islands, British Investment and Business Profile - Strategic, Practical Information and Contacts for Starting Business
Wake Atoll Investment and Business Profile - Strategic, Practical Information and Contacts for Starting Business
Wallis & Futuna Investment and Business Profile - Strategic, Practical Information and Contacts for Starting Business
Western Sahara Investment and Business Profile - Strategic, Practical Information and Contacts for Starting Business
Yemen Investment and Business Profile - Strategic, Practical Information and Contacts for Starting Business
Zambia Investment and Business Profile - Strategic, Practical Information and Contacts for Starting Business
Zimbabwe Investment and Business Profile - Strategic, Practical Information and Contacts for Starting Business

For additional analytical, business and investment opportunities information, Please contact Global Investment & Business Center, USA